The President as Party Leader

The President as Party Leader

James W. Davis

PRAEGER

New York
Westport, Connecticut
London

Library of Congress Cataloging-in-Publication Data

Davis, James W.
   The president as party leader / James W. Davis.
     p. cm.
   Includes bibliographical references (p.   ) and index.
   ISBN 0-275-94112-4 (pbk. : alk. paper)
     1. Presidents—United States. 2. Political parties—United
States. 3. Political leadership—United States. I. Title.
JK516.D39 1992b
353.03'23—dc20   91-35809

British Library Cataloguing in Publication Data is available.

A hardcover edition of *The President as Party Leader* is available from the
Greenwood Press imprint of Greenwood Publishing Group, Inc.
(ISBN 0-313-28007-X).

Library of Congress Catalog Card Number: 91-35809
ISBN: 0-275-94112-4

First published in 1992

Praeger Publishers, One Madison Avenue, New York, NY 10010
An imprint of Greenwood Publishing Group, Inc.

Printed in the United States of America

The paper used in this book complies with the
Permanent Paper Standard issued by the National
Information Standards Organization (Z39.48-1984).

10 9 8 7 6 5 4 3 2 1

Copyright Acknowledgments

The author and publisher wish to thank the following:

Table 4.1 is reprinted by permission of Westview Press from *The Electoral Origins of
Divided Government: Competition in U.S. House Elections, 1946–1988,* by Gary C. Jacobson.
Published by Westview Press, 1990, Boulder, Colorado; Table 5.1 is reprinted by per-
mission of Greenwood Publishing Group, Inc., Westport, CT, from *Presidents and Their
Parties: Leadership or Neglect?* edited by Robert Harmel; copyright by Robert Harmel and
published in 1984 by Praeger Publishers; Tables 7.4 and 7.5 are reprinted by permission
of the publishers from *The Decline of American Political Parties 1952–1988* by Martin P.
Wattenberg, Cambridge, Mass.: Harvard University Press, Copyright © 1991 by the
President and Fellows of Harvard College.

Contents

List of Tables **vii**

Preface **ix**

1 Introduction **1**

2 Emergence of the Party Leader: Nominating and General Election Campaigns **19**

3 Presidential–Congressional Party Interaction **43**

4 Party Leader in an Era of Divided Government **63**

5 The President and the National Committee **97**

6 The Presidential Party **119**

7 The Public President Overshadows the Party President **141**

8 Proposed Institutional Reforms to Strengthen the President's Hand **173**

9 Reassessing Presidential–Party Relations **193**

Selected Bibliography **213**

Index **221**

List of Tables

2.1 Presidential Coattails (1932–1988) **36**

2.2 Senate and Presidential Victory Margins, 1984 **39**

4.1 Public Opinion on Divided Control of Federal Government, 1981 and 1989 (percentages) **66**

4.2 Republican Representation in Congress after Republican Presidential Victories, 1952–1988 **74**

4.3 Conservative Coalition Votes and Victories, 1957–1988 **79**

4.4 Presidential Vetoes, 1789–1990 **81**

5.1 Factional Types of Presidential Partisanship **107**

6.1 Direct Campaign Expenditures by Presidential and National Party Committees, General Elections, 1912–1988 **134**

6.2 Presidential Spending: 1960–1988 **135**

7.1 Presidential Television from Kennedy to Reagan; First Nineteen Months in Office **144**

7.2 Public Support for Modern Presidents: A Summary **151**

7.3 Presidential Popularity and Presidential Elections **152**

7.4 Party Identification, 1952–1988 **162**

7.5 Trends in Split-ticket and Party-line Voting, 1952–1988 **164**

Preface

No aspect of American government fascinates the American public and academicians more than the presidency and the forty-one incumbents who have occupied the nation's highest office. Books and monographs come off the press in an unending stream, and the publication pace shows no signs of slowing down. However, no full-length study of the American president as party leader has appeared in the twentieth century. This scholarly neglect is difficult to explain because all great nineteenth- and twentieth-century presidents have been powerful party leaders. Chapters and sections of books have been devoted to the president's party role, but they have always been incorporated into broader studies of the American chief executive. This text endeavors to fill this gap in American political literature.

Former White House staffer George Reedy has argued that presidents are most effective when they understand the political process and are deeply immersed in it. On the other side of the coin, those presidents who shunned politics and their party leadership role, or who lacked the necessary political skills, have been labeled failures. History shows that strong twentieth-century presidents—Woodrow Wilson, Franklin D. Roosevelt, and Lyndon B. Johnson—all used their party leadership position to the hilt in winning approval of their programs. Passage of landmark legislation associated with Wilson's "New Freedom," FDR's "New Deal," and Lyndon B. Johnson's "Great Society" and civil rights legislation would not have been possible without huge presidential party majorities in Congress. In the opening chapters, the rise of the president as party leader is discussed as well as his emergence as legislative leader in the twentieth century.

Since 1968, however, and even during six years of Eisenhower's two terms in the 1950s, the nation has experienced divided government— the presidency controlled by the Republicans and one or both houses of Congress in the hands of the Democrats—for twenty of the past twenty-four years. No longer can the president count on a unified government to help him push his legislative programs through Congress. Even Democratic President Jimmy Carter, with the Democrats in control of both houses of Congress, was unable to win support for many of his legislative initiatives.

Clearly, the Washington scene has changed dramatically since the days of President Franklin D. Roosevelt and the Kennedy-Johnson years. Divided government, the fragmentation of power, especially the "subcommitteeization" of Congress, the decline of party influence, and the pervading influence of the mass media have all affected the role of the president as party leader and the nation's chief magistrate. This book devotes a full chapter to the president's party role in a system of divided government, which in recent years seems to have become the norm, rather than the exception. As a result, recent presidents, faced with an assertive Congress, have shifted their leadership tactics and strategy.

More and more, presidents prefer "going public," that is, taking their policies and programs to the nation via television and frequent personal appearances across the country at national meetings of interest groups, fraternal organizations, business conferences, veterans' groups, and so on, to win support for White House policies. The president's role as party leader surfaces only infrequently. Instead, the president conducts the affairs of state as if he were still running for office, not presiding over the nation's public business.

Frequently, the modern president will cloak his political goals by portraying himself as "leader of all the people," appealing to the general public rather than partisans to win backing for his key domestic and foreign policy proposals. As a change of pace, the president may sometimes pursue a policy of "fighting the special interests," in pursuing his goals. The steady growth of independent and split-ticket voters also makes his "above politics" strategy more effective in reaching his objectives. The president's role as the "public president" is also discussed at length.

Still, every president discovers that when decision-making time arrives on key domestic and foreign policy issues, his own political party is still his most reliable ally in defending his policies against opposition-party critics. Although Presidents Reagan and Bush have often found themselves outnumbered by the opposition Democrats, both have skillfully used their own party members in Congress to win crucial bargaining points in executive-legislative negotiations. Also, they know they can usually count on their own party members in Congress to sustain presidential vetoes. In the first twenty months of the Bush administration, for example, Republican members were a crucial factor in keeping President Bush's veto record unblemished, with sixteen out of sixteen vetoes sustained. Without the solid backing of his GOP colleagues on Capitol Hill,

President Bush would have, in all likelihood, found himself a captive of the Democratic majority in Congress.

Over the years, a variety of institutional reforms—parliamentary government, the responsible parties model, simultaneous election of the president and members of Congress, Corwin's legislative cabinet, direct election of president, among others—have been advanced to strengthen the president's hand. All these reforms are carefully assessed—and then rejected—by the author, chiefly because they either create more institutional or constitutional problems than they solve or else they merely substitute one set of problems for another.

Despite the checks and balances of our Madisonian system, several twentieth-century presidents with strong party majorities in Congress have been able to overcome, at least in their first terms, the formidable institutional barriers built into the American system—the separation of powers, staggered terms of office, numerous Congressional committees and subcommittees, shared appointment and treaty-making powers—to achieve major policy reforms. This opportunity, narrow though it may seem at the moment, still remains open for a future Teddy Roosevelt, Woodrow Wilson, or Franklin D. Roosevelt who can capitalize on his party leadership and coalition-building skills.

This book would not have been completed without the invaluable help of several colleagues. I would especially like to thank Professor Charles A. Hadley, Jr., University of New Orleans and retired Professor Hugh A. Bone, University of Washington, for their insightful suggestions at several points in the manuscript. Professor Bone, it might be noted, was an original member of the 1950 American Political Science Association's Committee on Political Parties, whose famous report *Toward a More Responsible Two-Party System*, still remains a classic in the field.

Also, I have deeply appreciated the warm support and encouragement of Professor Kenneth A. Hoover, Chairman, Political Science Department, Western Washington University, and Professor Michael A. Genovese, Loyola Marymount University, Los Angeles. Nor would this study have been completed without the assistance of Maurice L. Schwartz, Dean of the Graduate School, Western Washington University; Geri Walker, Bureau for Faculty Research; and the editorial skills and word processing of Gail Fox and Suzanne Scally, Bureau for Faculty Research. Lorraine Robinson was also helpful in the early preparation of the manuscript.

Finally, I would like to remember my doctoral advisor, Professor Charles H. Backstrom, University of Minnesota, for his continued support and inspiration over the years, to whom I have dedicated this book.

The President as Party Leader

Chapter 1

Introduction

Among the many hats the president wears, none is more important to his long-term success than that of party leader. To be sure, a president can assure his place in history by an outstanding performance as commander-in-chief, as a shrewd foreign-policy maker, or for his landmark reform legislation on the domestic front. But unless he is skilled in the management of party affairs, especially in dealing with members of the coequal legislative branch, the president will not be able to achieve that esteemed place in history reserved for all our great presidents. Except Washington, who served in the preparty era, Jefferson, Jackson, Lincoln, Wilson, and Franklin D. Roosevelt were all outstanding party leaders, though Wilson faltered toward the end of his second term.

This chapter traces the rise of the president as party leader, noting that the Constitution contains no mention of this demanding role. The emergence of the national nominating convention and its profound influence upon the establishment of the president's independent political base are carefully analyzed. The modern presidency, which evolved early in the twentieth century, and the president's new party-related role as "chief legislator" are also examined. Executive leadership in the presidential and parliamentary systems is contrasted, as are the limited powers of the president as party leader in a separation-of-powers system. Finally, a preliminary evaluation of the party leadership role of our two most recent presidents—Reagan and Bush—rounds out the chapter.

CONSTITUTIONAL JOB DESCRIPTION MISSING

The reader of the United States Constitution will search in vain for a description of the president as party leader. Indeed, the Constitution is silent concerning any relationship that might exist between president and party. The reason is simple: the Constitution does not address the matter because

political parties were nonexistent at the time the Framers met in Philadelphia in 1787. In retrospect, it is plainly evident from a review of James
Madison's *Notes* on the Constitutional Convention proceedings that the
Framers did not want a president who would gain office by popular election; who would be a tribune of the people, a champion of popular majorities. Clearly, the Framers abhorred political parties, "factions," as
they were called at the time. The Founders viewed them as instruments
of dissension and discord. Authors of the *Federalist*, James Madison and
Alexander Hamilton, warned about the damaging effects of "factions"
upon the political life of the new nation.[1] President Washington, in his
farewell address, warned his countrymen about the disruptiveness of
parties, arguing that they were the tools of designing men intent upon
subverting the will of the majority to achieve their own selfish ends. His
successor, John Adams, echoed Washington's dire admonitions and
declared that "division of the republic into two great parties . . . is to be
dreaded as the greatest political evil under our Constitution.[2]

Despite these warnings, a two-party system suddenly emerged within a
few years of Washington's inauguration. Differences over economic policy
and the role of the national government in the new republic led to the
formation of political parties. To Hamilton and Thomas Jefferson, two
key members of Washington's cabinet, belongs a major share of the credit
for the rise of parties. Hamilton and Jefferson brought conflicting philos-
ophies of government into Washington's inner circle as they competed
for the president's support. Hamilton, the staunch nationalist, insisted on a
broad definition of federal powers, especially in fiscal matters. Jefferson,
the strict constructionist, emphasized the importance of local autonomy
and of limiting the power of the central government. Hamilton's supporters soon became known as Federalists and Jefferson's backers as
Anti-Federalists or Democratic-Republicans.

Early in Washington's second term, Jefferson resigned from the cabinet,
believing that Washington had sided with Hamilton on most major issues.
Jefferson's departure, if anything, intensified the conflict between the
Federalists and the Anti-Federalists and hastened the arrival of the two-
party system. In 1800, Jefferson challenged John Adams's bid for a second
term. With a far superior political organization and a much broader base
of popular support, Jefferson and his Democratic-Republicans defeated
Adams, ending the Federalists' twelve-year reign. Within a short time,
the party role of the president became grafted onto the office.

Jefferson wasted no time in assuming the role of party leader and utilizing this position to take over leadership of Congress. Few presidents
have matched Jefferson's record as party chieftain; indeed, it might be
said that Jefferson established the model for all future presidents to follow. Not all presidents have been strong party leaders, but it is beyond
dispute that no president can be rated as a dynamic chief executive unless

he is a strong party leader. Clearly, Jefferson, Jackson, Lincoln, Teddy Roosevelt, Wilson, Franklin D. Roosevelt, Truman, Kennedy, and Reagan all fit this category.

PRESIDENT'S SEPARATE ELECTORAL BASE FROM CONGRESS'S

During that long hot summer in Philadelphia at the Constitutional Convention, no issue consumed more time or generated more conflicting proposals among the Framers than the structure, powers, and method of election of the president of the United States.

Four major proposals were debated extensively. One choice—the Virginia Plan—was to establish a president who would be chosen by Congress for one term only. This option would have probably made the president a pawn of the legislature or, in times of emergency, possibly would have spawned a proconsul. Another choice was to create a Council of States as a plural executive to run the new government. This type of weak executive would have undoubtedly assured a system of legislative supremacy. Alexander Hamilton offered still another plan: a president elected for a life term by electors chosen by people within each state. The fourth choice was to establish an independent chief executive with specified powers who might assume the functions, if not the form, of the British Crown. After long debate the Framers opted for the fourth choice—the independent chief executive. Though the Framers envisaged a nonpartisan president whose election and capacity to govern did not depend on "the popular arts" of winning public support, they must have been more than mildly surprised at the remarkable speed with which their design for the presidency was replaced by a chief executive dependent on popular election and popular approval.[3]

From 1800 to the 1820s, the nomination of presidential candidates was in the hands of the Congressional nominating caucus; in other words, the members of the legislative branch selected the nominee. As Theodore Lowi has noted, "the main impact of caucus nominations was to convert the formal separation of powers between the president and Congress into a *de facto* 'fusion of powers' not unlike such parliamentary systems as the British."[4] Indeed, under the prevailing one-party rule of the period, nomination of presidential candidates by the congressional caucus, in effect, handed the decision on presidential selection to the Congress. Thus, the Framers' original separation-of-powers plan to have the election decided by presidential electors for the express purpose of avoiding selection by Congress was for over two decades subverted by the congressional caucus system. But the demise of "King Caucus" in 1824 (caused by the unresolved rivalries in the dominant Democratic-Republican party) led to a major shift in presidential selection—the emergence of the national nominating convention.

NATIONAL CONVENTIONS ESTABLISHED REAL SEPARATION OF POWERS

Beyond doubt, the demise of the congressional nominating caucus not only altered the character of the young political parties but also fundamentally transformed the presidency and the constitutional system as well. The rise of the popular favorite, Andrew Jackson, and the emergence of presidential nominations by national conventions, gave Jackson and succeeding presidents a base of power totally independent of Congress, cutting Congress off completely from the presidential selection process. This is transformation, not evident at the time, "established for the first time an institutionalized *real* separation of powers."[5] Moreover, the evolution of the national convention as a nominating device is closely intertwined with the evolution of the president's independent power base. Indeed, these extraconstitutional party conclaves, consisting of delegations chosen by state party organizations throughout the nation, fulfill an indispensable role in helping enhance the stature of the president as chief executive and party leader.[6]

Over the past 150 years, the national convention has profoundly influenced the evolution of the modern presidency. Had the Congressional nominating caucus, by some quirk of fate, survived as a method for nominating presidential candidates, the odds are high that the presidency would have but a faint resemblance to the powerful institutional chief executive that has emerged in the twentieth century.

POPULAR ELECTION CONFERS LEGITIMACY FOR EXERCISE OF EXECUTIVE POWER

The Framers, in drafting the Constitution, endeavored to protect the executive branch from popular democratic control. After prolonged debate, the men of 1787 decided on an indirect method—the electoral college—to select the president. Under this system, each state's electoral vote was determined by its number of U. S. representatives and senators: for example, a state with six representatives and two senators had eight electoral votes. These presidential electors, originally chosen by state legislatures, were expected to be men of property and stature within their states. It was anticipated that their presidential choice would be limited to a few well-qualified men, and it was presumed that the best man would be selected.

As the Framers envisaged the operation of the electoral college system, they believed that no candidate was likely to receive the Constitutional majority of electoral votes needed to win the presidency. Instead, they thought that with only a plurality winner in the electoral college, the final choice for president would actually be made by the House of Representatives, as stipulated in the Constitution, with each state (no matter how large or small) casting one vote. (This arrangement was especially pleasing to the small states since they would regain the equality they gave up in the electoral college.) While this procedure operated successfully in the Washington-Adams nonparty era, the emergence of political parties and the rise of popular democracy, especially in the new frontier states, soon changed the operation of the electoral college. Instead of their state legislatures handpicking presidential electors, the constitutions of most new states required that the electors be popularly elected. By the late 1820s, all states except South Carolina had switched to popularly elected presidential electors. Thus, the rapid expansion of manhood suffrage and the spread of popular election of presidential electors transformed presidential selection into a form of popular democracy.

Within a few years the presidential nominating process, too, went through a metamorphosis. Following the demise of "King Caucus" in 1824, states began experimenting with several decentralized presidential nominating methods: (1) state legislative caucuses; (2) state conventions; (3) "mixed" conventions composed of party members of the state legislature and independently elected delegates from counties and towns not represented in the legislature by the party holding the convention; and (4) public meetings or mass rallies. None of these decentralized nominating practices, however, met the needs of the young nation. Within a decade, the emergent parties turned to the national convention system, first used by the small Anti-Masonic party in 1831, to pick presidential candidates. When the newly formed Whig party held a national convention in 1840 to select its candidate—William Henry Harrison—the national nominating convention became a permanent element of the American party system.

By 1848, the national nominating convention had become completely divorced from the Congressional caucus, and that year marked the last time the Democratic congressional caucus issued a "call" for the party's convention. Henceforth, the newly established Democratic national committee issued the call for delegates and determined the time and place for the conclave. The Republican party, which held its first convention in 1856, soon copied this same party structure and plan for convening its national conclaves.

Beyond question, the national nominating convention was well suited for the young nation because

1. It divorced presidential nominations from congressional control.
2. It concentrated the party strength behind a single presidential ticket.
3. It reconciled personal rivalries and group or sectional interests.

4. It provided for a broad-based formulation of a party program.

5. It was representative in character.[7]

From the start, national conventions have made it possible for the peculiarly decentralized American parties to have their own national existence. Most important, the national convention system has concentrated the electorate behind the two major-party nominees, thus keeping the final presidential selection away from Congress and giving the president a base of support independent of the legislative branch. Clearly, the national convention has strengthened the nominee's ability not only to lead his party, but also—if successful at the polls—to lead the nation as well. Thus, it can be said that the national convention, though it has escaped constitutional regulation, has profoundly shaped the nature of the presidency as much as the party system itself.[8]

EARLY RISE OF PRESIDENT AS PARTY LEADER

Only four nineteenth-century presidents—Jefferson, Jackson, Polk, and Lincoln—can be classified as strong party leaders. It is significant that all four were elected before the outbreak of the Civil War. It seems doubtful, however, that any of these presidents would have achieved greatness simply on the basis of party stewardship alone. But party leadership was an important factor in their historical ratings. Because the presidential office was not endowed with constitutional authority for party leadership, the necessary powers evolved through forceful action of dynamic presidents whose position within the government was reinforced by the emergence and development of political parties.

Undoubtedly, Jefferson ranked as the foremost party leader of the nineteenth century. No president in the nineteenth or twentieth centuries worked more assiduously through his party to achieve his programmatic goals. Jefferson met almost daily with his congressional leaders to chart the legislative agenda. In the evenings, he dined with his leaders to discuss activities on Capitol Hill and to map party strategy for upcoming bills. Also, the door to his office was open for rank-and-file members as well to discuss legislative business. Still, Jefferson was careful to preserve, at least to outward appearance, the separation of powers between the executive and legislative branches. But his role as leader of the Democratic-Republican (later simply Democratic) party enabled him to bridge this wall of separation almost as often as needed by the exigencies of the day.

Andrew Jackson ranks near the top of all presidential party leaders. The "Hero of New Orleans" in the War of 1812, Jackson became a strong Democratic party leader even before he reached the White House. Jackson was denied the presidency in 1824, even though he won a plurality in the electoral college, by the so-called "corrupt bargain" between John

Quincy Adams and Henry Clay. Jackson and his supporters claimed that
Clay agreed to have his state supporters in the House of Representatives
(each state casts one vote as required by the Constitution in the event no
candidate has received a majority of votes in the electoral college) vote
for Adams for president. In return, Adams agreed to choose Clay as
secretary of state in the new administration. Thoroughly incensed by the
Adams-Clay deal, Jackson and his adherents immediately began organizing support, especially in the South and West, for his 1828 White House
drive. So successful was Jackson in the 1828 election campaign that he
overwhelmed President Adams, winning the electoral college vote 178
to 83.

The Jacksonian inaugural festivities were still winding down when
Jackson and his managers began a wholesale removal of Adams's officials—"throwing the rascals out"—to be replaced by staunch Jacksonian
partisans. This "spoils system," first developed by Jefferson, reached a
new high in the Jackson administration; and abetted by his dedicated
supporters in the House and Senate, Jackson dominated the federal government to a degree few successors have matched.

Jackson viewed himself as the "tribune of the people." The foundation
for this conception of the presidential office rested heavily on his powerful
hold over the dominant Democratic party and the rapidly expanding
electorate. As head of both party and government, Jackson persuaded
Congress to follow his lead, thus allowing him to assume even greater
control over government and public affairs. "Old Hickory," as he was
affectionately called by the party faithful, assumed that his popular mandate gave him the authority to define issues, set the national agenda,
and to push his pet legislation through Congress.

Derided as "King Andrew the First" by his political enemies, Jackson
nevertheless let Congress know that he considered himself the true and
sole representative of all the people and stated further that his responsibility lay with the American people. As Robert V. Remini, the Jacksonian
scholar, put it,

With Jackson, the chief executive no longer served simply as the head of a coordinate branch of the government; no longer was he restricted in his actions by
what the Congress would allow him. Henceforth, he could assert himself as the
spokesman of all the people and by the skillful use of his powers force the legislature to follow his lead. This did not free him from the political necessity of working
with Congress to accomplish the public will, but it did allow him to assume greater
control of the government and to dominate and direct public affairs.[9]

Jackson's "plebiscitarian" conception of the presidency unquestionably
expanded the power and influence of the nation's highest office. However, critics have pointed out that the Jacksonian presidency contained
the seeds of what historian Arthur M. Schlesinger, Jr. later termed "the

Imperial Presidency.''[10] Be that as it may, Jackson demonstrated that a charismatic president, with the united backing of his party and a dominant majority in Congress, can overcome the barriers and obstacles of the formidable separation-of-powers system constructed by the Founding Fathers.

President James K. Polk, often overlooked by party historians, demonstrated during his single term in the White House that a president with firm control over his party can compile a remarkable record of achievement. The ''Sly Polk,'' as he was called by his critics, was nominated by the 1844 Democratic Convention on the ninth ballot as a dark-horse candidate over former President Van Buren. Frequently underestimated by his rivals, Polk had earlier served as speaker of the House—the only occupant of that position ever to reach the White House. A former Jackson lieutenant, Polk soon proved his firm grasp of the power levers in Washington. Faced with the mounting slavery controversy and border disputes with newly independent Mexico, as well as Great Britain in the Oregon territory, Polk relied on his party leadership in Congress to back his expansionist policies. His bold tactics led to a victorious war with Mexico—one of the more sordid chapters in American history. In the subsequent peace treaty, the Mexican government was forced to cede a land tract almost the size of the Louisiana Purchase, which included the states of California, Arizona, New Mexico, Nevada and portions of Utah and Colorado. In the Pacific Northwest, Polk and his emissaries negotiated a successful settlement of the Oregon territory with Great Britain, which established the northern boundary at 49 degrees north latitude, not the natural boundary of the Columbia River. His fiery rhetoric and skillful negotiating meant that the territory that now constitutes the entire state of Washington remained under the Stars and Stripes rather than the Union Jack. Polk, long a victim of ill health, retired after a single term and died only three months after leaving office. He was only fifty-five years old.[11]

While President Abraham Lincoln is always remembered for having saved the Union during the nation's bloodiest conflict, his party leadership talents have often been overlooked. But, as the late political scientist Wilfred E. Binkley has noted: ''No president entered the great office more adept in the high art of politics than Abraham Lincoln.''[12] Indeed, no president in the nineteenth century spent more time reviewing patronage requests than Lincoln. A survey of his correspondence and official actions shows that the Civil War president spent a sizable share of each working day on patronage matters. Even the relentless demands of the war effort did not prevent him from dealing with political appointments.

Soon after the outbreak of the Civil War, the composition of the Republican party began to change as more War Democrats came over to the GOP. For the duration of the conflict, the Republicans and northern Democrats, with Lincoln's full endorsement, adopted the name the

Union party. Lincoln had no hesitancy in using party patronage extensively to help cement ties with the Union party in states, cities, counties, and precincts. Post office appointments were generously distributed to Union partisans, and when the supply ran low, Lincoln turned to the creation of captains, colonels, and brigadier generals to keep them out of the Democratic party. In Lincoln's mind, preservation of the Union justified his utilizing military patronage to achieve this supreme goal.

Even in the midst of the bloody Civil War, Lincoln managed to keep an eye on the 1864 election. He did not hesitate to ask generals in the field to furlough soldiers to go home to vote in close elections in those states that had not authorized their soldiers to cast ballots in the field. In a letter to General William T. Sherman, sent by a special messenger, Lincoln suggested: "Anything you can safely do to let [Indiana's] soldiers, or any part of them to go home and vote at the state election will be greatly in point. They need not remain for the presidential election, but may return to you at once."[13] Sherman obliged not only by granting wholesale furloughs to Indiana's soldiers but also by sending two of his generals, Blair and Logan, home to make campaign speeches. Union party victories in the October state elections heralded Lincoln's reelection in November.

In 1864 Lincoln also used party patronage blatantly to help secure ratification of the Thirteenth Amendment, which abolished slavery. Lacking one state to obtain the needed two-thirds vote, Lincoln sent his emissary, Charles A. Dana, on a special mission to win the support of two congressmen whose votes were necessary to get Nevada admitted to the Union—and to provide the extra votes required for ratification of the new amendment. As Dana recounted the event some years later, Lincoln declared: "Whatever promise you make to them I will do."[14] Subsequently, Nevada was admitted to the Union and the Thirteenth Amendment was ratified.

ABSENCE OF PARTY LEADERSHIP DURING THE "POSTAGE STAMP" PRESIDENCY ERA

As indicated in the previous section, only a handful of presidents before the Civil War displayed notable ability as party leaders. In the post–Civil War era, weak party leadership characterized all the presidents, with the possible exception of Grover Cleveland. That the "postage stamp" presidents failed to assume the reins of power is not surprising. Lincoln's assassination removed a powerful leader and gave the Radical Republicans in Congress the needed opening to reassert their influence over both the legislative and executive branches. Andrew Johnson's impeachment trial (he avoided removal by a single vote) and Grant's scandal-ridden two terms provided congressional leaders an unmatched opportunity to dominate the government. Nor were the presidents of the Gilded Age perceived as leaders of public opinion or chief legislators. In contrast to the twentieth century, with its frequent diplomatic confrontations among the great powers, foreign affairs played only a minor role in the nation's capital. America's destiny focused on internal development, building factories, expanding the railroad system, and exploiting the land; presidents were content to stand by passively as congressional leaders handled most of the decision making. It was therefore not coincidence that political scientist Woodrow Wilson, the future twenty-eighth president of the United States, called his first major treatise *Congressional Government*.[15] Furthermore, state party leaders at the national nominating conventions were not looking for charismatic leaders. They preferred "safe" candidates who would not upset the status quo.

America's emergence as a world power following victory in the Spanish-American War (1898), however, opened the door for several presidents who were willing to face the mounting challenges of the twentieth century.

THE MODERN PRESIDENCY AND PARTY LEADERSHIP

Theodore Roosevelt might be described as the first modern president. The supercharged former Rough Rider never hesitated to utilize the full powers of the office to face the problems of an emerging industrial society and the highly competitive international community. Not only did President Theodore Roosevelt invent the "stewardship theory," that the president should take whatever action is necessary to meet the nation's problems so long as it did not conflict directly with the Constitution, but he also developed the modern roles of the president as leader of public opinion in the "bully pulpit" and chief legislator. To accomplish his goals, however, Roosevelt used his position as party leader to help push his priority legislative measures through Congress.

The model party leader in the White House before the New Deal, however, was Woodrow Wilson. Five years before his inauguration, Wilson, then president of Princeton University, had noted in observing Teddy Roosevelt in action the growing popular tendency to recognize the president "as the unifying force in our complex system, the leader both of his party and the nation."[16] A warm admirer of the British parliamentary system, Wilson had this advice for the White House occupant: "He must be the leader of his party. He is the party's choice and is responsible for carrying out the party platform. He therefore should have a large influence in determining legislation."[17] Furthermore, Wilson stated that the president "cannot escape being the leader of his party except by incapacity and lack of personal force because he is at once the choice of the party and nation."[18]

To be sure, Wilson's leadership task was simplified by a huge Democratic congressional majority, consisting mostly of first-term congressmen who were especially responsive to party discipline. His handling of the Underwood Tariff Act was particularly noteworthy. At his urging, the Ways and Means Committee began working on the bill weeks before the inauguration. Within three weeks after moving into the White House, Wilson had a complete draft of the bill and announced his full support of the proposed legislation. He consulted with the Democratic caucus, and after a thorough study there, the membership took it to the floor of the House. Without even a motion to limit debate, the bill passed virtually intact by a large majority. Unlike his predecessors, Wilson then personally addressed the Senate, urging passage of the tariff bill.

In keeping with his views on party responsibility, Wilson reportedly twice considered resigning during his presidency, in the fashion of the British prime minister, if Congress rejected two major administrative measures—the repeal of the exemption of American vessels from Panama Canal tolls and the McLenmore Resolution warning American citizens against traveling on armed vessels of belligerents. But he was sustained in Congress both times.[19]

Two decades later, in the midst of the Great Depression, Franklin D. Roosevelt entered the White House as the most adept politician of his time. Blessed with solid Democratic majorities in both houses of Congress, FDR mounted the famous "Hundred Days" legislative program in 1933, which produced more social and economic legislation than the country had ever seen before. When bills dealing with the economic crisis were pending, congressmen came to the White House seeking patronage rewards—but FDR held them off with the coyly whispered information: "We haven't got to patronage yet!"[20] FDR was not prepared to dispense jobs and federal contracts until the lawmakers had earned them with their votes.

Roosevelt's party leadership became more systematic after the Hundred Days, but by the time he was ready to announce his second-term reelection plans in 1936, his legislative accomplishments included the Social Security Act, the Wagner Act (authorizing collective bargaining), the Securities Exchange Act, the Federal Deposit Insurance Corporation, and a host of other New Deal measures. But as other chief executives before him have discovered, a president's party leadership influence seldom carries far into his second term.[21]

Roosevelt's "court-packing" plan, announced early in 1937 after the Supreme Court had invalidated more than a dozen of his pet New Deal measures, led to a rapid deterioration of his party influence on Capitol Hill. Many Democratic legislators, especially from the South, deserted the Roosevelt ranks. Indeed, the only major bill passed during Roosevelt's second term bearing FDR's special stamp of approval was the Fair Labor Standards Act of 1938 (which established a minimum federal wage and, in effect, abolished child labor).[22] From that point on, Roosevelt shifted his major attention abroad to battle Nazism, Fascism, and the Japanese militarists.

Even so, FDR left a mark on the Democratic party that remained for nearly four decades. He had inherited a badly tattered minority party, consisting of big city bosses and southern and western farmers, held together by states' rights doctrine and periodic spurts of Progressivism. From this base he built an alliance of northern city bosses, labor unions, blacks and other minority groups, intellectuals, and low-income farmers into a majority coalition that dominated the American scene, except for the Eisenhower presidency, until the Vietnam War.

Ronald Reagan, though not generally concerned with the intricacies of day-to-day party management, nevertheless displayed a firm grasp of party matters and legislative leadership. Although faced with a Democratically controlled House of Representatives, Reagan used his political skill and the GOP-controlled Senate to obtain passage of three high-priority items—tax cuts, a reduced domestic budget, and increased military spending—during the first eight months of his administration.[23] Though Reagan was unable to maintain this legislative momentum in subsequent years, especially after the GOP lost control of the U. S. Senate in the 1986 mid-term elections, he nevertheless continued to work effectively as party leader. With the support of the GOP national committee and extensive use of sophisticated political technology—satellite broadcast hookups with congressional candidates across the land and computerized direct-mail fundraising—Reagan, in the 1982 off-year election, lent a helping hand to the Republican party whenever needed. He did dozens of television and radio spots for congressional candidates, and he also helped with party fundraising.

CONTRAST OF EXECUTIVE LEADERSHIP IN PRESIDENTIAL AND PARLIAMENTARY SYSTEMS

In recent years several presidential nominees have become the nation's chief executive without a congressional majority of their party in either chamber. Since 1952, American presidents have been saddled with a divided government (with one or both houses held by the opposition party) for twenty-six out of forty years.

By contrast, the British prime minister is assured a party majority in Parliament. Indeed, it is impossible to split a ballot in the parliamentary system because each British voter casts a ballot not for prime minister but for a single member in the House of Commons. The prime minister, at least in the Conservative party, is selected by a majority in the House of Commons. (The Labour party formerly used this system, but recent reforms give trade unions and party constituents a partial voice in the leadership selection process.) Moreover, the prime minister is the team captain, and he or she calls all the signals in the huddle. Thus, the prime minister enters office as the leader of a united party with a strong commitment to party programs and a mandate from the electorate. Equally important, the prime minister is in a position to carry out these policies. It is also noteworthy that when the Conservatives are the opposition party, the Conservative party leader is acknowledged as the chief spokesman and organizational leader of "Her Majesty's Loyal Opposition" as the prime minister is of the governing party.[24]

Americans choose a president, not a party. As the British observer Anthony King has noted, the American governmental system permits the accession to office by presidents who may have had little national political experience and minimal or no acquaintance with, to say nothing of preexisting support among, members of the legislative branch.[25] The newly elected president of the United States in the fragmented, decentralized American party system usually wins office not through an effective nationwide party organization but by virtue of a personally recruited, independent campaign organization. This team, consisting mostly of media specialists, advance men, TV schedulers, pollsters, and accountants, has worked for him on the "long march" through the primary season, to the convention, and through the general election campaign. More often than not, the victorious presidential nominee will have had limited contact with his party leaders in Congress. The new White House occupant owes them virtually nothing for his victory. Members of Congress, in turn, owe him nothing, since usually they have polled larger electoral majorities in their states and districts than the presidential candidate. Unlike the collective discipline that the prime minister enjoys in Parliament, the president has to build his governing coalition from scratch.[26]

Most Western democracies, it might be noted, do not elect their chief executives independently from the legislature. Instead, the executive occupies his or her ruling position in the government by virtue of party leadership in the legislative branch or, in a coalition government, by bargaining with the leaders of the other coalition members. Furthermore, a parliamentary leader's tenure, unlike the fixed term of the American president, depends upon the support of the party members.

Under the American separation-of-powers system, the president has only a limited means for imposing his will on members of his party in Congress. First of all, the president and members of Congress answer to different constituencies. The presidential constituency covers the entire country, but a representative's constituency is restricted to a single district within a state and a senator's to a single state. On paper at least, none owe their election to their fellow officeholders, even though the president's constituency overlaps the other two. Frequently, the voters within

a state or congressional district may vote for a president from one party
and members of Congress from the other. This split-ticket voting clearly
undermines the president's influence over members of Congress. Nor
does the president have any direct control over the selection of the party
leaders in Congress. Both houses function through their own party
organizations. The speaker of the House and the majority leader of the
Senate, as well as their minority party counterparts, are elected by their
colleagues in each chamber, not appointed by the president.

LIMITED POWER AS PARTY LEADER

Presidential scholar Richard M. Pious has concluded that "no president
is an effective party leader."[27] The separation of powers and the confederate nature of the American party organization are, in Pious's view,
"anti-presidential" for they prevent incumbents from dominating Congress, and they decentralize power throughout the federal system. The
thesis espoused throughout this book, however, is that while the president faces numerous constraints in our Madisonian system of checks
and balances, he nevertheless can, if he has the inclination and leadership
drive, use his party ties to lead the nation to new heights. But the president often finds the political cards stacked against him. Although it is a
common practice to refer to the president as leader of his political party,
the fact is that the president has no formal position in the party structure.
Even though he is considered the titular leader, the president's influence
over his party does not extend to congressional campaign committees or
to state and local parties. His dominance is confined to the national committee—he personally chooses the national chairman, and the committee
invariably ratifies his choice without dissent.

The constitutional separation of powers denies the president the tools
of discipline that are always available to prime ministers in parliamentary
systems, and party discipline in the United States is therefore of limited
utility to the president. A prime minister operates in a system in which
discipline and unity are indispensable elements. If the prime minister
fails to carry his party in a vote of confidence, he or she resigns and asks
the monarch or other head of state to call new elections. But rarely does
a prime minister lose confidence votes. Consequently, he is in full command, not only of the executive branch or cabinet but also of the legislative
branch. Unlike the prime minister, the president as party leader has no
power over the nomination of any candidate for Congress, nor can he
block the renomination of any recalcitrant member of Congress. He lacks
the powerful sanctions or appealing rewards with which to influence the
voting behavior of individual federal legislators. Patronage appointments,
which formerly served as bargaining chips to reward congressional party
loyalty to the administration, have almost dried up as a result of repeated
expansion of civil service job protection and greater emphasis on merit

hiring in the federal service. Occasionally, however, the president will find an appointive position in the executive branch for a defeated senatorial or congressional candidate or a lame duck member.

One veteran president watcher has observed: "At most, the president can be only a quasi-party leader."[28] A combination of forces and pressures has dictated that the president can be only a quasi-leader. The decentralized confederate party system in the United States, in which the bulk of power rests in fifty state parties, means that the president has no influence over the nomination of congressional candidates or prospective governors who might be willing to follow the president's lead in party or government affairs. They are all nominated in their districts or states by direct primary elections.

When an incumbent president loses his reelection bid, his influence over his party usually evaporates overnight. Former President Jimmy Carter soon learned that he was an unwanted guest at national and state party conclaves after his defeat in 1980. Not until the 1988 Democratic National Convention, held in Atlanta, Georgia—Carter's home state—did the national party organization put out the welcome mat for the former president. Since then, friends and foes alike have praised Carter's public service contributions: monitoring elections in Panama, personally doing carpenter work in constructing houses in the New York slums, and offering his services as a mediator in the Middle East. Nor has he engaged in the blatant commercialization of the presidential office as former Presidents Ford, Reagan, and to a lesser extent, Richard Nixon have done through exorbitant speaking fees and huge book contracts.

PRESIDENTS TURN TO POPULAR APPEAL

Deprived of a strong party organization in the decentralized American party system, the president must depend heavily upon public support, his personal magnetism, and his ability to work with congressional leaders if he is to achieve his political and legislative goals. Actually, recent presidents seem to have become resigned to the decline of party influence. Instead, they have turned to television to win popular support for their programs and develop heavy pressure on Congress to endorse their initiatives. Presidential speeches today are not really directed to the local audiences they are addressing but rather to millions of Americans viewing the TV clips on the network evening newscasts, or the twenty-four-hour, around-the-clock Cable News Network (CNN). No president has been more adept than Ronald Reagan, with the possible exception of Kennedy, before the TV cameras. His ability to clarify complex issues through a simple, straightforward, smoothly delivered message has made him one of the most effective party leaders since Franklin D. Roosevelt. Similarly, his successor, George Bush, has followed in his mentor's footsteps in relying on television far more than his party in dealing with

Congress. Early in 1990, President Bush, facing Democrats in control of both houses of Congress with their knives out to cut the $295-billion defense budget, especially in light of rapid disintegration of the Soviet empire in Eastern Europe, did not turn to his Republican colleagues on Capitol Hill to save the day. Instead, he jumped on Air Force One for a cross-continental junket to address and review U.S. Army troops on their war-game maneuvers at Fort Irwin, California, in the Mojave desert. This "photo opportunity" was, of course, intended to demonstrate his staunch support of the Pentagon's budget and to forestall sharp cuts. On the return trip, he stopped off at the huge Strategic Air Command (SAC) base in Nebraska, clambered into the cockpit of a B-1 bomber and sat at the controls, to reemphasize his point. Incidentally, President Bush combined some party business on his 6,000-mile tour; he addressed major party fundraising events for gubernatorial candidates in both of these states.[29] Clearly, the chief purpose of the trip was to forestall cuts in the Pentagon budget, not to help the GOP contenders.

Once again, President Bush demonstrated how television has largely replaced party negotiation between the president and Congress. In Bush's case, since he faced an opposition Congress, his only real hope of winning the battle of the military budget was to go over the heads of the Capitol Hill lawmakers and plead his case to the American people on the televised newscasts. As Thomas E. Cronin has put it, "Presidents are instructed by their pollsters and marketing managers to rely on popular appeal and encourage popular leadership rather than party leadership."[30]

Under such circumstances, it is no surprise that the role of the president as party leader has been heavily discounted. Especially for Republican presidents, they have had to turn to popular leadership, not to their party, to win approval of their programs. During the twenty-eight years the GOP has controlled the White House since 1952, presidents have operated under divided government for twenty-six. Only President Eisenhower, in the first two years of his first term (1953–1955), had a Republican congressional majority in both houses to back his programs. Small wonder Republican presidents have turned to alternate avenues for implementing their programs. They are, in effect, forced to operate in a "no-party" context. Unless Republican presidents can attract Democratic votes to build cross-coalition majorities, they will be forced "to go public" and take their case directly to the American people via national telecasts.

SUMMARY

The president as party leader is in an extraconstitutional position. Since the Founders drafted the Constitution during the preparty era, no mention is made of this presidential responsibility that usually holds the key to his success or failure. All the great presidents, except Washington, have been outstanding party leaders.

More than anything else, political parties have enabled strong presidents to establish their independent power base and to combine their party leadership role and chief executive duties into a dominant force in American government. Transformation of the electoral college from an elite decision-making body into an instrument of popular democracy has bestowed upon the president a level of legitimacy and power not far below that of a Roman proconsul. As leader of the nation and his party, the president has become the "tribune of the people." Still, the separation of powers, especially Congress's power of the purse, serve as an institutional check upon excessive presidential ambition. Also, the fact that party leaders in the legislative branch operate independently and are in no way beholden to the president has often restrained presidential leadership. Unlike the British prime minister who, through his or her party leadership, can control the executive and legislative functions in the parliamentary system, the president is at best, in Louis Koenig's words, a "quasi-party leader."

Frustrated by the separation of powers and fragmented party system, modern presidents have turned increasingly to nationwide televised addresses and numerous public appearances to plead their case and try to overcome congressional resistance to presidential initiatives.

The next chapter focuses on the emergence of the president as party leader in the age of party reform.

NOTES

1. *The Federalist* (New York: New American Library, 1961), No. 51.
2. Robert V. Remini, "The Emergence of Political Parties and Their Effect on the Presidency," in Phillip C. Dolce and George H. Skau, eds., *Power and the Presidency* (New York: Scribner's, 1976), p. 25.
3. Robert A. Dahl, "Myth of the Presidential Mandate," *Political Science Quarterly* 105 (Fall 1990), p. 366.
4. Theodore J. Lowi, "Party, Policy and Constitution in America," in William Nisbet Chambers and Walter Dean Burnham, eds., *The American Party System* (New York: Oxford University Press, 1967), p. 248, as cited by Austin Ranney, *Curing the Mischiefs of Faction* (Berkeley: The University of California Press, 1975), p. 173.
5. Ibid., 173–174.
6. James W. Davis, *National Nominating Conventions in an Age of Party Reform* (Westport, CT: Greenwood, 1983), pp. 30–31.
7. Eugene H. Roseboom, *A History of Presidential Elections* (New York: Macmillan, 1957), p. 106.
8. Davis, *National Conventions in an Age of Party Reform*, p. 31.
9. Robert V. Remini, *The Life of Andrew Jackson* (New York: Penguin, 1990), p. 270.

10. Arthur M. Schlesinger, Jr., *The Imperial Presidency* (Boston: Houghton Mifflin, 1973).

11. David M. Pletcher, "James K. Polk," in Henry F. Graff, ed., *The Presidents: A Reference History* (New York: Scribner's, 1984), pp. 183–205.

12. Wilfred E. Binkley, *The Man in the White House*, rev. ed. (New York: Harper and Row, 1958), p. 102.

13. Ibid., p. 102.

14. Charles A. Dana, *Recollections of the Civil War* (New York, 1898), p. 174, as quoted by Wilfred E. Binkley, "The President as Chief Legislator," *Annals of the American Academy of Political and Social Science* 307 (September, 1956), pp. 92–105.

15. Woodrow Wilson, *Congressional Government* (Boston: Houghton Mifflin, 1885).

16. Woodrow Wilson, *Constitutional Government in the United States* (New York: Columbia University Press, 1908), p. 54.

17. Ibid., pp. 60–61.

18. Ibid., p. 67.

19. Binkley, *The Man in the White House*, p. 108.

20. Ibid., p. 109.

21. James W. Davis, *The American Presidency: A New Perspective* (New York: Harper and Row, 1987), p. 288.

22. Frank Freidel, *Franklin D. Roosevelt: A Rendezvous with Destiny* (Boston: Little, Brown, 1990), pp. 281–282.

23. See Barbara Kellerman, *The Political Presidency* (New York: Oxford University Press, 1984), Chap. 11.

24. Richard Rose, *The Postmodern President* (Chatham, N.J.: Chatham House, 1988), pp. 104–107.

25. Anthony S. King, "How Not to Select Presidential Candidates: A View from Europe," in Austin Ranney, ed., *The American Elections of 1980* (Washington, D.C.: American Enterprise Institute, 1981), pp. 303–328.

26. Austin Ranney, "The President and His Party," in Anthony S. King, ed., *Both Ends of the Avenue* (Washington, D.C.: American Enterprise Institute, 1983), p. 143.

27. Richard M. Pious, *The American Presidency* (New York: Basic Books, 1979), p. 120.

28. Louis W. Koenig, *The Chief Executive*, 4th ed. (New York: Harcourt Brace Jovanovich, 1981), p. 149.

29. *The New York Times*, February 7, 1990.

30. Thomas E. Cronin, "Presidents and Political Parties," in Thomas E. Cronin, ed., *Rethinking the Presidency* (Boston: Little, Brown, 1982), p. 291.

Chapter 2

Emergence of the Party Leader: Nominating and General Election Campaigns

Over the past three decades, the presidential nominating system has undergone a major transformation. Indeed, early twentieth-century commentators would, if they could see it, shake their heads in disbelief over the remarkable shift from the old-fashioned "brokered" system of state delegation leaders picking presidential nominees in "smoke-filled" rooms to the new system of participatory democracy that finds rank-and-file voters selecting the party nominee in the presidential primaries and caucuses.

This development and the shifting role of the national convention from a decision-making body to a coronation ceremony anointing the victor in the primaries is closely examined in the opening section of the chapter. Under this "freelance" nominating system, incumbent presidents are no longer automatically guaranteed renomination, though so far they have successfully warded off their challengers. Major attention is focused on the emergence of the candidates' television-dominated national election campaign, fully funded by federal taxpayer dollars ($46.1 million in 1988) since passage of the Federal Election Campaign Act of 1974.

Under the new system of candidate-centered campaigning, the party nominees operate almost as if the party were nonexistent. Federal matching funds help underwrite the candidate's nominating race, and the full tab for his general election campaign—if he agrees not to accept private funding—is picked up by Uncle Sam, not party supporters. Under these circumstances the reasons for the decline of party influence are understandable. Moreover, because the presidential candidates reach most voters via television, the candidates no longer have to depend upon party regulars and precinct captains to deliver the campaign message. Finally, it is emphasized that the plebiscitary nominating system and the "non-party" campaign of the president-elect is more likely to produce better campaigners than chief executives.

RISE OF THE PLEBISCITARY NOMINATING SYSTEM

Until the early 1970s, presidential candidates captured the nomination the old-fashioned way: they won the support of state party leaders and their delegations through a "mixed" caucus–primary system that sometimes involved smoke-filled-room deliberations. To be sure, a dozen or so states had held presidential primaries since 1912, permitting rank-and-file voters to express their individual preference for president and also to elect delegates to the national conventions. But most of these popularly elected delegates were unpledged. Nearly three-quarters of the states still used the insider, caucus-convention system. Thus, a candidate such as Senator Estes Kefauver in 1952 could win twelve out of fourteen primaries and still lose the nomination because state party leaders and big city bosses decided that he was "unsafe" and that Governor Adlai E. Stevenson of Illinois would be a more dependable, middle-of-the-road candidate.[1] In short, both the Republican and Democratic parties still selected nominees in the same traditional manner that national conventions had used to nominate such leaders as Abraham Lincoln, Teddy Roosevelt, Woodrow Wilson, and Franklin D. Roosevelt, and other, less well known nominees.

With the rapid spread of television and the growing nationalization of the two-party system, this traditional system was transformed in less than a decade into a vast national popularity contest. John F. Kennedy, in 1960, was among the first national contenders to recognize that the limited number of presidential primaries could be used to demonstrate widespread popular support to convince state party leaders that he—a young war hero, a Pulitzer Prize winner, a member of a famous family, and a Roman Catholic—deserved the nomination over more senior challengers, including Senate Majority Leader Lyndon B. Johnson.[2] Kennedy also had broad support in a number of caucus states, but his bold new campaign strategy of running strong in the primaries pointed the way toward revision of the nominating system.

In 1968, however, when Vice President Hubert H. Humphrey was nominated even though he had not contested a single primary, the uproar from party reformers, especially the followers of defeated candidate Eugene McCarthy, led to major nomination reforms in the Democratic party. By 1972, seven additional states had adopted presidential primaries; four years later, another seven states joined the presidential primary club. By 1980, more than thirty states, including nine of the ten most populous, were using primaries. Equally important, optional delegate pledges were changed to mandatory pledges. Thus, presidential contenders could no longer strike deals with state party leaders. Under the pledged delegate system, the leaders no longer controlled their delegations. Instead, the rank-and-file voters determined which candidates state delegates would be pledged to support. Under this new system, the popular choice in the primaries became the party nominee. Briefly, then, participatory democracy has become the watchword, and the number of Americans involved in the presidential nominating system has risen steadily.

Between 1968 and 1984, the number of participants in the Democratic primaries increased from twelve million to nearly eighteen million.[3] Also, the Republicans experienced comparable turnouts in several of the nominating races. As a result, the transformation of the presidential nominating system has shifted the decision making from an insider's game to one of participatory democracy, indeed, almost a plebiscitarian system. No longer can a leading contender rely on state party leaders to tip the nomination in his direction. Instead, a serious contender now forms his own self-contained campaign organization, complete with fund-raisers, pollsters, accountants, media specialists, and schedulers, to mount his drive for the White House.

By contrast, in the British parliamentary system the leader of the Conservative party is chosen by party members in the House of Commons, and the leader of the largest party in Parliament becomes the prime minister.

In this "nonparty" era the two major American parties have virtually no role in nominating races, except to convene the national conventions, which in effect anoint the winners of the primaries as party standard-bearers.[4] Nor is the nominee necessarily the choice of a majority of voters in the primaries. Four of the five most recent Democratic nominees have been the choice of far less than a majority of voters. In 1976, for example, Jimmy Carter received only 39 percent of the popular vote in the primaries. Four years earlier, Senator George McGovern, the Democratic nominee, was the choice of only 30 percent of the Democratic voters. More recently, Walter Mondale, in 1984, collected only 39 percent of the primary votes; and in 1988, Massachusetts Governor Michael Dukakis received 43 percent. Only in 1980, when President Carter was seeking renomination, did the Democratic nominee—Carter—receive a majority of the votes in the primary.

What is the explanation for this plebiscitarian phenomenon? The reason is that in a crowded field of candidates, the more contenders there are, the more likely that the nominee will be the first choice of a minority of primary voters. Thus, in the six-candidate Democratic field in 1984,

Mondale eventually emerged the victor with less than 40 percent of the Democratic vote.[5] In this type of round-robin competition, some candidates drop out of the race after a few primaries, meaning that their primary vote goes for naught. Furthermore, voters in primary states holding their elections in late April, May, or early June may find that the nominating race is, in effect, over because the popular favorite has already collected a majority of the convention delegates.

Amendments to the Federal Election Campaign Act of 1974, which provides federal matching dollars in the nominating campaign to candidates who qualify, may have speeded up the "winnowing out" of weak candidates relatively early in the race. Under the revised Federal Election Commission (FEC) rules, a presidential candidate who receives less than 10 percent of the popular vote in two successive primaries loses eligibility for federal matching funds. The only way a candidate can regain eligibility is to collect 20 percent or more of the popular vote in a subsequent primary. Thus far, only one candidate—Jesse Jackson in 1984—has overcome this FEC-imposed hurdle.[6] Over the past two presidential elections, this drying up of federal matching funds has helped convince several candidates to throw in the towel early and leave the nominating race to more affluent contenders.

Within the Republican party, there have been far fewer minority nominees. Twice in the past five races, GOP presidents—Nixon and Reagan—have easily won renomination. In 1976, the appointed president, Gerald Ford, seeking his first regular nomination, defeated his only challenger, former California Governor Ronald Reagan, in a tight race. In 1980 and 1988, the front-runners, Reagan and Bush, lapped the field by impressive showings in the early primaries and thus knocked out all other rivals long before convention time.

TELEVISION AND PRINT JOURNALISTS INHERIT THE INFLUENCE OF PARTY POWER BROKERS

The vacuum left by the "decomposition" of political parties has been filled by the mass media. Indeed, the mass media have absorbed or taken over a number of the democratic functions traditionally performed by political parties: handicapping the political contenders, elevating key issues, promoting new leaders, and criticizing the administration's performance or the role of the political opposition. Unlike yesteryear's parties, the media inform voters about who the candidates are, their personalities, and stands on the issues. Formerly, the voters were contacted by the party's ward heelers; now voters acquire their information about upcoming elections from television, radio, and the print media.

Presidential candidates and their managers know that in a high-stakes race their future prospects depend heavily on network and local television rather than on their party's efforts. To reach millions of prospective voters in this vast nation, candidates turn to network and local television because it is the only way to reach this huge electorate. Political parties in the fifty states—many of them in various stages of disrepair—simply do not have the trained personnel or funds to perform this gargantuan task.

THE NATIONAL CONVENTION AND THE PRESIDENTIAL NOMINEE'S INDEPENDENT POWER BASE

Before the rise of national conventions, in the first quarter of the nineteenth century, presidents were beholden to the congressional nominating caucus because they owed their nomination to members of Congress.

During the transitional period (1824–1836) the decentralized nomination system, which relied on state legislative caucuses, state conventions, "mixed" caucus–public meetings, and mass meetings to nominate candidates added little to the stature of the president as an independent national leader. In 1836, the newly emergent Whig party (formed mainly from elements of the defunct National Republican party and anti-Jackson Democrats) could not agree on a unified strategy to oppose the Democratic nominee, Martin Van Buren, Jackson's hand-picked successor. Instead of convening a national convention, the Whigs decided to run several strong state and regional leaders for president. The "divide and rule" strategy was to nominate several candidates in hopes of preventing Van Buren from winning a majority of electoral votes, thus forcing the presidential election into the House of Representatives. According to the plan, Senator Daniel Webster was to capture New England; the Northwest was to unite behind General William Henry Harrison; and Tennessee's Hugh White was expected to hold down the Southwest. The Whig plan almost succeeded. Van Buren's majority was only 25,688 out of the popular vote of 1,505,290 in a highly competitive race. But Van Buren carried the electoral college vote, 170 against a combined total of 125 votes for the three rivals.

The Whigs did not use the "divide and rule" strategy again. Instead, they copied the Jacksonian convention system in 1840 and nominated an old war hero, General William Henry Harrison. Indeed, since 1836 no major party has failed to use the national convention to pick its nominee. Clearly, the national convention has become the one truly nationalizing political institution in an otherwise highly decentralized and fragmented fifty-state party system. By independently selecting the presidential nominee, the national convention enhances the strength and grandeur of this high office. Had the congressional caucus, by some quirk of fate, survived as the method for nominating presidential candidates, the odds are high that the presidency would have faint resemblance to the powerful institutional chief executive that has emerged in the twentieth century.

INCUMBENT PRESIDENTS NO LONGER AUTOMATICALLY GUARANTEED RENOMINATION

Until the late 1960s, incumbent presidents could have renomination merely for the asking. Most potential challengers considered it the better part of wisdom to avoid the challenge, since no sitting president in the twentieth century has been denied renomination. Yet, in 1912, former President Theodore Roosevelt, increasingly disenchanted with the conservatism of his hand-picked successor, President William Howard Taft, decided to throw his hat in the ring and challenge Taft. Though far more popular than Taft, Teddy was no match for the incumbent president whose vast patronage authority enabled him to control the GOP "post office" delegates from the one-party Democratic states of the then solid South. These delegates consisted mostly of patronage-seekers, hoping for a GOP presidential victory that would assure them of jobs as postmasters, federal marshals, and collectors of customs. These 200-plus loyal delegates provided Taft with his margin of victory at the convention.[7] Frustrated by Taft's insider control of the GOP nominating machinery, Teddy and his delegates marched out of the convention, formed their own Progressive party, and mounted a furious third-party presidential challenge. As a result of the three-way race and split vote between Taft and Roosevelt, the Democratic nominee, Woodrow Wilson, captured the White House with only 44 percent of the popular vote.

Even saddled with the Great Depression and faced with almost certain electoral defeat in November 1932, Herbert Hoover encountered no serious opposition for renomination. For a party to deny renomination to its incumbent president is an open admission that it mistakenly chose a loser four years earlier.

After World War II, the certainty of renomination began to erode. Though most historians now rank Harry S. Truman among the "near great" presidents, it has been largely forgotten that Truman had to wage an uphill battle and overcome major intraparty opposition to claim the 1948 Democratic nomination for his full term. During the early months of 1948 anti-Truman Democrats—led by President Roosevelt's three politically minded sons (James of California, Franklin D., Jr., of New York, and Elliott of Texas), Mayor William O'Dwyer of New York, Cook County Democratic Chairman Jake Arvey of Chicago, Mayor Frank ("I Am the Law") Hague of Jersey City, and CIO labor chieftains Philip Murray and Jack Kroll—all joined an "Eisenhower for president" drive.[8] Two major roadblocks, however, stood in their way. First, the former supreme allied commander had declined to identify himself with any political party; second, General Ike said he was not available for any high political office. Still, the coalition continued its pursuit of the retired general. When James Roosevelt and nineteen well-known party leaders sent a telegram to all Democratic national convention delegates inviting them to a preconvention meeting to select ''the ablest and strongest man available'' as the party nominee, Eisenhower once and for all cleared the air, announcing, ''No matter under what terms, conditions, or premises a proposal might be couched, I would refuse to accept the nomination.''[9] Faced with this flat-out refusal from the popular general and having no viable alternative candidate, the Roosevelt-led organizers called off the meeting. Mayor O'Dwyer and Chicago boss Arvey belatedly jumped on the Truman bandwagon.

Meanwhile, several Americans for Democratic Action (ADA) leaders had tried unsuccessfully to persuade Supreme Court Justice William O. Douglas to leave the bench and become a candidate. When this desperate last-ditch effort failed, the stop Truman movement collapsed. Southern Democrats nevertheless remained cool to Truman and nominated one of their own, Senator Richard B. Russell of Georgia. Truman forces, however, were in full control of the convention. On the first ballot he defeated Russell by 947.5 to 263 votes.[10] A review of the balloting showed that except for North Carolina, Truman received no votes from the eleven southern states of the old Confederacy. But Truman's rousing acceptance speech, especially his blistering attack on the ''do-nothing Eightieth Congress,'' controlled by the Republicans, helped bring many dissident Democrats back into the party fold. Moreover, Truman's willingness to forgive wayward Democrats also helped heal party wounds and unite the Democratic party for the long-shot campaign against the front-running Dewey, considered by many commentators and pollsters to be a shoo-in winner in the November election.

In early 1952, President Truman was still undecided about seeking another term (he was still eligible to run under the newly adopted Twenty-second Amendment) when Senator Estes Kefauver, a maverick southerner from Tennessee, upset him in the first-in-the-nation New Hampshire primary. Though Truman discounted the primaries as so much ''eyewash,'' he nevertheless announced, less than three weeks later, his retirement and withdrawal from the race.

In 1968, President Lyndon Johnson faced a severe challenge from Senators Eugene McCarthy and Robert F. Kennedy. He was still an unannounced candidate when the primary season opened, but he did permit his name to go forward in the New Hampshire primary, and most Washington pundits assumed he would run again. However, when Senator McCarthy came within an eyelash (49 percent to 42 percent) of upsetting Johnson in the opening-round New England primary, and only two days away from an impending defeat in the Wisconsin primary, Johnson suddenly announced his withdrawal from the Democratic race.

Clearly, in this age of participatory democracy, we have reached a point where an incumbent president can no longer count on winning renomination automatically, and thus would be well advised to maintain personal and organizational support within his party in order to reduce the chances of being challenged for renomination. In 1976, for example, President Gerald Ford came within 120 delegate votes of losing his nomination for a full term to former California Governor Ronald Reagan at the Kansas City convention. To justify his challenge against Ford, Reagan and his managers argued that Ford, an appointed—not elected—president, had no clear mandate from the American people. (Ford was elevated to the presidency in August 1974 after President Nixon, threatened with an impending impeachment trial, resigned.) The bitter Ford–Reagan pre-convention battle, in the eyes of many campaign professionals, led to Ford's defeat in the general election.

Four years later, Democratic President Jimmy Carter faced a heavy renomination challenge from Senator Ted Kennedy, the youngest brother of the slain president. Starting out in the unusual position, for an incumbent at least, of being an underdog, Carter managed to overtake Kennedy shortly after the Iranian hostage takeover in early December 1979. Even the famous Kennedy name could not match the aura of a president who, although running low in the polls, was dealing with a delicate international problem from a position of strength. Carter won renomination, but he had been badly wounded by the long months of primary campaigning. Like Ford, four years earlier, Carter lost the general election—part of the price of a heated nominating contest. In retrospect, President Lyndon B. Johnson's bitter observation about his own plight and growing vulnerability in the early months of 1968 before he renounced seeking another term may be closer to the mark: "The old belief that a president can carry out the responsibilities of his office and at the same time undergo the rigors of campaigning is, in my opinion, no longer valid."[11]

In this age of participatory democracy and declining party influence, a president can no longer count on undivided support from his own party in seeking renomination. Unlike yesteryear, many members of his own party believe that they have the right to conduct a referendum on his first-term stewardship rather than bestow an automatic renomination endorsement. This is not to say, however, that all modern-day presidents will encounter renomination fights. In 1984, President Reagan, riding the crest of nationwide popularity, was the unanimous choice of the GOP convention in Dallas. But in this age of mass democracy, self-generating candidates, public subsidies for candidates in the primaries, and television, the likelihood of contested renominating races is several times greater than it was in the period when party insiders clearly controlled the presidential selection process.

PRESIDENTIAL NOMINEE ASSUMES PARTY LEADERSHIP
EVEN BEFORE ELECTION

Presidential leadership of the national party commences the moment the nominee receives his party's nomination from the national convention. By custom, the national party chairman, who heads the national committee, is the personal choice of the presidential nominee; the party's national committee rarely refuses automatic approval of his selection. Just as the 1932 Democratic national committee routinely approved Roosevelt's choice of James A. Farley as national chairman, so did the 1952 GOP national committee automatically approve Arthur Summerfield as General Eisenhower's choice for party chair.

Generally, there is wholesale turnover of the party's national committee staff as the new nominee takes over the party reins and replaces the personnel with some of his own campaign staff. While a smooth transition is still the norm, there have been exceptions. In 1984, for example, former Vice President Mondale had indicated before the San Francisco convention that he wished to replace Democratic National Party Chairman Charles Manatt with his own choice, Bert Lance, former President Jimmy Carter's Office of Management and Budget (OMB) director. But this announcement aroused a hornets' nest of opposition, especially among the host California national committee members who came to the defense of fellow-Californian Manatt. To these Californians, Mondale's proposed replacement of Manatt bordered on rank ingratitude, especially since the convention was being held in Manatt's home state, and because many committee members felt that Manatt had done a creditable job during his watch at the Democratic national headquarters. Furthermore, Lance's brief tenure as President Carter's director of the OMB had been tarnished by alleged irregularities with Lance's banks in Georgia. Also, some members thought that Lance's appointment would tie Mondale too closely to the unpopular former president. The end result was that Mondale reversed himself and, at the Democratic national committee meeting held the day after the convention, endorsed the reappointment of Manatt for the six-month term established for presidential election years.[12]

FEDERAL LEGISLATION REQUIRES SEPARATE
CANDIDATE ORGANIZATION TO FUND CAMPAIGN

Intentional or not, the president's role as party leader has been reinforced by the Federal Election Campaign Act of 1974. Under this legislation, which provides for full funding of both major party candidates in the general election campaign, the Federal Election Commission (FEC) is authorized to disburse funds ($46.1 million in 1988) to underwrite each candidate's campaign. Each of the major candidates, in turn, agrees not to accept any private funding during the general election campaign. Congressional intent in passing the 1974 law was to remove some of the worst abuses associated with the Watergate scandals ($2-million individual contributions, slightly disguised corporate donations, etc.) and to equalize campaign funding between the two major parties.

The net effect of turning this federal money over to the two presidential candidates instead of the two major parties, however, makes the candidates—especially the president-elect—virtually free of any party obligation, responsibility, or accountability.[13] No longer does the president-elect have to ask state parties to contribute to his campaign. And the state parties, in turn, feel little sense of obligation to the president-elect. As a result, presidential campaign funding is now highly centralized in the candidates' national headquarters, with all disbursements handled by the presidential candidates' accountants. Under this system, it is understandable why state and local parties feel almost totally excluded from the national campaign. In 1976, for example, Democratic nominee Jimmy Carter and his staff decided to spend virtually all the federal funds on national television, leaving no money for the state parties to distribute lawn signs, bumper stickers, or campaign buttons to local partisans, since these items would have to be charged to the Carter national campaign and thereby would be likely to push it over the federally imposed spending limit. To correct this problem, Congress, in 1979, amended the law to permit state and local parties to raise up to $4.5 million for "grass roots" party-building activity, without this money being charged against the candidate's national limit.[14]

CANDIDATES APPEAL TO PARTY ELECTORATE RATHER THAN PARTY ORGANIZATION

Prior to the age of television, media specialists insisted that most of the public was influenced by a "two-step flow" process of communication, that is, the message must be directed to the community leaders or influentials who, in turn, would influence the rank and file.[15] But the rise of television has discredited this older theory of communication. Today, influence flows directly through the televised message from the candidates to millions of individual voters in their own living rooms. No longer do presidential candidates spend much time urging local partisans to doorbell and distribute campaign literature to get out the vote because they believe that televised campaign messages are far more cost-effective and efficient than the old-fashioned ward-heeling activities.

Presidential candidates focus their attention on the party electorate rather than the party organization for another good reason. They know that to win the presidential election they need more than the support of the party organization and the party faithful because neither party enjoys the support of a majority of the electorate. To win, the candidate must attract a substantial portion of the independent voters, who now constitute almost one-third of the electorate.[16] Since the proportion of the populace who identify strongly with a political party is declining, it can be expected that future candidates will direct even less attention toward the party organization—and more toward the party electorate and the growing number of independents.

TELEVISION-DOMINATED PRESIDENTIAL CAMPAIGN LEAVES PARTY OPERATIVES AS OUTSIDERS

More than anything else, the ability to communicate instantly with millions of viewers via television differentiates twentieth-century presidential candidates from their nineteenth-century counterparts. Indeed, no invention in the past forty years has had a more profound effect on the American political environment than network television. Presidential chronicler Theodore H. White has described television's influence in far stronger terms: "Television in modern politics has been as revolutionary as the development of printing in the time of Gutenberg."[17]

Census data show that television now reaches almost every home in America—over 98 percent of all American households now have at least one TV set, and nearly half have two or more sets. According to *The World Almanac*, the United States has 170.8 million TV sets in operation in over 89 million households—far more than any other nation. On a typical evening, the three major television network news programs attract more than 43 million viewers. Over and above this huge audience, the recently expanding Cable News Network (CNN) offers 24-hour news service to more than 53.9 million cable television subscribers.[18] It is no wonder that presidential campaign operatives devote far more time to poring over viewer data in the 167 Standard Marketing Area (SMA) TV market audiences in the metropolitan areas across the country and buying TV time in these areas than they do to, say, appearing at a party rally in Cuyahoga County (Cleveland), an airport in Memphis to please the mayor, or a suburban shopping mall in the Oakland–San Francisco Bay area as a favor to a senator. Maintenance of good relations with TV network executives or their traveling reporters rates as a far higher campaign priority than the care and feeding of national committee members or a host of Congress members intent on saving their seats in the House of Representatives.

RELATIONS WITH SENATE AND HOUSE CAMPAIGN COMMITTEES

Cooperation between a presidential candidate and his party's campaign committees on Capitol Hill is minimal during a national election campaign. While control of both the executive and legislative branches of the federal government would seem to be the common goal of both the president and the Capitol Hill committees, their operations during the general campaign seldom mesh.

Clearly, the independent, candidate-centered presidential selection process, with its heavy emphasis on media advertising, discourages close cooperation between the presidential candidate team and their congressional counterparts. Bolstered by a $46.1-million FEC grant to fund his general election campaign, the presidential candidate is usually so heavily involved with his own campaign that he rarely coordinates his schedule with Capitol Hill committees. Similarly, the House and Senate campaign committees, with their own staffs and funding, have usually targeted a short list of Senate contests and not more than 40 or so marginal House seats. Synchronization of their campaigns with the presidential candidates' seldom seems to occur. The pressing time demands of the presidential candidates' nationwide 50-state campaign usually drains away the time they might wish to devote to some joint campaign appearances.

The White House–Capitol Hill record of campaign coordination between the Hill committees and incumbent presidents seeking a second term is not much better, and sometimes worse, than that of first-time campaigners. In 1972, for example, President Nixon asked his assistants to form a completely autonomous campaign reelection committee to manage his reelection drive. Officially known as the Committee to Re-Elect the President, better known as CREEP, this committee was totally independent of the party's national committee, raised its own funds (over $62 million) and used White House operatives to staff itself. Accountable only to the president, CREEP soon became involved in under-the-table fundraising and other shady activities. Exposure of its activities came to light during the Watergate committee hearings. Investigation testimony prompted Congress to pass legislation in 1974 intended to reduce the influence of money in federal elections. Congress enacted a new, complex subsidy-matching fund scheme for presidential candidates in the primaries and authorized underwriting the full cost of the party nominee's general election campaign.[19]

With plenty of money in the till, President Reagan's White House reelection campaign staff in 1984 passed up numerous opportunities to campaign on behalf of GOP senatorial and congressional candidates locked in tight races. Instead, Reagan concentrated his campaign on building up his own electoral majority, ''running up the score,'' as the traveling press put it. Indeed, as his Gallup poll lead widened over his challenger, former Vice President Mondale, during September and early October, the president and his staff seemed far more intent on trying to sweep all fifty states for the presidential ticket than in helping Republican congressional candidates involved in close contests. After the election, one of Reagan's staunchest supporters, House Minority Leader Robert

Michel (R-Ill.), complained about the White House indifference to other 1984 GOP races and blamed Reagan's personal campaign for the Republican's disappointing showing in the House elections: "He never really, in my opinion, joined that issue of what it really means to have the numbers in the House . . . . Here the son-of-a-buck ended up with 59 percent and you bring in [only] fifteen seats."[20]

Presidents sometimes, however, have had more than a passing interest in the Capitol Hill campaign committees. In 1982, for example, the Reagan administration worked behind the scenes to have Senator Robert Packwood of Oregon replaced as chairman of the Republican Senate Campaign Committee. Packwood had been in the White House doghouse for several months after he accused the president of turning the Republican party into "an assemblage of white males over 40."[21] According to one source, Reagan encouraged Senator Richard Lugar of Indiana to challenge Packwood for the chairmanship and let it be known that he would be more confident with Lugar overseeing the Republican Senate Campaign Committee in 1984, when nineteen GOP senators were up for reelection. Senator Paul Laxalt of Nevada, a close Reagan advisor, nominated Lugar and worked successfully for his election.

Packwood's loss was attributed by some observers to his tendency to use the chairmanship to enhance his own political visibility more than the party's. Packwood's pro-choice stand on abortion was also viewed as a negative by the White House. Some of Packwood's colleagues also felt that six years as committee chairman was more than enough. In any event, as political scientist Roger G. Brown noted, "Reagan's behind-the-scenes support for Lugar underscored emphatically the White House perception that workable ties must be maintained with party organizations inside the government as well as outside it. Furthermore, it was an unusually clear attempt by the president to enforce a unified point of view among Republican leaders in Congress."[22] Two years later, it should be noted, Packwood was back in the good graces of the White House after he successfully shepherded the 1986 tax reform bill through the Senate and thence to the Oval Office for President Reagan's signature.

PRESIDENTIAL CANDIDATES' GOALS MAY NOT COINCIDE WITH THOSE OF CONGRESSIONAL LEADERS

Because the president and Congress run on different timetables, a presidential candidate knows that if he is elected, he must get his programs off the ground in a hurry, usually during his first year in office. Lyndon Johnson, who knew the inner workings of Congress better than almost any president, understood the need to get moving early in his term, for he believed that a president's impact is short-lived. This is how he put it in his memoirs:

The President and Congress run on separate clocks. The occupant of the White House has strict tenancy. . . . A president must always reckon that his mandate will prove short-lived. . . . For me, as for most active presidents, popularity proved elusive.[23]

Congress, by contrast, has a much slower timetable. Most members view their congressional service, if they continue successful at the polls, as a lifetime career; hence, they lack the burning compulsion to push proposed legislation through the congressional machinery quickly. Also, because the two branches represent such diverse constituencies, their electoral goals may diverge widely. Members of Congress often subscribe to the view that, "What's good for Seattle is good for the nation"; potential presidents are more likely to say, "What's good for the nation is good for Seattle."

Since most congressional districts tend to be homogeneous—urban, suburban, or rural–small town—congressmen know that their reelection success depends heavily on representing a few major interest groups in their districts. Since a victorious presidential candidate will have to represent a wide diversity of interests—and frequently competing groups—he cannot afford to become beholden to any single one. Therefore, his messages must be couched in general, not specific, terms that offer something to almost every group without alienating potential supporters.

Over the past two decades, the vast changes in the presidential nominating system have widened the gap between the nominating process and the presidential election to a point where candidates are often better campaigners than future chief executives. The rapid spread of presidential primaries to more than 30 states, the direct linkage between the popular vote and pledged delegates, and the rise of independent campaign organizations by each of the major contenders all require that a candidate become a top-notch campaigner long before he can seriously contemplate the tasks of governing.

Formerly, presidents were nominated at the national conventions by state party leaders who were frequently acquainted with the individual candidates, knew their strong points and weaknesses, their ability to work with various constituencies within the party. But this traditional "brokered" nominating system, used for more than a century, has been replaced by a presidential lottery. To be sure, vice presidents, leading U.S. senators, and well-known governors continue to remain major contenders for the nomination in this new system; but since the party's nominee is, in effect, chosen by the millions of voters participating in more than thirty primaries, there is no assurance that the nominee selected will be skilled in the art of government.

Several persuasive reasons can be advanced why presidential nominees should be carefully scrutinized by state and local party leaders as well as designated delegates meeting in a national convention, not exclusively by millions of voters in the primaries or the mass media. As one former presidential contender has noted:

Participation in primaries can tell us something about a candidate's electability—his or her fund-raising or organizational talents—and how a candidate comes across in a television commercial. On the other hand, it may tell us only that a candidate has been willing to quit work and devote two full years or more to full-time campaigning for the presidency.[24]

Victory in the primaries does not necessarily tell the party whether the candidate can appeal to a larger constituency—party identifiers, some weak party identifiers of the opposition party, and independents—that will determine ultimate victory in the general election. Primaries do not tell how well a candidate will delegate authority. Nor do they demonstrate his ability to choose the best-qualified people for top government posts—everything from the cabinet, the White House staff, the Supreme Court—and even the vice presidency. Primaries also do not tell the party how well a candidate will conduct our foreign policy or relate personally with the heads of foreign nations. Primaries do not tell the party how effective a candidate will be in dealing with Congress, how capable he will be in moving the national power structure, or how good an "educator" of the American public he would be as president. And, most important, primaries do not tell us how good a candidate would be at presidential decision making—the ultimate test of a good president.

Meanwhile, the transformation of the nominating process has, in the words of the perceptive British observer, Richard Rose, "made it more likely that Americans will elect a president who is an amateur in government."[25] Rose continues, "By definition, the winner of a presidential nomination is a professional campaigner. By the time a candidate reaches the White House, he is certain to know a lot about Iowa and very little about Iran, a lot about Super Tuesday, but very little about super budgets and super weapons."[26]

So far, however, these apprehensions may be somewhat exaggerated. To be sure, President Jimmy Carter arrived in Washington inexperienced in the ways of the federal government and unskilled in dealing with members of a coequal branch of government—Congress. But, the two most recent incumbents—Reagan and Bush—have not moved into the White House as political neophytes. Reagan served as the governor of California, the most populous state in the Union (more than 28 million inhabitants) with a budget that exceeds those of all but six countries of the Western world. President Bush's candidate resume is undoubtedly one of the longest in the nation's history. It reads: eight years as vice president, chief American representative to the People's Republic of

China in Beijing (before the official exchange of ambassadors); director of the Central Intelligence Agency (CIA), ambassador to the United Nations, Republican national chairman, two terms in the House of Representatives, and unsuccessful candidate for the Senate.

While the dangers of a plebiscitarian-type presidential candidate reaching the White House have grown over the past two decades, the fact remains that so far American voters in the primaries have not been easily swayed by charismatic political practitioners—televangelists, demagogues, or third-party spellbinders.

IMPACT OF NONPARTY CAMPAIGN ON PRESIDENT-ELECT

To measure the impact of the ''no-party'' politics on a new president cannot yet be done systematically, but one means might be to contrast the way President Franklin D. Roosevelt (1933) and President George Bush (1989) approached their new responsibilities. In forming his cabinet, Roosevelt sought to give a voice to most of the constituencies in his winning coalition. For secretary of state, he selected Senator Cordell Hull of Tennessee, a former national party chairman. Another southern senator, Claude Swanson of Virginia, was appointed secretary of the navy. The secretary of war, George Dern, was governor of Utah. The new secretary of the interior was Harold Ickes, an old Bull Moose Progressive; in 1932 Ickes served as chairman of the Western Committee of the National Progressive League for Franklin Roosevelt. Roosevelt elevated his campaign manager, James A. Farley of New York, to the postmaster generalship (this position was not dropped from the cabinet until Congress transformed the Post Office Department into a government corporation in 1970). This short list does not exhaust the number of high-level positions filled by straight political appointments, but it does illustrate how closely Roosevelt followed traditional political folkways in rewarding supporters and spreading high-level jobs to all regions of the country.

President-elect Bush concentrated on putting members of his independent campaign organization in top-level positions. He appointed his senior campaign adviser, James Baker III, President Reagan's former secretary of the treasury, as his secretary of state. He appointed New Hampshire Governor John Sununu, who almost single-handedly rescued Bush's faltering New Hampshire primary campaign after his disastrous Iowa caucus loss, to be chief of staff in the White House. A wealthy Texan, Robert Mosbacher, his chief fundraiser throughout his long quest for the White House, became secretary of commerce. Also, Bush selected his campaign manager in the nominating race, Lee Atwater, to be the GOP national committee chairman. But most of his other cabinet appointees were personal friends or holdovers from the Reagan administration.

Whereas Roosevelt huddled frequently with Democratic congressional leaders before inauguration day to map New Deal strategy, Bush gave only passing attention to Congress, since the leadership in both houses was controlled by the Democrats. President Roosevelt had over 75,000 patronage jobs to fill in the early months of his first administration, and he decreed that the only criteria for all these Democratic appointees was "FRBC" (For Roosevelt Before Chicago). In short, nothing was too good for original Roosevelt supporters. Those who became late-inning Roosevelt converts after the 1932 Chicago Convention were treated less generously.[27]

By contrast, President-elect Bush had only 4,000 or so policy-making positions to fill after inauguration day. Nor were the applicants lined up on Pennsylvania Avenue for appointments, since many of these positions paid less than Republican applicants could make in private industry. During the early months of the Bush administration, dozens of the policy-making positions remained vacant, and the president and his White House staff seemed in no rush to fill them. Because Bush had won the presidency with minimal support from his party and owed few political debts to party leaders, neither governors nor members of Congress had much reason to expect patronage payoffs. Actually, President Bush and his staff seemed far more concerned about the impact the names of prospective appointees would have upon right-wing, pro-life groups within the Republican party. Intent on preserving the conservative Reagan legacy, leaders of these groups scrutinized every prospective Bush appointee to be certain that he or she met the rigorous pro-life criteria established by these groups.[28] In their eyes, Bush had always been suspected of being a "closet" eastern liberal of the "Rockefeller wing" of the GOP. Consequently, President Bush frequently seemed to lean over backwards to placate the conservatives.

PRESIDENTIAL COATTAILS

For many years, "presidential coattails"—the ability of a presidential candidate to pull into office along with him many fellow Senate and House members, governors, and other state officials on the party ticket—provided an important incentive for lawmakers and state party leaders to work closely with the president during the campaign. Since their fortunes were tied closely with those of the presidential candidate, party leaders and elected officials at the national convention invariably sought to nominate a contender who would help the entire party ticket. The names of McKinley, Wilson, and both Roosevelts helped party candidates ride into office on the president's coattails. But this phenomenon has declined somewhat in recent years (see Table 2.1). Indeed, as Austin Ranney has commented: "A president running for reelection these days

Table 2.1
Presidential Coattails (1932–1988)

| | | | Gains or Losses of President's Party | |
Year	President	Party	House	Senate
1932	Roosevelt	Dem.	+90	+ 9
1936	Roosevelt	Dem.	+12	+ 7
1940	Roosevelt	Dem.	+ 7	- 3
1944	Roosevelt	Dem.	+24	- 2
1948	Truman	Dem.	+75	+ 9
1952	Eisenhower	Rep.	+22	+ 1
1956	Eisenhower	Rep.	- 2	- 1
1960	Kennedy	Dem.	- 20	- 2
1964	Johnson	Dem.	+37	+ 1
1968	Nixon	Rep.	+ 5	+ 6
1972	Nixon	Rep.	+12	- 2
1976	Carter	Dem.	+ 1	0
1980	Reagan	Rep.	+33	+12
1984	Reagan	Rep.	+15	- 2
1988	Bush	Rep.	- 3	- 1

Sources: Updated from Congressional Quarterly, *Guide to U.S. Elections*, 928; Norman J.
Ornstein, Thomas E. Mann, and Michael J. Malbin, *Vital Statistics on Congress 1989–1990*,
Washington, D.C. Congressional Quarterly, Inc., 1990, and post-election data for 1984
and 1988 from *Congressional Quarterly Weekly Reports*, 42 (November 17, 1984), pp. 2901
and 2947; 46 (November 12, 1988), pp. 3264–3269.

leads his party's ticket only in the sense that he is its best-known candidate, not in the sense that the electoral fate of his party's congressional
candidates depends heavily on how well or how badly he does."[29]

The chief reason for the unraveling of the president's coattails is that
incumbent members of Congress, especially in the House of Representatives, have become increasingly entrenched in their constituencies—over
90 percent of the incumbents in the House seeking reelection, no matter
who is sitting in the White House, have consistently won in recent decades.
In 1988, for example, the return rate of both Democratic and GOP incumbents was over 98 percent, virtually unchanged from 1986.[30] The return

rate for House incumbents has fallen below 90 percent only four times in the past twenty elections.

The advantages of incumbency—high visibility, a large taxpayer-supported staff, and several cost-free district offices; huge amounts of political-action-committee (PAC) money for the reelection campaign; and the high cost of campaigning—have all sharply reduced the number of competitive congressional districts. As a result, members of Congress are less susceptible to the electoral influence of the president. Federal lawmakers no longer believe that their electoral fortunes are closely tied to the president's, or even to those of their own party. Whether or not they win reelection will depend largely on their own success in providing what Morris P. Fiorina calls "nonpartisan, non-programmatic constituency service" and much less on national trends.[31]

With the decline of party identification and the rise of a large bloc of independent voters, incumbency becomes a major factor in affecting congressional attitudes toward the president. The declining influence of presidential coattails is reflected in data that show the percentage of congressional districts carried by a president of one party but electing a member of the opposite party in the House rising from 19.3 percent in 1952 to 44.1 percent in 1972.[32] Indeed, some recent research suggests that, whatever the reasons, "the incumbency advantage in House races has increased to such a level during the last decade that the electoral outcomes for president and Congress have become virtually independent."[33] Democratic presidential candidates often run behind congressional candidates and usually receive a lower percentage of the two-party vote. Small wonder that few members of the Democratic congressional party regard the president as responsible for their own electoral success.

As a matter of fact, when John F. Kennedy squeezed into the White House in the 1960 election, House Democrats lost 20 seats—an unusual political phenomenon; many of the defeated Democrats blamed the presidential campaign for their losses. Sixteen years later, Carter won the presidency with slightly over 50 percent of the vote, while 208 of 292 House Democrats received more than 60 percent of the total vote in their districts—a clear demonstration of greater enthusiasm for the legislative party.[34]

Republican coattails appear to be stronger than Democratic ones, but usually not strong enough to aid the party for any length of time. In 1952, General Eisenhower's coattails were long enough to enable the GOP to gain a narrow control of both the Senate and the House. But these wafer-thin majorities melted away two years later; Eisenhower's coattails in 1956 were not long enough to enable the GOP to regain control of either house of Congress. In 1972, Nixon's landslide victory over George McGovern helped House Republicans gain twelve seats, though not enough to control the chamber.[35] Nixon's coattails failed to help in GOP senatorial contests; the Republicans lost two seats.

Eight years later, Reagan's coattails helped the GOP win control of the Senate for the first time since 1954. The Republicans picked up twelve Senate seats for a five-vote margin. In the House, the Republicans gained thirty-three seats, not enough to overcome the almost two-to-one margin the Democrats enjoyed at that time. Thus, over the past thirty years, the data show that Democratic congressional candidates do not need a strong presidential candidate but the GOP can be helped to some extent by presidential coattails. Still, in 1984, Ronald Reagan's great popularity failed to prevent the net loss of two Senate Republican seats. Of the seventeen GOP senators reelected, eleven won by margins greater than the president's; four others had sizable winning margins ranging from 59 percent to 72 percent, indicating again the absence of presidential coattails (see Table 2.2). In the 1986 off-year election, despite Reagan's fourteen-state, 25,000-mile campaign on behalf of incumbent Republican senators, the GOP suffered a net loss of eight Senate seats, losing control of the chamber for the first time since 1980.

In 1988 George Bush's coattails were virtually nonexistent. The GOP lost three House seats and one Senate seat (see Table 2.1).

One study on presidential coattails in Senate races, however, indicates that presidential coattails exert a modest but significant influence on Senate votes. In a study covering presidential election years 1972 to 1988, political scientists James W. Campbell and Joe A. Sumners report, "A 10-percentage-point gain in a party's presidential vote in a state . . . adds about two percentage points to the vote for a Senate candidate. Put differently, about 18 percent of the presidential vote carries over to the Senate vote."[36]

In off-year elections, presidents are of little value in helping House members retain marginal seats. Except in 1934, the party in the White House has always lost seats. Presidents Wilson, Roosevelt, Johnson, Nixon, Ford, and Reagan have all discovered that their White House occupancy does not translate into off-year congressional victories for their parties. One longtime Capitol Hill observer has put it even more bluntly: "National trends don't affect Congressional races anymore."[37]

SUMMARY

Since the rise of political parties early in the nineteenth century, the method of electing presidents by the electoral college has remained essentially unchanged. But the process of nominating presidents has undergone a complete transformation. The demise of "King Caucus" in 1824, which ended congressional selection of presidential nominees, was followed by a short transition period of decentralized nominations by state legislatures, state conventions, and a mixture of caucuses and mass rallies. But soon the emergence of national nominating conventions cen-

Table 2.2
Senate and Presidential Victory Margins, 1984

State	Winning Party (Senate)	Percentage	Winning Party (Presidential)	Percentage
Alabama	Dem.	62%	Rep.	60%
Alaska	Rep.	71	Rep.	67
Arkansas	Dem.	58	Rep.	61
Colorado	Rep.	64	Rep.	63
Delaware	Dem.	60	Rep.	60
Georgia	Dem.	80	Rep.	60
Idaho	Rep.	72	Rep.	73
Illinois	Dem.	50	Rep.	57
Iowa	Dem.	56	Rep.	54
Kansas	Rep.	77	Rep.	67
Kentucky	Rep.	50	Rep.	60
Louisiana	Dem.	x	Rep.	61
Maine	Rep.	74	Rep.	61
Massachusetts	Dem.	55	Rep.	51
Michigan	Dem.	53	Rep.	59
Minnesota	Rep.	58	Dem.	51
Mississippi	Rep.	61	Rep.	62
Montana	Dem.	57	Rep.	60
Nebraska	Dem.	53	Rep.	71
New Hampshire	Rep.	59	Rep.	69
New Jersey	Dem.	65	Rep.	60
New Mexico	Rep.	72	Rep.	60
North Carolina	Rep.	52	Rep.	62
Oklahoma	Dem.	76	Rep.	68
Oregon	Rep.	66	Rep.	55
Rhode Island	Dem.	73	Rep.	62
South Carolina	Rep.	67	Rep.	64
South Dakota	Rep.	74	Rep.	63
Tennessee	Dem.	61	Rep.	63
Texas	Rep.	59	Rep.	64
Virginia	Rep.	70	Rep.	63
West Virginia	Dem.	52	Rep.	55
Wyoming	Rep.	78	Rep.	71

Source: Congressional Quarterly Weekly Report, 42 (November 10, 1984), 2923–2931.
x = no opponent.

tralized the nominating process and produced presidential nominees who enjoyed the united backing of the vast majority of state party delegations meeting in convention.

Except for a brief flurry of presidential primaries passed during the heyday of the Progressive era in the early 1900s, the presidential nominating process remained basically an insiders' game, dominated by the state party leaders and their tightly controlled delegations, for another

60 years. But the post-1968 party reforms, especially in the Democratic party, led to a widespread proliferation of presidential primaries and the selection of mandatory pledged delegates chosen by the voters in each of the primary states. Delegates were thus no longer tied to state party leaders but linked directly to presidential candidates. Under this open system, the various contenders competed for popular favor and the winner of the primaries became, in effect, the nominee even before the national convention assembled. Under this new system, incumbent presidents were no longer automatically guaranteed renomination, though, so far, sitting presidents have held off all intraparty challengers.

With full federal funding of general elections since the passage of the Federal Election Campaign Act of 1974, presidential nominees now rely heavily on huge TV campaigns in their quest of the White House and largely ignore state and local organizational help. Nor do most presidential candidates work closely with the Capitol Hill congressional and senatorial campaign committees during the general election campaign. Formerly, a president-elect often carried a raft of congressional and state-wide candidates into office on his presidential "coattails." But in recent years presidential coattails have almost vanished because the power of congressional incumbency shows that most House and Senate victors outpoll the president. By and large the plebiscitary nominating system, the candidate-centered campaign organizations, and the public funding of general elections, has, most critics agree, produced better campaigners than chief executives.

NOTES

1. James W. Davis, *Presidential Primaries: Road to the White House* (New York: Thomas Y. Crowell, 1967), pp. 61–62.

2. Ibid., pp. 62–64.

3. James W. Davis, *The American Presidency: A New Perspective* (New York: Harper and Row, 1987), p. 49.

4. James W. Davis, *National Nominating Conventions in an Age of Party Reform* (Westport, CT: Greenwood, 1983), pp. 128–129.

5. Gary R. Orren, "The Nomination Process: Vicissitudes of Candidate Selection," in Michael Nelson, ed., *The Elections of 1984* (Washington, DC: Congressional Quarterly Press, 1985), p. 36.

6. Herbert E. Alexander and Brian A. Haggerty, *Financing the 1984 Election* (Lexington, MA: Heath, 1987), p. 151.

7. George E. Mowry, *Theodore Roosevelt and the Progressive Movement* (Madison: University of Wisconsin Press, 1947), p. 246.

8. Harold F. Gosnell, *Truman's Crises: A Political Biography of Harry S. Truman* (Westport, CT: Greenwood, 1980).

9. Ibid., p. 375.

10. Ibid., p. 379.

11. Quoted by Cyrus R. Vance, "Reforming the Electoral Reforms," *New York Times Magazine* (February 21, 1981), p. 16.

12. *The New York Times*, July 21, 1984.

13. David E. Price, *Bringing Back the Parties* (Washington, DC: Congressional Quarterly Press, 1984), pp. 242–243.

14. Frank J. Sorauf, *Money in American Elections* (Glenview, IL: Scott, Foresman, 1988), p. 42.

15. Paul Lazarsfeld, Bernard Berelson, and Hazel Gaudet, *The People's Choice* (New York: Columbia University Press, 1944).

16. Norman H. Nie, Sidney Verba, and John R. Petrocik, *The Changing American Voter* (Cambridge, MA: Harvard University Press, 1976).

17. Theodore H. White, *America in Search of Itself* (New York: Harper and Row, 1982), p. 165.

18. *The World Almanac and Book of Facts 1991* (New York: Pharos Books, 1990), p. 318.

19. See Frank J. Sorauf, *Money in American Elections*, pp. 34–43.

20. *The New York Times*, November 12, 1984.

21. Roger G. Brown, "The Presidency and the Political Parties," in Michael Nelson, ed., *The Presidency and the Political System* (Washington, DC: Congressional Quarterly Press, 1984), p. 322.

22. Ibid.

23. Lyndon B. Johnson, *The Vantage Point* (New York: Holt, Rinehart, and Winston, 1971), pp. 411 and 443.

24. Senator Alan Cranston, Address to California Democratic Convention, Sacramento, California, January 17, 1981. Copy of speech furnished to author by Senator Cranston.

25. Richard Rose, *The Postmodern President* (Chatham, NJ: Chatham House, 1988), p. 115.

26. Ibid.

27. Cornelius P. Cotter and Bernard C. Hennessy, *Politics without Power: The National Party Committees* (New York: Atherton, 1964), p. 139.

28. Michael Duffy, "Courting the Conservatives," *Time* 134 (October 16, 1989), p. 33.

29. Austin Ranney, "The President and His Party," in Anthony King, ed., *Both Ends of the Avenue* (Washington, DC: American Enterprise Institute, 1983), p. 140.

30. Ross K. Baker, "The Congressional Elections," in Gerald M. Pomper, ed., *The Election of 1988* (Chatham, NJ: Chatham House, 1989), p. 158.

31. Morris P. Fiorina, *Congress: Keystone of the Washington Establishment* (New Haven, CT: Yale University Press, 1977), p. 37.

32. Walter Dean Burnham, *Critical Elections* (New York: W.W. Norton, 1970), p. 109. For data on ticket-splitting between 1920 and 1976, see *Congressional Weekly Report*, April 22, 1978, p. 972; see also Randall L. Calvert and John A. Ferejohn, "Coattail Voting in Recent Presidential Elections," *American Political Science Review* 77 (June 1983), pp. 407–419.

33. Calvert and Ferejohn, "Coattail Voting," p. 408.

34. For additional data on presidential coattails, see George C. Edwards III, *The Public Presidency* (New York: St. Martin's, 1983), pp. 83–93.

35. Richard M. Pious, *The American Presidency* (New York: Basic Books, 1979), p. 134.

36. James A. Campbell and Joe A. Sumners, ''Presidential Coattails in Senate Elections,'' *American Political Science Review* 84 (June 1990), p. 517.

37. Paul Pendergast, executive director of the Democratic Congressional Committee in *Congressional Quarterly Weekly Report* 35 (March 19, 1977) p. 489.

Chapter 3

Presidential–Congressional Party Interaction

Without political parties in the United States, there would be no institutional bridge between the executive and legislative branches. Despite the construction of a checks-and-balances system, the Framers, as we best can tell today, thought that good will and necessity would produce the cooperation needed to make the separation-of-powers system operate successfully. But government life is not that simple.

In this chapter we discuss the dependence of the president upon congressional party leaders to make the separation of powers function. It is noted, however, that even if the president's party constitutes a legislative majority, it does not follow automatically that cooperation is guaranteed between the two branches. Members of the president's own party in Congress may not always follow his leadership, as recent presidents Kennedy and Carter learned to their dismay. "Working majorities" in Congress, not merely "legislative majorities" are still the key to presidential success. That presidents and Congress frequently operate on different timetables, meaning that the president strives to get his pet legislative proposals passed early in his administration while Congress prefers to deliberate on legislative matters at length, is discussed in detail. The importance of party channels to overcome potential presidential–congressional deadlock is also given close attention. Finally, the president's priority need for coalition building—collecting the needed votes—and the frequent reliance on bipartisan leadership and support to make the separation-of-powers system viable also is carefully examined.

PARTY SERVES AS INSTITUTIONAL BRIDGE BETWEEN EXECUTIVE AND LEGISLATIVE BRANCHES

Under the separation of powers originally constructed by the Founding Fathers, no bridge between the two branches was constructed. Instead, the Founders concluded that a variety of powers shared by the two branches would force them to cooperate. Just what mechanism would grease the wheels to make this happen is left unmentioned in the Constitution. But within a decade political parties emerged fortuitously as the magic lubricant for helping the separate institutions mesh together. To be sure, parties have not always been able to provide the lubrication needed between the branches. Indeed, the parties were unable to avert a breakdown of the national government before the Civil War. Yet, before the first postwar election in 1868, Southern Democrats had rejoined their Northern brethren to help the party mount a formidable, but losing, campaign against the Republican war hero, General U. S. Grant. By 1876, the Democrats, fully reunited, launched a furious campaign to capture the White House and seemed to have victory within their grasp. But in the disputed electoral college vote between Democrat Samuel B. Tilden and Republican Rutherford B. Hayes, a special electoral commission, consisting of eight Republicans and seven Democrats, awarded contested electoral votes from three states to Hayes, giving him a margin of 185 to 184 in the electoral college.[1] In the behind-the-scenes bargaining, however, the Southern Democrats had obtained an agreement to have the remaining federal troops withdrawn from the old Confederacy and the Reconstruction brought to an end. Moreover, the Republicans in Congress guaranteed the Southerners that a southern transcontinental railroad route would be built, linking the South to the Pacific.[2] With full two-party competition restored by 1880, the nation has now seen more than a century of healthy, uninterrupted rivalry between Republicans and Democrats.

Until the end of World War II, cooperation between the executive and legislative branches was generally assured because, with few exceptions (1910–1912, 1918–1920, and 1930–1932), the same party controlled both branches. Since then, however, divided government has almost become the norm. Between 1952 and 1992, for instance, the country has experienced a split government for 26 out of 40 years. With the executive branch controlled by the Republicans and the legislative branch by the Democrats, or with each of the parties controlling one house of Congress, the federal government has continued to function, but with less effectiveness than in the earlier era.

PRESIDENTIAL DEPENDENCE ON CONGRESSIONAL PARTY LEADERS

Since President Thomas Jefferson's first term, presidents have relied heavily on their congressional party leaders to implement White House–sponsored policies. Not all presidents, however, have been as skillful as Jefferson in dealing with congressional leaders. But all strong presidents— Jackson, Polk, Lincoln, the two Roosevelts, Truman, Johnson, and

Reagan—have demonstrated a firm understanding of the need to consult with congressional leaders throughout their years in the White House.

Andrew Jackson, however, was far less concerned with the sensibilities of congressional leaders; indeed, he often treated them as subordinates. Yet, he saw to it that his staunch supporters were elevated to leadership posts in both houses. Also, he utilized the "spoils system" effectively to see that Jacksonians were placed in nearly every federal office across the land. In the process Jackson made certain that congressmen receiving federal appointments for their constituents would toe the "party line" in Congress. Jackson's relations with Congress, however, did not always run smoothly. During his second term, he became involved in a bitter controversy with Congress over his veto of the proposed rechartering of the Second Bank of the United States. Known widely as the "Bank War," this dispute was the most dramatic issue to arise in his two administrations. Furthermore, Jackson's veto served as warning to Congress that the president would have to be recognized as a coequal branch of government.[3]

President John Tyler, elevated to the nation's highest office after William Henry Harrison's sudden death only a month after he assumed office in 1841, is perhaps our best example of what happens to the national government when parties are unable to negotiate a compromise between the two branches. Tyler's obstinate refusal to work with Congress led to virtual governmental deadlock that was not broken until the new president, Democrat James K. Polk, assumed office. Polk, a former speaker of the House, was thoroughly familiar with the mores of Capitol Hill, and though facing volatile border disputes with Mexico in Texas and with Great Britain in the Oregon territory, and the ever growing slavery controversy, he managed to rally Congress behind him. Before he left office, he had defeated Mexico, grabbed over two million square miles of territory in the seven states of the Southwest in the peace treaty, resolved the British–United States border dispute in the Oregon territory, and held off the pro-slavery hotheads in Congress.[4]

Abraham Lincoln, throughout his years in the White House, maintained a bilevel party relationship with Congress. In his role as commander in chief, Lincoln operated much of the time as if Congress did not exist. On the civilian level, however, according to historian John A. Carpenter,

Lincoln, in true Whig fashion, scarcely interfered with that body, maintaining correct relations with almost all the leading Republicans and dutifully signing virtually every bill placed before him. Most of the important legislation of the war years, such measures as the Homestead Act, the chartering of the transcontinental railroad, and the banking and tariff acts, were enacted through the initiative of Congressional leaders.[5]

In the last quarter of the nineteenth century, the so-called Gilded Age, presidents performed more as symbolic heads of state than active political leaders. The times did not call for strong presidential leadership, and the chief executives responded accordingly. Parties counted for more than the presidents; the electorate was evenly divided—no president from Hayes to Cleveland won reelection. Furthermore, none carried a majority of his own party into both the House and Senate during his full four years in office.[6] Under these conditions, presidents from both parties tended to avoid controversial issues and concentrated on trying to retain the White House. Congress dominated the national government during this era, and presidents seemed content to defer to the wishes of the Capitol Hill lawmakers.

If medals were to be awarded to twentieth-century presidents who excelled in ''the care and feeding'' of congressmen, Teddy Roosevelt would qualify for a gold or at least a silver. Few presidents surpassed him in consulting with congressional party leaders. Teddy often spent evenings talking politics with Speaker Joe Cannon and double-checking his legislative agenda. The crusty, tobacco-chewing Cannon, who ruled the House with an iron hand, took a special liking to the flamboyant Rough Rider, striking political bargains that few outsiders would have thought possible. With the conservative GOP barons in the Senate—Nelson Aldrich of Rhode Island, Thomas C. Platt of New York, and John C. Spooner of Wisconsin—Roosevelt walked a delicate tightrope to retain their support for his railroad reform legislation.[7]

Woodrow Wilson, the first modern president to be an active lobbyist on Capitol Hill, was regularly found in the president's room near the Senate chamber discussing legislative matters with the lawmakers. Two decades later, President Franklin D. Roosevelt built close working relationships with leaders on Capitol Hill. Though his party held heavy one-sided majorities during his first term, Roosevelt was always careful to cultivate close ties with the Speaker, Senate and House majority leaders, and committee chairmen.[8] A generation later, President Eisenhower, though saddled with a divided government for six out of his eight years in the White House, demonstrated that it is possible to maintain a generally harmonious relationship with congressional leaders, even if they are from the opposition party. Democratic House Speaker Sam Rayburn and Senate Majority Leader Lyndon B. Johnson found that they could do business with General Ike across party lines with minimal disruption.[9]

Other Republican presidents—Nixon, Ford, Reagan, and Bush—have been much less successful, though Reagan managed for a brief time to coopt nearly fifty southern ''boll weevil'' Democrats to push through his tax and budget cuts in his first year in the White House.

President Johnson, clearly one of the most knowledgeable chief executives on Capitol Hill matters in the nation's history, maintained daily contact with congressional party leaders. Indeed, he extended these contacts far beyond normal working hours, frequently inviting groups of lawmakers and their wives to the White House for dinner and dancing—and some extra LBJ politicking on his priority legislation.

President Bush, whose 135,000 miles of globe-trotting took him to sixteen countries during his first year in office, still spent considerable time cultivating his own party's leaders on Capitol Hill. Early in 1990 he demonstrated his ability, despite Democratic majorities in both chambers, to sway most Republican senators to avert a veto override of a bill that banned the deportation of Chinese students to Communist China. (Bush preferred to handle this question through the Department of Justice and the State Department.) Two days before the Senate vote on the veto override, GOP assistant minority leader, Alan Simpson of Wyoming, conceded that chances to block the override were almost nil; the House had already voted to override, 390 votes to 25. But Bush's personal phone calls and furious White House lobbying produced enough GOP votes to block the override 62 to 37—four votes short of the needed two-thirds majority.[10]

PARTY MAJORITY IN CONGRESS IS NO GUARANTEE OF PRESIDENTIAL SUCCESS

Most presidents quickly learn the distinction between a "party" majority in Congress and a "working" majority. John F. Kennedy, for example, had party majorities in both houses of Congress during his brief tenure, but the southern Democrat–Republican coalition usually controlled the votes on most domestic issues. Like his predecessors, Roosevelt (after his first term) and Harry S. Truman, Kennedy often found his domestic proposals stalled or blocked by the Democrat–GOP conservative coalition.

President Jimmy Carter enjoyed solid Democratic majorities in both houses of Congress almost as large as those President Johnson had. But, for a variety of reasons, Carter squandered most of this advantage during his one term. Unskilled in "inside the Beltway" politics, Carter failed repeatedly to get his priority proposals approved by Congress. Anxious to "hit the ground running," during his first six months, Carter sent an impressive collection of complex legislative proposals to Capitol Hill: a major tax-cut package, a substantial budget revision, executive reorganization authority, election-law reform, a new Department of Energy, an antiinflation package, food stamp policy revision, hospital cost containment, an ethics in government bill, social security reform, and welfare reform, not to mention a sweeping energy-conservation plan.[11] Except for the energy plan, which Carter extolled on national television, there were no clear-cut presidential priorities—all seemed to be top priority items.[12] Many of these proposals were referred to the House Ways and Means Committee where, in the words of one commentator, "A kind of gridlock resulted." Several measures—including the widely-publicized $50 individual tax rebate—were later withdrawn, abruptly and without advance notice. Carter's inability to work with his own party leaders in both houses of Congress came through repeatedly. Upon reaching the

White House, for example, the former Georgia governor had announced that he was beholden to no political interest group, since he had won the election as the anti-Washington candidate. Reports of his failure to curry the favor of congressional leaders or to cultivate closer social ties with them surfaced repeatedly. According to one report, Carter failed to provide Democratic Speaker Thomas P. (Tip) O'Neill, Jr., with tickets to his inauguration. Another report had it that Carter invited congressional leaders to a White House breakfast and then, in his frugal fashion, billed them for their meals.[13]

Whether the stories were true or not, Carter's political maladroitness cost him dearly on Capitol Hill. With party majorities of seventy or more in the House and six or seven in the Senate, Carter managed to dissipate his political advantage. During his first two years, a watered-down energy bill was all he had to show for his efforts. To add to his congressional problems, he ordered the Office of Management and Budget to remove from the budget nearly two dozen planned dam and irrigation projects, mostly in the West, as an economic measure. As all Capitol Hill insiders know, nothing is closer to the hearts of western lawmakers—or any lawmakers, for that matter—than public works projects for their districts and states. Before the dust had cleared on Capitol Hill, the irate legislators had restored eighteen of these untouchable projects to the budget. Meanwhile, Carter's stock with the Democratic lawmakers plummeted even further.[14]

FRAGMENTATION OF POWER IN CONGRESS WEAKENS THE PRESIDENT'S HAND

Recent institutional changes in Congress have weakened the president's hand in dealing with lawmakers. Congressional reforms in the 1970s led to the establishment of a host of subcommittees and subcommittee chairs. As a result, these subcommittees have a far more important role in handling legislation than formerly. Individual legislators have larger personal and subcommittee staffs available for assistance. All these additional resources, as Edwards, Wayne, and others have pointed out, make it easier for members to challenge the White House.[15]

To add to the president's burden, split and joint-committee referrals on many bills make it far more difficult for the president to influence members because it is not easy to lobby several committees simultaneously with only a limited White House staff. President Carter's 1977 energy package, embracing more than a hundred separate legislative initiatives, was referred to five different House committees and one ad hoc body.[16]

With the growing fragmentation in Congress has come a decline of party discipline to hamper the president's efforts on bridge-building on Capitol Hill. One former Johnson assistant described the changes this way:

In 1965, there were maybe ten or twelve people who you needed to corral in the House and Senate. Without those people, you were in for a tough time. Now I'd put the figure upwards to one hundred. Believe it, there are so many people who have a shot at derailing a bill that the President has to double his efforts for even routine decisions.[17]

THE CARE AND FEEDING OF CAPITOL HILL LAWMAKERS

In this age of the civil service merit system, most old-fashioned patronage jobs that presidents formerly distributed through congressional and party leaders—postmasterships, customs office jobs, port commission jobs, and the like—have virtually disappeared. Still, the care and feeding of Capitol Hill lawmakers remains high on the list of every president's party business. With only a handful of decent-paying patronage jobs still remaining, presidents must therefore rely on more subtle symbolic means of influencing Congress.

President John F. Kennedy was an ardent suitor of Congress. In his first year in office, the young president held thirty-two Tuesday-morning breakfasts with the party leadership, ninety private conversations with congressional leaders that lasted an hour or two, coffee hours with five hundred lawmakers, and bill signing ceremonies with a like number of legislators. During his abbreviated presidency he had twenty-five hundred separate contacts with members of Congress, exclusive of correspondence.[18]

President Reagan, like Lyndon Johnson, was a past master at keeping the lines open to Capitol Hill. Frequent invitations to breakfast at the White House, special guest seats in the president's box at Kennedy Center, a White House appointment for a senator's out-of-town supporter were all part of Reagan's repertoire for maintaining influence on Capitol Hill. Nor did he confine his good will efforts to his own Republican party. Democratic Speaker Thomas P. (Tip) O'Neill twice received dinner invitations to the White House during Reagan's first months in office. Southern "boll weevil" Democrats also found a sympathetic ear in the White House to their special requests.

During President Reagan's first hundred days, his Capitol Hill liaison chief, Max Friedersdorf, arranged sixty-nine Oval Office sessions in which 467 congressmen participated. Also, he brought 60 Democratic lawmakers for a personal White House visit with Reagan in the week before a crucial vote on the Reagan-proposed budget cuts.[19]

BACKDOOR LOBBYING

For independent-minded congressmen from safe districts, standard lobbying efforts by the White House staff are usually futile. To win their vote on a crucial bill, presidents often have their staff resort to "backdoor lobbying," that is, contacting a lawmaker's key financial backers and organizational supporters back home to have them build a fire under his feet and pressure him to vote for a measure. Backdoor lobbying is not a new phenomenon. During the 1940s, Presidents Roosevelt and Truman often found that the only way to collect a vote from crusty Representative Clarence Cannon (D-Mo.), chairman of the House Appropriations Committee, was to contact his long-time supporters in his "Little Dixie" district in Missouri to urge his support for the administration bills.

President Reagan's highly successful lobbying campaign to win congressional approval of his budget and tax-cut proposals in 1981, even though the Democrats controlled the House of Representatives, was a more recent case of effective backdoor lobbying. To be sure, Reagan's well-honed televised speech to Congress following his narrow brush with death from a failed assassination attempt in late March 1981 was an important factor in winning congressional and public support for his economic program. But it seems highly doubtful that these proposals would have passed without a skillful backdoor lobbying drive to supplement his televised speeches.

To soften up potential Democratic congressional defectors, White House aide Lyn Nofziger coordinated a "Southern Blitz" by Republican National Committee officials to put pressure on those Democratic representatives whose districts had gone heavily for Reagan the previous November to support President Reagan's budget program. Two days before a critical House vote on the budget cuts, the White House enlisted the support of major business allies, including the Chamber of Commerce, with its huge computerized mailing list and high-speed communications system. The amazing results of this privately financed blitz campaign surprised even veteran White House staffers. Within twenty-four hours, according to a presidential staff member, one congressman reported receiving between 75 and 100 phone calls from down-home businessmen in his district. Trade associations, corporations, and local campaign contributors sympathetic to President Reagan's economic program were recruited to put the heat on their congressmen. Letter-writing campaigns were launched and corporations were asked to place ads in magazines and newspapers endorsing the administration's budget-cutting plan. The final vote on the budget cut package—the Gramm-Latta bill—showed that nearly four dozen boll weevil Democrats had deserted their party to support President Reagan and hand him a six-vote victory—217 to 211 votes. Even before the showdown vote, one exasperated Democratic party leader, anticipating the bad news, complained, "We've got about twenty Democrats who would vote for sun worship if Reagan came out for it."[21] A few weeks later, the well-coordinated White House campaign to drum up legislative support for the Kemp-Roth tax cut bill was a repeat performance of the budget reduction story. A combination of a televised presidential speech urging public support of the Kemp-Roth tax cuts and strong backdoor lobbying produced another deluge of phone calls to Capitol Hill. One Democratic congressman from Kentucky reported receiving 516 phone calls from his district on the day after the president's speech, and a West Coast Democrat recorded 400 phone messages from his constituents; each lawmaker then changed his mind and voted for the Reagan-endorsed Kemp-Roth tax cut bill. On the final vote on the bill, forty-eight Democrats, mostly southerners, abandoned their party and backed the Republican president, giving Reagan his widely publicized victory.[22] To nail down this triumph, it seems clear in retrospect, the president and his staff conducted the budget and tax-cut campaign as if it were a national political campaign—and they were just as successful as the Reagan general election campaign had been against President Jimmy Carter in 1980.

In the present era when special-interest politics often replaces partisan politics, we can expect to see more and more backdoor lobbying.

OFFICE OF CONGRESSIONAL RELATIONS

Presidents, since Washington's first administration, have always maintained informal contacts with Congress to help steer their priority legislation through the two houses. President Washington often dispatched Alexander Hamilton, his favorite cabinet officer, to consult with lawmakers.

In more recent times, President Franklin D. Roosevelt frequently sent top-level aides such as Tommy "the Cork" Corcoran, Ben Cohen, and James Rowe to Capitol Hill to lobby for his New Deal measures. But it was not until 1949 that any president established an office on Capitol Hill to maintain ties with Congress. Truman's congressional liaison unit consisted of two persons inexperienced in legislative politics. Since then, however, White House liaison with Congress has become far more formalized. President Eisenhower institutionalized the president's legislative role by establishing an office and staff to help carry out this responsibility— the White House congressional liaison office. Modeled after General George Marshall's liaison office during World War II, the office staff, working through congressional leadership, endeavored to explain the president's programs to Congress.[23] General Wilton B. Persons, an Eisenhower aide, was the first White House assistant formally assigned to Capitol Hill.

Lawrence (Larry) O'Brien, special assistant to the president for congressional affairs under John Kennedy and Lyndon Johnson from 1961 to 1965, perfected the bridge-building activities first formalized by Persons. O'Brien and his staff spent half their time prowling the corridors of the Capitol. O'Brien centralized the liaison activities of the agencies and departments. He required his staff to give Monday morning reports of the previous week's legislative lobbying and to make projections on the forthcoming week's activities. O'Brien's staff analyzed and condensed these reports on Monday afternoons and presented them to President Kennedy for his review Monday evenings. These reports provided agenda items for the Tuesday morning meetings between congressional leaders and President Kennedy.[24]

Lobbying on Capitol Hill during the Carter administration was generally rated below average. First of all, Carter selected an untutored fellow Georgian to be his congressional liaison chief. Most of the other members of the Carter liaison staff also lacked a basic knowledge of the legislative process. Poor coordination between the White House staff and congressional leaders frequently led to a breakdown in communication. Among the early errors committed by the Carter Administration was structuring the congressional liaison office along issue lines, instead of regional geographical blocs, in each chamber. As one observer noted, "Instead of having specialists for the Senate and for various blocs within the House, there would be specialists for energy issues, foreign policy issues, health issues, environmental issues and so on."[25] By the time this error had been corrected, precious time was lost, and because the general caliber of the Carter lobbyists on Capitol Hill was below average, President Carter's effectiveness with Congress remained low throughout his single term in the White House.

President Reagan's lobbying staff, on the other hand, received excellent grades from the start. Unlike President-elect Carter's, whose problems with Congress began during the transition period, President-elect Reagan's transition period was smooth and efficient. Mr. Reagan appointed Max Friedersdorf, who managed the entire Capitol Hill operation for the Ford administration in 1975–1976, to head the Reagan congressional office. During the transition, Mr. Reagan took an active interest in building support with members of Congress and spent considerable time on Capitol Hill stroking Republicans and Democrats alike. In fact, one Reagan transition leader reported in an interview, "We had to lasso him to keep him off the Hill."[26]

INFORMAL METHODS OF PRESIDENTIAL LOBBYING

Since the emergence of the president as legislator-in-chief in the twentieth century, however, no chief executive has assumed that members of his own party in Congress will automatically follow his leadership. Presidents must frequently court and persuade lawmakers, whose constituency interests may conflict with those of the president, to go along with him. Sometimes the president succeeds, sometimes not. President Kennedy, for example, found most of his legislative proposals stalled by conservative southern Democrats in alliance with the Republicans. It was not until Democratic Speaker Sam Rayburn won a crucial vote on increased membership of the powerful House Rules Committee that the Kennedy legislative programs began to show movement—only to be cut short by the assassination of the young president.

Few presidents have matched Reagan's skills in using personal relationships with congressional leaders to win support for his proposals. Unlike Carter, who did not understand the personal equation in winning congressional support for his legislative proposals, Reagan built up a reservoir of good will through his personal consultations and visits to Capitol Hill to help him win bipartisan congressional support for his tax and budget cuts as well as congressional backing for his huge military buildup.

Personal accessibility to congressional leaders of both parties is especially beneficial to a president if he is to be an effective leader. Despite the major constraints on their time, presidents Kennedy, Johnson, Ford, and Reagan all maintained an "open presidency," even with members of the opposition party. While cordial personal relationship are no guarantee that the lawmakers will automatically rally around the president, presidential popularity helps keep the lines of communication open and may win enough doubtful votes to tilt the outcome in the president's favor.

PARTY CHANNELS TO OVERCOME PRESIDENTIAL–CONGRESSIONAL DEADLOCK

While the decline of party influence in this country continues, a president may still find that when all else fails, he can still turn to inside channels within his own party, and sometimes within the opposition party as well. Meetings between the president and congressional leaders are, of course, the standard way for trying to overcome deadlocks. Seated in the Oval Office or strolling in the Rose Garden, congressional leaders often find it difficult to resist the president's overtures. That so many compromises are negotiated in this quiet fashion suggests that direct contacts via party leaders will not go out of fashion soon.

President Johnson, aware that he could not always count on a united front in his own Democratic party, especially on civil rights issues, routinely courted the Republican Minority Leader, Everett Dirksen. This special attention was not limited to legislative matters. If Senator Dirksen were vacationing in Florida, LBJ would send Air Force One to Miami to pick the Illinois senator up and return him to the nation's capital. David Broder has recounted the unique Johnson–Dirksen relationship: "Johnson felt more, far more, affinity for the cynical, showboating opposition leader—who was always ready to cut a deal—than he did for the prim, proper and painfully honest majority leader, Mike Mansfield."[27] It was Dirksen who was endlessly flattered and courted and allowed to take a large share of the credit for such measures as the civil rights acts of 1964 and 1965. (To overcome the Southern filibuster of the 1964 civil rights bill, Dirksen supplied the needed Republican votes on the cloture motion to cut off debate.)[28] Dirksen always maintained one of the longest "wish lists" at the White House—a federal judgeship for down-state Illinois, a new post office for Peoria, a research station in the Chicago suburbs, and so on. Actually, Dirksen's close relationship with Democratic presidents did not start with Johnson. President Kennedy also maintained close ties (but not in the Johnson style) with the flamboyant Senate minority leader. While he was out stumping for Democrats across the country in 1962, the highly partisan Kennedy nevertheless went out of his way to avoid endorsing Dirksen's Democratic opponent, Sidney Yates, in the Illinois senatorial race. Dirksen did not forget the favor.

President Reagan, who preferred to stay above congressional insider politics, nevertheless managed to achieve some of his top legislative goals by letting the Republican majority leader, Howard Baker of Tennessee, negotiate compromises with Democratic Speaker O'Neill and his fellow Democrats during the first six years of his White House tenure. But he lost this bargaining chip after the Democrats recaptured the Senate in the 1986 mid-term election. Thereafter, Reagan found his programs frequently stalled in Congress, and more and more he had to resort to veto to hold off the Democrats. To be sure, there were other reasons for Reagan's loss of clout—the Iran–Contra affair, the Senate rejection of Judge Robert Bork for the Supreme Court vacancy, and his lame-duck status. But his inability to use Senate Republicans to extract concessions from the Democrat-controlled House seriously weakened his hand.

COALITION BUILDING—COLLECTING NEEDED VOTES

The fragmentation and growing "subcommitteeization" of Congress in the 1970s has meant the president must work harder than ever to put together legislative coalitions for his proposed programs. Straight party majorities seldom exist in this age of party decomposition. Indeed, most issues involved in major legislation defy partisan categorization. In other words, a number of pressing issues such as toxic-waste management, acid rain, air pollution, and care of the elderly are not partisan issues. Therefore, the president must become a master coalition builder if he is to see his programs reach fruition. To pass environmental bills will require both Democratic and Republican votes. Farm bills will invariably be supported by rural Republicans and Democrats alike. But revision of a minimum wage law will require a different bipartisan coalition. The best that most presidents can do under the circumstances is to retain most of their own support and try to attract enough votes from the opposition party to carry the day.

Traditionally, political parties served to moderate conflicting group demands in order to build a government coalition. But with the decline of political parties in recent years, these relatively stabilized coalitions have given way to ad hoc coalitions. Indeed, recent presidents have increasingly turned to interest groups to help build support for White House policy initiatives. In other words, the White House staff has assumed a role formerly performed by the political party. A half-century ago, President Franklin D. Roosevelt relied on the Democratic National Chairman James A. Farley and his committee staff to keep the lines open to ethnic groups, veteran organizations, the elderly, minorities, and numerous other voluntary associations.[29] Over the years, however, presidents have shifted this liaison responsibility to their White House staff. As the nation's population grew and the number of interest groups expanded, this task became more important. In the Nixon White House this task was organized as the Office of Public Liaison, with Charles Colson as its head. His assignment was to maintain liaison with various groups— veterans, labor, youth, Catholics, Jews, women, the elderly, blacks, and Hispanics. Under presidents Ford and Carter the Office of Public Liaison continued to expand. Its chief function has been "to lobby the lobby- ists."[30] By reaching out to important nongovernment constituencies, this White House office has endeavored to sell the president's policies and build ad hoc coalitions in support of them. Clearly, the Office of Public Liaison aims to serve as a substitute for political party coalition building. Since its heyday in the Carter administration under Anne Wexler—she maintained contact with over 800 separate organizations— the Office of Public Liaison has been less visible. In the Reagan White House it was subsumed under the Office of White House Communica- tions. Even so, the public liaison function with nongovernmental groups has continued to expand; its function is now well-established as an impor- tant part of White House staff work—not the task of the party's national committee, as was the case in the FDR era. More is said on this subject in Chapter 6.

BIPARTISAN LEADERSHIP

The president's commander-in-chief role can sometimes serve as a readily available excuse to shift from a partisan to an "above politics" or at least a bipartisan chief executive. Thus, during World War II President Franklin D. Roosevelt shed his partisan armor, somewhat belatedly, when he declared that the American body politic was no longer to ministered to by "Dr. New Deal," but by "Dr. Win-the-War."[31] Earlier, in 1940—just four days before the opening of the Republican National Convention—

FDR demonstrated a broad streak of bipartisanship by appointing two
widely respected Republicans to cabinet posts directly involved in military
affairs. He selected former Secretary of State Henry Stimson to be secretary of war (the Department of Defense was not established until 1947),
and Colonel Frank M. Knox, the GOP vice presidential nominee in 1936
and one of Teddy Roosevelt's original "Rough Riders" in the Spanish–
American War, became secretary of the navy. Also, in 1941, shortly before
the United States entered the war, FDR elevated Associate Justice Harlan
F. Stone, President Calvin Coolidge's attorney general and a former
dean of the Columbia University Law School, to be Chief Justice of the
United States. That Justice Stone had been one of FDR's law professors
when he attended Columbia early in the twentieth century may have
weighed heavily in his choice of this Republican to head the high court,
but Roosevelt reaped a rich harvest of good will from this popular appointment—a clear demonstration of bipartisanship.

In this era of divided government, presidents have little choice but to
rely on bipartisan leadership. But this is not a new phenomenon. President
Harry S. Truman, it is sometimes forgotten, was a skilled practitioner of
the bipartisan approach. Though he has often been tagged as one of our
most partisan presidents, Truman demonstrated his mastery of bipartisan
politics after the Republicans won control of both houses of Congress in
1946. The Marshall Plan, which provided the money and resources for
the economic reconstruction of Western Europe after World War II, and
the special military aid package to Greece and Turkey were both enacted
during Republican control of Congress. Truman's secret weapon was
his alliance with his old friend, Republican chairman of the Senate Foreign
Relations Committee, Arthur Vandenberg of Michigan, a former isolationist turned internationalist after World War II.[32]

To obtain Vandenberg's support and that of a number of other internationalist-minded Republicans for the huge Marshall Plan, Truman
permitted Vandenberg to name the administrator—Paul Hoffman, a
leading industrialist—for the new program. Moreover, Truman agreed
that the European Recovery Administration would be established as an
independent agency rather than a bureau in the State Department, and,
further, that "businessmen" rather than diplomats would administer
the program.[33]

President Dwight D. Eisenhower, who spent his entire career as a
military officer, also proved to be sure-handed in his selective bipartisan
initiatives with the controlling Democrats in Congress. The vast interstate
highway system, the St. Lawrence Seaway project, which opened up
the Great Lakes to ocean-going shipping, and NASA (National Aero-
nautics and Space Administration) were all products of Eisenhower's
bipartisan leadership.

President-elect John F. Kennedy, who had waged a strong partisan campaign in the 1960 election, felt that his wafer-thin victory over Vice President Nixon gave him only a narrow mandate; consequently, he sought to strengthen his new administration by putting a strong bipartisan polish on his New Frontier cabinet appointments. Two of the three top cabinet posts went to Republicans. With C. Douglas Dillon, a New York investment banker and the treasury secretary holdover from the Eisenhower administration, and Robert S. McNamara, former president of the Ford Motor Company, at the defense department as key advisors, Kennedy endeavored to reassure the eastern business community that his new administration would follow prudent management policies. Serious consideration was also given to appointing another Republican, John J. McCloy, a New York lawyer and former high commissioner for Germany, to be secretary of state. But Kennedy reminded former Secretary of State Dean Acheson, who was McCloy's chief advocate, that it would ill become a Democratic president to imply that his own party had nobody capable of being secretary of state and add still another Republican to a top-level cabinet post. (The state department assignment went to Dean Rusk of the Rockefeller Foundation.) Even so, JFK appointed another Republican, Dean McGeorge Bundy of Harvard University, who had twice backed Eisenhower against Stevenson, to be his special assistant for national security affairs.[34] Faced with this solid bipartisan lineup of New Frontiersmen, Republican critics were hard-pressed to find fault with the young president's new administration, which was to last only one thousand days.

President Reagan, one of the most ideologically focused chief executives in the twentieth century, was nevertheless willing, if the circumstances dictated, to cut a deal with the opposition Democrats. The long list of bills he signed into law in 1986—tax reform, heavy subsidies for American farmers, immigration reform, and others—was the result of bipartisan bargaining between the White House and Democratic lawmakers on Capitol Hill.

President Reagan also came up with another presidential stratagem to obtain bipartisan support for some seemingly intractable problems. In 1982, congressional Democrats and Republicans were at loggerheads over the means to be used to keep the social security system from becoming bankrupt (without direct appropriations) before the end of the twentieth century. Faced with the prospect of insolvency within fifteen years (since benefit payments then continued to be made in excess of contributions and anticipated income), Reagan appointed a bipartisan commission on social security, headed by Alan Greenspan, President Ford's chief economic advisor and current chairman of the Federal Reserve Board, to come up with an acceptable compromise approach.

To the surprise of many Capitol Hill watchers, Greenspan's bipartisan task force, after considerable sparring among the members, came up with a package of recommendations acceptable to both Democratic and Republican lawmakers. The final version of the 1983 Social Security bill recommended by the bipartisan commission moved through Congress with only a few minor hitches. President Reagan's ready acceptance of the commission's major recommendations won him plaudits across the land. Once again, Mr. Reagan could proudly claim that he had resolved a politically charged issue through bipartisan cooperation.[35]

President Bush, though he maintained close social ties with a number of Democrats on Capitol Hill, did not include bipartisanship high on his list of priorities during his first two years in office. But in June 1991 he demonstrated a masterly stroke of bipartisanship by nominating a popular Democrat, Robert S. Strauss, former Democratic national party chairman and U.S. trade representative in the Carter administration, to be the new United States ambassador to the Soviet Union.

PRESIDENTIAL SANCTIONS

Especially since the disappearance of a huge federal patronage list—the number of politically appointed federal jobs has declined from more than 75,000 to approximately 4,000 over the past half-century—the president's political clout within his party has lost much of its punch.

Since presidents now frequently operate within a divided government system, they have additional reason to avoid straight power plays against recalcitrant congressmen and senators. The president needs every party vote he can lay his hands on; therefore, it would ill serve him to punish an uncooperative lawmaker by denying him a federal judgeship or a new federal project in his state. Thus, Senator Jesse Helms (R-N.C.) could thumb his nose at President Bush with impunity on the proposed confirmation of some second-echelon State Department appointments or a proposed treaty on intermediate nuclear forces and know that the president will not engage in retribution because, most likely, next month the president will need his vote on another measure. Nor did President Bush seriously entertain the idea of finding a more compliant Republican to run in the 1990 North Carolina GOP senatorial primary against Helms. Not since President Franklin D. Roosevelt sought unsuccessfully to "purge" more than a dozen conservative Democratic senators and representatives in the 1938 off-year primaries, has a president openly attempted to replace maverick lawmakers from his own party who oppose his policies.[36] Such ventures are considered counterproductive. In plain terms, the American president in the late twentieth century is sometimes a paper tiger, since he cannot control how individual senators and congressmen vote on administration measures. Nor can he prevent the renomination of dissident party incumbents who have refused to play on his team. No wonder one leading presidential scholar has commented, "At most, the President can be only a quasi-party leader."[37] This is not to say, however, that the president is without formidable resources to achieve many of his goals in our separation-of-powers system. But they exist in other public forums, a matter discussed in Chapter 7.

SUMMARY

When the Framers launched the Constitution and its unique separation-of-powers system, they failed to delineate a process that would assure reasonable cooperation between the legislative and executive branches. Fortunately, the rise of political parties shortly after Washington's retirement provided an institutional bridge between them. This bridge, however, has sometimes been shaky.

History shows that the separation-of-powers system operates most effectively when both the president and the majorities in both houses of Congress are from the same party. Strong twentieth-century presidents—Teddy Roosevelt, Wilson, FDR, and Johnson—demonstrated that strong party leadership from the White House could produce landmark legislative programs. But executive leadership is often fleeting. Strong presidents find that the fragmented power structure in Congress can stall even the most determined leaders. Presidents operate on fast timetables, but longtime congressional leaders, who see presidents come and go, are less inclined to be in a hurry in considering presidential initiatives.

To improve presidential–congressional relations, post–World War II presidents have established an Office of Congressional Relations to maintain daily contact with members of Congress. With the continued subcommitteeization and fragmentation of leadership on Capitol Hill, however, presidents find that they and their staffs must resort to constant coalition building, including bipartisan approaches, to collect the votes needed for passage of almost every major piece of administration-sponsored legislation. Party channels, however, are still the best tried-and-tested means for developing sound executive–congressional relations. But with the rapid growth of divided government—twenty years out of twenty-four years between 1968 and 1992—the future prospects for an era of high-level executive–congressional cooperation do not seem bright.

NOTES

1. Ian Polakoff, "Rutherford B. Hayes," in Henry F. Graff, ed., *The Presidents: A Reference History* (New York: Scribner's, 1984), pp. 309–310.

2. C. Vann Woodward, *Reunion and Reaction*, (Boston: Little, Brown, 1951), passim.

3. Edward Pessen, "Andrew Jackson and the Strong Presidency," in Philip C. Dolce and George H. Skau, eds., *Power and the Presidency* (New York: Scribner's, 1976), pp. 35–43.

4. David M. Pletcher, "James K. Polk," in Henry F. Graff, ed., *The Presidents: A Reference History* (New York: Scribner's, 1984), pp. 183–203.

5. John A. Carpenter, "Abraham Lincoln and Use of the War Power," in Philip C. Dolce and George H. Skau, eds., *Power and the Presidency* (New York: Scribner's, 1976), p. 49.

6. Richard Harmon, "The Presidency in the Gilded Age," in Philip C. Dolce and George H. Skau, eds., *Power and the Presidency* (New York: Scribner's, 1976), p. 59.

7. George E. Mowry, *The Era of Theodore Roosevelt* (New York: Harper and Row, 1958), pp. 165–180.

8. Frank Freidel, *Franklin D. Roosevelt: A Rendezvous with Destiny* (Boston: Little, Brown, 1990), pp. 165–180.

9. Stephen E. Ambrose, *Eisenhower* (New York: Simon and Schuster, 1984), 2:488–489.

10. *The New York Times*, January 26, 1990.

11. Norman J. Ornstein, "Assessing Reagan's First Year," in Norman J. Ornstein, ed., *President and Congress* (Washington, DC: American Enterprise Institute, 1982), p. 94.

12. Paul Light, *The President's Agenda: Domestic Policy Choice from Kennedy to Carter* (Baltimore: The Johns Hopkins University Press, 1982), p. 31.

13. James W. Davis, *The American Presidency: A New Perspective* (New York: Harper and Row, 1987), p. 160; Austin Ranney, "The President and His Party," in Anthony King, ed., *Both Ends of the Avenue* (Washington, DC: American Enterprise Institute, 1983), pp. 152–153, n. 15.

14. Betty Glad, *Jimmy Carter in Search of the Great White House* (New York: W. W. Norton, 1980), pp. 419–420.

15. George C. Edwards III and Stephen J. Wayne, *Presidential Leadership* (New York: St. Martin's, 1985), p. 323.

16. Roger H. Davidson and Walter J. Oleszek, *Congress and Its Members* (Washington, DC: Congressional Quarterly Press, 1981), pp. 435–436.

17. Cited in Light, *The President's Agenda*, p. 211.

18. John F. Manley, "Presidential Power and White House Lobbying," *Political Science Quarterly* 93 (Summer 1978), p. 270.

19. "A Win for 'Blue Max'," *Newsweek*, May 18, 1981, p. 40.

20. Samuel Kernell, *Going Public: New Strategies of Presidential Leadership* (Washington, DC: Congressional Quarterly Press, 1986), p. 116.

21. "Tax Cuts: Reagan Digs In," *Newsweek*, June 15, 1981, p. 27.

22. Kernell, *Going Public*, p. 120.

23. Davis, *The American Presidency*, p. 160.

24. Ibid., p. 159.

25. Eric L. Davis, "Legislative Liaison in the Carter Administration," *Political Science Quarterly* 95 (March 1979), p. 289.

26. Stephen J. Wayne, "Congressional Liaison in the Reagan White House: A Preliminary Assessment of the First Year," in Norman J. Ornstein, ed., *The President and Congress*, p. 50.

27. David S. Broder, *The Party's Over* (New York: Harper and Row, 1971), p. 67.
28. Ibid.
29. Cornelius P. Cotter and Bernard C. Hennessy, *Politics without Power: The National Party Committees* (New York: Atherton, 1964), p. 139.
30. John Hart, *The Presidential Branch* (New York: Pergamon, 1987), p. 112.
31. David M. Kennedy, "Franklin D. Roosevelt," in Henry R. Graff, ed., *The Presidents: A Reference History* (New York: Scribner's, 1984), p. 527.
32. Cabell Phillips, *The Truman Presidency* (Baltimore: Penguin, 1966), pp. 184–190.
33. Davis, *The American Presidency*, p. 223.
34. Herbert S. Parmet, *JFK: The Presidency of John F. Kennedy* (New York: Penguin, 1984), pp. 66–68.
35. Davis, *The American Presidency*, p. 223.
36. Freidel, *Roosevelt*, pp. 280–287.
37. Louis W. Koenig, *The Chief Executive*, 4th ed. (New York: Harcourt Brace Jovanovich, 1981), p. 145.

Chapter 4

Party Leader in an Era of Divided Government

Between 1968 and 1992 the United States has experienced divided government for twenty out of twenty-four years, with the presidency in the hands of one major party—the Republicans—and one or both houses of Congress controlled by the opposition party Democrats. By contrast, the country experienced divided government for only six years out of thirty-six between 1910 and 1946. What accounts for this amazing change in federal government power balance?

This chapter investigates the causes and impact of divided government upon the president's role as party leader. Various strategies developed by presidents for operating under a divided government system are discussed. The president's use of his veto power in a divided government system is also examined. Undoubtedly the most important by-product of divided government has been the emergence of the "independent" or "separated" president, who frequently seeks to conduct his executive duties without working through the two major parties, except as a last resort. The long-term implications of this growing development also receive detailed consideration. With the steady growth of divided government in recent decades a new form of competition between the president and Congress over pressing national issues has sometimes led to "policy escalation" and a new form of bipartisan accommodation between Republican presidents and the Democrat-controlled Congress. This new phenomenon is discussed in the final section of the chapter.

The Founding Fathers who drafted the United States Constitution did not perceive—or perhaps chose to ignore—the threat of divided government. Living in an era before the existence of political parties, the Framers envisaged a government managed by well-established leaders with no formal party identification. Though organized into separate legislative and executive branches, each with a check on the other, the government was expected to function without partisan rivalry.

EARLY STRAIGHT-TICKET VOTING

With the emergence of two political parties by 1800, however, divided government, theoretically at least, became a potential danger. For the nation's first 150 years, however, leadership of the executive and legislative branches tended to rotate in tandem between the major parties. Only infrequently before World War II did the American voters choose a president from one party while the opposition controlled one or both houses of Congress. Moreover, the occasional periods of divided government were short-lived. Voters usually cast their ballots for a straight ticket, which meant support for the presidential and congressional candidates of the same party. Indeed, in 110 years, between 1854 (the birth year of the Republican party) and 1964, only twice did incoming presidents confront either house of Congress under the control of the opposition party. In 1877, Rutherford B. Hayes faced a Democratic House; less than a decade later Grover Cleveland began the first of his nonconsecutive terms in 1885 with a Republican Senate.[1]

In a dozen other cases, the mid-term election resulted in the opposition party controlling at least one house. Yet, through President Eisenhower's first term, a president could generally count on having his party control both houses of Congress, at least through his first two years in office. Indeed, in the fifty-eight years from 1897 through 1954, the country experienced divided government during only eight years—all in the final half of a presidential term—or 14 percent of the time.[2] But all this changed soon after mid-century.

EMERGENCE OF THE DIVIDED-GOVERNMENT ERA

Since 1954, divided government has almost become an endemic feature of our political system. From Eisenhower's inauguration to 1992 (forty years), the country has experienced divided government almost two-thirds of the time. Thus, by the end of President Bush's first term, the same party will have controlled the presidency and both houses of Congress for just fourteen of the past forty years.

Presidents Nixon, Reagan, Bush, and Ford (who assumed office near mid-term when Nixon resigned) have all begun their terms facing at least one house of Congress controlled by the opposition party. Nor does the return of "party government" seem imminent, since Republicans have won five out of the last six presidential elections, and the Democrats have dominated the House of Representatives for an unbroken string of thirty-eight years; in fact, over the past sixty years the Democrats have kept control of the House of Representatives for all but four years (1946–1948 and 1952–1954). In few countries of the western world has one party kept virtually continuous control of a legislative body for a comparable period of time. The reasons are fairly clear. The incumbent's ability to win reelection has been enhanced by congressional "perks" approved in the 1970s: enlarged congressional staffing; rent-free local offices in each district; increased budgets for travel to a member's district (thirty-six paid round-trips a year); and virtually unlimited long-distance phone service to the district. All these special benefits have been used to form a "taxpayer-financed political organization." Capitol Hill veterans have estimated that these public-funded campaign resources for incumbents would cost as much as $1 million a year on the open market.[3]

Over the decade from 1980 to 1990, incumbents in the House have been reelected approximately 95 percent of the time, thus reinforcing the Democratic stranglehold on the House. Of this huge crop of incumbents, in 1989 only twenty-one members were reelected with 55 percent or less of the vote.

Other factors have seemingly conspired to weaken united party control and to produce divided government. The presidential primary movement has encouraged the growth of self-generated independent candidates who find little need to work with their party to win the White House. The emergence of television has given candidates an invaluable tool, enabling them to short-circuit the party organization and reach millions of voters directly. Also, the rise of the independent voter (now more than 30 percent of the electorate) and the popularity of split-ticket voting has helped produce more bifurcated elections. Nor is divided government confined to the national level. State governments have also encountered divided government, with the two parties frequently splitting control of the governorship and the legislature. In 1971, for example, twenty-three of forty-nine states had a governor of one party and a legislature controlled wholly or in one chamber by the opposition party.[4] More recently, thirty-one states out of forty-nine experienced divided government in 1990 (eighteen with the split between the governor and the legislature, thirteen with a split between the two chambers of the legislature). Nebraska has a nonpartisan, unicameral legislature.

THE PUBLIC SEEMS COMFORTABLE WITH DIVIDED GOVERNMENT

Shortly before the 1988 general election, an NBC News/*Wall Street Journal* poll found that voters, by a five to three margin, thought it better for different parties to control the White House and Congress.[5] According to the survey, a majority of respondents preferred a divided government—with the Democrats looking after the domestic needs in Congress and the state capitals while the Republicans manage foreign policy, defense, and the economy.

The *New York Times*/CBS News pollsters asked about fifteen hundred respondents nationwide this question in September 1989:

Do you think it is better for the country to have a president who comes from the same political party that controls Congress, or do you think it is better to have a president from one party and Congress controlled by another?

The results showed that 45 percent favored different parties controlling the executive and legislative branches; 35 percent favored the same party in charge of both branches; 20 percent were listed as "don't know" (see Table 4.1).[6]

Do voters deliberately choose to divide control of the executive and legislative branches between the two parties? While polls show that majorities endorse divided government, there is little evidence that many voters consciously split their presidential and congressional votes between the parties in order to achieve ideological balance in government. Indeed, it taxes the imagination to conjure many voters who, while wavering between Bush and Dukakis in 1988, simultaneously vacillated in the opposite direction between Democratic and Republican House and Senate candidates.[7] Still, it is possible that some voters found it easier to vote for Reagan or Bush because they felt confident that Democrats would retain control of Congress.

More likely, however is Gary C. Jacobson's view that "divided control of the presidency and Congress is more a by-product of the electorate's self-contradictory preferences than the fulfillment of sophisticated ideological balancing."[8] According to Jacobson, voters want different, mutually

Table 4.1
Public Opinion on Divided Control of Federal Government, 1981 and 1989 (percentages)

1. Do you think it is better for the country to have a president who comes from the same political party that controls Congress, or do you think it is better to have a president from one political party and Congress controlled by another?

	November, 1981	September, 1989
Same party	47%	35%
Different parties	34%	45%
Don't know	19%	20%

Source: New York Times/CBS News Poll surveys, cited in Gary C. Jacobson, *The Electoral Origins of Divided Government* (Boulder, Colorado: Westview Press, 1990), p. 121.

exclusive items from presidents and members of Congress. As Jacobson explains, "Presidential and congressional votes thus express different, often contradictory preferences that pit the president against Congress as each tries to satisfy its constituents."[9]

During the 1980s, partisan and institutional differences combined to give the electorate an opportunity to express their contradictory preferences on election day. Voters could cast their ballots for Republican presidential candidates who were committed to lower taxes, reduced spending, deregulation, and a strong defense. Simultaneously, they could vote for congressional Democrats who promised to protect their favorite domestic programs—social security benefits, environmental protection measures, farm subsidies, highway construction—from budgetary cuts. This split-ticket voting is generally consistent with the public's view that Republicans do a better job at reducing deficits, ensuring prosperity, and maintaining a strong national defense, while congressional Democrats do better at protecting social security benefits, the unemployed, minorities, women, and the environment.

Split-ticket voting is also consistent with the differences in the duties the electorate assign to presidents and members of Congress.[10] Presidents are expected to concentrate on broad national interests, such as peace and prosperity. Members of Congress, in contrast, are expected to protect constituents from damaging government policies or budget cuts to popular domestic programs.

Under these circumstances it is not surprising that divided government—political scientist Charles O. Jones calls it "co-partisan government"—continues to thrive as we approach the twenty-first century.

PRESIDENTIAL STRATEGIES FOR DEALING WITH DIVIDED GOVERNMENT

Harry S. Truman

Although President Truman led the nation to final victory over Germany and Japan in 1945, his "honeymoon" with Congress soon came to a sudden halt. Within a year the complex problems connected with the demobilization of several million troops and the huge American war machine, coupled with rampant inflation, caused many voters to desert the Democratic party. In the 1946 off-year elections, the Republicans gained control of both houses of Congress. The GOP increased its membership in the Senate from 38 to 51 members and in the House from 190 to 246. Faced with the threatened collapse of the war-torn countries of Western Europe and a possible Communist takeover of Italy and France, Truman did not let divided government discourage him from taking decisive action to speed European reconstruction and contain the spread of Soviet Communism. Nor did the long odds ever discourage the plain-spoken man from Independence. Initially, the nationwide polls in 1947 showed that only 14 percent of the respondents supported loans and grants to Western Europe. Outnumbered by Republicans in both houses, Truman turned to bipartisanship to meet the threat of European collapse. Though archconservative Republican Senators Robert Taft (Ohio), Joseph McCarthy (Wisconsin), and Homer Ferguson (Michigan) stood in his path, Truman was able, as mentioned earlier, to recruit his old Republican seatmate Arthur Vandenberg, Chairman, Senate Foreign Relations Committee, to carry the battle and win congressional approval of both the Marshall Plan and special aid to Greece and Turkey. In the House he turned to Republican Representative Charles A. Eaton (Ohio), Chairman of the House Foreign Affairs Committee, to carry the fight for his foreign aid program. When GOP resistance stiffened in the House over threatened excessive foreign spending, Truman urged the Republicans to form a bipartisan fact-finding commission and send the members abroad to see firsthand if the crisis in Western Europe was as critical as the president had portrayed it. Led by Republican Representative Christian A. Herter (Massachusetts) (who served as secretary of state in the second Eisenhower administration), the bipartisan commission returned six weeks later convinced that the plight of Western Europe was desperate. Even the vocal Illinois Representative Everett M. Dirksen, a longtime isolationist, became a new convert to the proposed Marshall Plan, as did most similarly oriented members within the Republican party. Still, several GOP opposition leaders remained adamantly opposed to the huge $17 billion outlay to save Western Europe. Senator Robert A. Taft, in a West Coast speech, complained:

Certainly we wish to help, but an international WPA would fail to solve the problem. . . . We cannot afford to go on lending money on a global scale. I believe our loans should be made to specific countries for specific purposes and only to pay for goods shipped from the United States.[11]

So persistent were the critics about "the Marshall gap" that Truman decided to call a special session of Congress to convene on November 17, 1947, to deal with the threatened rejection of the Marshall Plan. (Republicans, sensing victory in the 1948 presidential election, were increasingly restive about rescuing a Democratic incumbent.) Truman, however, won approval by substantial margins in both houses in December for a stopgap measure until the full Marshall Plan budget could be hammered out. The final Marshall Plan draft was approved in early April 1948, by a vote of 318 to 75 in the House and by an overwhelming voice vote in the Senate. Historians rank the Marshall Plan as one of the most remarkable and successful foreign policy initiatives of the century—a program that rescued post–World War II Western Europe from chaos and near destruction. Four decades later, Truman's reputation as one of the nation's most formidable presidents has continued to grow as a result of his political leadership in meeting one of America's foremost postwar challenges.

On the domestic scene, President Truman more than held his own with the Republican-controlled 80th Congress, even though the law-makers overrode his vetoes of the Taft-Hartley labor relations act and several other measures. Before calling Congress back into a special session in November 1947, however, Truman demanded inflation-control legislation, which he did not expect to get.[12] By so doing, Truman publicly linked the Republican party with the high cost of living—and also created an issue that would help him retain the White House in the 1948 election. Indeed, from mid-1947 through the special session early in 1948, Truman's escalating demands for expanded social security benefits, including Medicare, an increased minimum wage, rural electrification, and other Fair Deal proposals, coupled with his vetoes, helped frame the issues to be debated—on his terms—throughout the fall campaign. Not only did Truman pull the upset of the century in defeating Dewey by 303 electoral votes to 189 (with a popular vote margin of more than two million), but the man from Independence helped the Democrats gain 9 seats in the Senate for a 54 to 42 seat margin and a 75-seat gain in the House to a 263 to 171 Democratic majority. Truman retained Democratic majorities in both houses during his first full term, but few of his legislative victories were as sweet as those he won against the Republican-controlled Eight-ieth Congress.

Dwight D. Eisenhower

For six of his eight years in the White House, President Eisenhower faced a Democrat-controlled Congress. But to observe his generally cordial relations with the opposition Democrats, some outsiders might have thought that General Ike's party held control on Capitol Hill. To be sure, Eisenhower had his differences with the Democrats, but his adroit handling of relations with Speaker of the House Sam Rayburn and Democratic Majority Leader Lyndon B. Johnson was more remindful of President James Monroe's "Era of Good Feelings" than any twentieth century Republican presidency. Some historians report that President Eisenhower found it easier to work with the Rayburn–Johnson duo than with his own slow-witted Republican Senate leader, William Knowland of California, who seemed far more interested in advancing his own conservative agenda and thinly disguised presidential ambitions. In his first months in the White House, however, Eisenhower also developed a surprisingly close personal relationship with Senator Taft, his leading opponent for the 1952 GOP presidential nomination. Always the diplomat, General Ike personally assured the veteran Ohio senator, who had been a three-time loser for the Republican nomination, that he should always feel free to enter the Oval Office unannounced.[13] He also used patronage to satisfy the Taft regulars. But Taft's sudden death six months after Eisenhower's inauguration abruptly ended this cordial working relationship.

Throughout his presidency, General Eisenhower continued his efforts to "broaden, unify, strengthen and modify the Republican party, not-withstanding his simultaneous efforts to convey the impression of non-partisanship."[14] Especially he tried to strengthen the influence of moderate or centrist Republicans within the party by putting his "citizen" activists from the Citizens for Eisenhower–Nixon campaign committee in leading party positions at both the national and state level.

Richard M. Nixon

Before he reached the White House, Richard M. Nixon was viewed by many political insiders as the quintessential politician. But once Nixon stepped into the Oval Office, he seemed to leave these talents at the door. While serving as vice president, Nixon performed innumerable political chores for President Eisenhower, campaigning in the off-year elections, fundraising for GOP candidates across the land, and attacking Democratic officeholders. Though he temporarily dropped out of politics after his narrow loss to John F. Kennedy in the 1960 presidential election and his loss in the 1962 California gubernatorial election, Nixon assumed the role of a senior party insider in the 1966 off-year election, campaigning for congressional and senatorial candidates in nearly forty states. Nixon received plaudits from grateful GOP candidates and credit within the party for the resurgence that saw the GOP recapture forty-four congressional seats. In his victorious drive for the GOP presidential nomination two years later, Nixon had locked up support from so many state GOP leaders that he froze out Governor Nelson Rockefeller before the primary race opened. So far ahead was Nixon that his chief opponent, Governor George Romney of Michigan, the early GOP frontrunner, decided to pull out of the first-in-the nation New Hampshire primary ten days before the voting and withdraw from the race, even though he had invested $3 million in advance organizational work. But once Richard Nixon reached the White House, party matters were relegated to the back burner. The first newly elected president since the Whig Zachary Taylor in 1848 to confront a Congress controlled by the opposition party, Nixon soon decided to downplay his party leader role.

Columnists Rowland Evans and Robert Novak also point out that Nixon, in spite of his reputation as a professional politician, was never a keen student of Congress.

Despite his own four years in the House of Representatives, two in the Senate and eight as the Senate's presiding officer, Nixon knew remarkably little about the workings of Congress and cared less. . . . During his four years in the House, he had been uninterested in the team play of passing bills, concentrating instead on the investigation of Communism that made his rise so rapid.[15]

Outnumbered by the Democrats on Capitol Hill 58 to 42 in the Senate and 243 to 192 in the House, Nixon relied heavily on a veto strategy for his first two years. He spent less time trying to get his own bills passed. But veto overrides of a Hill–Burton hospital-construction bill and an Office of Education bill weakened Nixon's hand in dealing with Congress. Veto overrides, it has been suggested, undermine the president's credibility with Congress and the public. Richard E. Neustadt has argued that the veto is actually a sign of presidential weakness, not strength, because it usually comes into play when Congress has refused to go along with the president's proposals.[16] Moreover, sustained vetoes add little to the president's public standing. Nixon felt his veto strategy would help Republicans recoup seats in the 1970 off-year elections. But the record showed mixed results: the GOP lost 12 seats in the House but picked up two in the Senate. In the state governorships, however, the Republicans took a licking, losing a net of eleven state executives.

Nixon's ability to lead his own party in Congress was severely hampered by his intense dislike of several liberal Republicans—senators Charles Percy of Illinois, Mark Hatfield of Oregon, Hugh Scott of Pennsylvania, and Charles Goodell of New York. While Nixon observed the normal courtesies in his day-to-day contact with these so-called "phony liberals," the president bitterly denounced them repeatedly in private. Nor could he count on their support in any close votes on Capitol Hill. Unlike Presidents Reagan and Bush, who maintained solid relationships with both left- and right-wing GOP lawmakers, Nixon's hard-line campaign style inhibited him from developing close teamwork with the Republican moderates.

Gerald R. Ford

"A man of the House," Gerald Ford was first elected to Congress in 1948. He served continuously until President Nixon selected him to be the new vice presidential nominee after Vice President Spiro Agnew resigned under a cloud in the fall of 1973. At the time Ford was the minority leader in the House and thus would have been in direct line to be speaker if the Republicans won control of the House. With twenty-five years' experience in the House and well respected on both sides of the aisle, Ford was ideally suited for working with his former colleagues on the hill. But Ford was never able to bridge the gap between 1600 Pennsylvania Avenue and Capitol Hill, despite his personal friendships with many members of the Democratic opposition. Unable to push his own legislative proposals through Congress and determined to hold off the Democrats until the 1976 presidential election, Ford turned to the veto sixty-six times during his twenty-nine-month tenure in the White House.[17] In twelve instances, the Democratic-controlled Congress overrode his vetoes—tying him with John Tyler for second place with the most veto overrides in the nation's history (President Andrew Johnson was the leader with fifteen overrides). Whether Ford would have done better if he had been an elected, not an appointed, president is impossible to say. Ford was caught in the Watergate scandal riptide—the Democrats picked up forty-four House seats in the 1974 off-year election—and it is doubtful that he could have used his role as party chieftain much more effectively under the circumstances.

Ronald Reagan

Next to Dwight Eisenhower, Ronald Reagan confronted the issue of divided government more effectively than other recent Republican presidents. Indeed, in his first year, when the Republicans controlled the Senate and the Democrats the House of Representatives, Reagan successfully pushed through the main features of his legislative package— budget and tax cuts, the defense buildup, and aerial surveillance planes (AWACs) for Saudi Arabia—with the aid of more than forty southern House Democrats known as boll weevils.[18] But Reagan was unable to go back to the well a second time in 1982 for further legislative support for his budget-cutting proposals. Indeed, in the 1982 off-year elections, the Republicans lost twenty-six House seats; many commentators believed that GOP losses might have been twice as high if President Reagan had not campaigned extensively for House members and ordered the Republican National Committee to pour huge sums into more than twenty close House contests. Reagan's record as party leader hit another high in 1986, when he grabbed the tax reform issue away from the Democrats to win the first major overhaul of the tax structure in forty years. When the bipartisan farm bill, with a budget-raising price tag of more than $25 billion, reached his desk late in 1985, Reagan's first inclination was to veto the bill, since it violated almost every tenet of Reagan's conservative political philosophy. But Republican Senate Majority Leader Robert Dole advised him that a farm-bill veto would cost the GOP control of the Senate. Reagan swallowed hard and signed the huge farm bill. Even so, Reagan was unable to stem the Democratic tide in the 1986 off-year election—the Democrats won control of the Senate fifty-five to forty-five and retained their huge majority of more than seventy members in the House. Reagan, however, could not be accused of failing to play his party leader role to the hilt. He personally campaigned over 25,000 miles, visited more than twenty states, and raised more than $6 million to help beleaguered Republicans, but to little avail.

Confronted with a Democratic Congress in his final two years, Reagan shifted his major focus to foreign affairs and the reduction of the nuclear warfare threat. Many observers, who thought Reagan's strident anti-Communist posture and description of the Soviet Union as an "Evil Empire" would never permit him to negotiate a nuclear-forces reduction treaty with the Soviets, were astounded when the Soviet Union and the United States signed the INF (Intermediate Nuclear Forces) Treaty in December 1987. When President Reagan toasted Soviet leader Mikhail Gorbachev at the White House during the treaty-signing ceremonies, longtime Reagan watchers must have felt the arrival of a new millennium. Insofar as party politics and nuclear weapons reduction were concerned, Reagan gained widespread bipartisan support. The Senate approved the INF Treaty by a vote of ninety-three to five.[19] Indeed, the only serious reservations to the treaty came from the Republican Senate Minority Leader Robert Dole, Senator Jesse Helms, the arch-right-wing conservative GOP senator from North Carolina, and a handful of other conservative Republicans.

That divided government led to presidential–legislative gridlock in the waning days of the second Reagan administration (1987–1991) seems more myth than reality. Legislative specialists Roger H. Davidson and Walter J. Oleszek remind us that during the One-hundredth Congress (1987–1988) 714 public laws were put on the statute books—the joint product of a Democratic Congress and a Republican president.[20]

George Bush

Every time President George Bush sits at his Oval Office desk, he is confronted with the fact that he entered the White House with proportionately fewer copartisans than any president in history.[21] As Table 4.2 shows, Bush faced a far more divided government than did Eisenhower, Nixon, or Reagan.

To confront the divided-government dilemma and the Democratic congressional majorities, Bush has pursued a dual-pronged strategy. In foreign policy he followed an accommodationist approach in his first few months in office. For example, he and Secretary of State James Baker III decided to seek an early end to Nicaraguan Contra aid—an issue that had been a major bone of contention between President Reagan and the congressional Democrats for more than five years.

After the first few months of the so-called "honeymoon" period between a new president and Congress, however, Bush became much less conciliatory. By mid-June 1990 he had vetoed twelve measures ranging

Table 4.2
Republican Representation in Congress after Republican Presidential
Victories, 1952–1988

Year	President	House	Senate
1952	Dwight D. Eisenhower	221	48[a]
1956	Dwight D. Eisenhower	201	47[a]
1968	Richard M. Nixon	192	42
1972	Richard M. Nixon	192	43
1980	Ronald Reagan	192	53
1984	Ronald Reagan	182	53
1988	George Bush	175	45

Source: Gary C. Jacobson, "Congress: A Singular Continuity," in Michael Nelson, ed.,
The Elections of 1988 (Washington: Congressional Quarterly Press, 1989), p. 147.
[a] The Senate had ninety-six members in 1952 and 1956.

from an increased minimum wage bill and increased federal financing of
abortions in the District of Columbia to a bill that would have allowed
mainland Chinese students to stay in the United States after their visas
expired. Since none of these vetoes was overridden, it seems fair to say
that President Bush more than held his own on policymaking with the
Democratic-controlled Congress during his first seventeen months in
office. Moreover, his willingness to retract his 1988 "read my lips, no
new taxes" campaign pledge in June 1990 suggested his willingness to
negotiate with Congress on the huge, persistent annual deficit that was
still running at a rate of $220 billion in fiscal year 1990.

Since his dramatic 100-hour victory in the Persian Gulf War early in
1991, however, President Bush has been much less willing to compromise
with the opposition Democrats, a majority of whom opposed his military
action.

CROSS-PARTY COALITIONS

Astute presidents have long known that they cannot always count on all
their party members in Congress to back them on critical votes. Therefore,
every president, even though his party controls one or both houses of
Congress, usually goes out of his way to cultivate a select number of
opposition party members whose votes can save the day when the parties
are almost evenly divided. President Franklin D. Roosevelt, for example,

never let his partisanship reach a point that drove all Republican law-makers away from supporting a Democratic-sponsored measure he wanted passed. To be sure, Roosevelt enjoyed solid majorities in both houses of Congress throughout his years in the White House, but wide-spread defections by southern Democrats after his first term seriously eroded FDR's labor–urban–black–poor farmer Democratic coalition. Most New Deal–sponsored domestic measures in his second term were throttled by the emerging southern Democratic–Republican coalition that informally dominated Congress on many issues after 1937. In one of the most critical votes, taken shortly before World War II—the extension of the Selective Service Act of 1940—the House of Representatives, on August 10, 1941, voted 203 to 202 to extend the military draft beyond its one-year limit.[22] This bill, it was clear, would not have passed if FDR's Capitol Hill leaders had not rounded up more than twenty internationalist-minded Republicans, mostly from New England, to offset defections on the part of a group of isolationist urban (mostly Irish) Democrats. In other words, without this cross-coalition support—less than four months before Pearl Harbor—the United States would have faced the Nazi–Fascist–Imperial Japanese war machine with a standing army of less than 200,000 federal troops. "As late as 1939," Roosevelt historian William E. Leuch-tenburg reminds us, "the American army ranked eighteenth in the world, behind the forces of Greece and Bulgaria."[23]

President Dwight D. Eisenhower, though considered a political novice when he was elected in 1952, showed more political savvy than many more experienced presidents during the six years he headed a divided government. One of his most notable foreign policy victories came in 1955 when he persuaded the Democratic majorities in both houses to back his Formosa Straits Resolution, giving him virtually blank-check authority to protect the Chinese Nationalist Government on Formosa (Taiwan) from Chinese Communist attack by interposing the United States Seventh Fleet between the Chinese mainland and Formosa. The vote in favor of the joint resolution was 410 to 3 in the House and 83 to 3 in the Senate. As Eisenhower's biographer, Stephen E. Ambrose, notes, "For the first time in American history, the Congress authorized the President in advance to engage in a war at a time and under circumstances of his own choosing."[24]

Richard M. Nixon

In the history books, President Richard Nixon has been consigned to the presidential failure list. But President Nixon's use of the Republican–Dixiecrat cross-coalition majorities during his first term was remarkably successful. The conservative-coalition legislative victories approached the level of the GOP–Dixiecrat alliance of the 1940s and 1950s. In the

Ninety-second Congress (1971–1972), the cross-party coalition in the House joined hands with Nixon in 40 percent of the contested votes and won on eight out of ten key votes. In the Senate, approximately 37 percent of the major roll-call votes were contested, and the GOP–Dixiecrat coalition won 75 percent of these votes.[25] During Nixon's first term, the cross-party coalition was on the winning side of voting on the Safeguard ABM, closing Job Corps centers, granting governors veto power over legal services programs, military aid to Greece, the defeat of the Hatfield-McGovern amendment limiting American troops in Vietnam, the Lockheed Aircraft "bailout" loan, confirmation of William H. Rehnquist to the Supreme Court, uniform school desegregation, defeat of efforts to strengthen enforcement powers of the Equal Employment Opportunity Commission, killing the Family Assistance Plan, confirmation of Richard Kleindienst as attorney general, and twenty of twenty-seven amendments dealing with tax reform.[26] Though the GOP–Dixiecrat coalition victories were impressive, they did not win all the time. The coalition failed to confirm Clement Haynesworth or G. Harrold Carswell to the Supreme Court, and lost on expansion of the food stamp program, providing twenty-six additional weeks of unemployment compensation to unemployed workers, and various amendments to set a timetable for withdrawal of troops from Vietnam.[27]

President Nixon's landslide reelection in 1972—he carried all eleven states of the old Confederacy—suggested that the GOP–Dixiecrat alliance would continue to function effectively during his second term. But the gathering clouds of the emerging Watergate scandals badly undermined the alliance and halted further legislative collaboration with the Nixon White House until his resignation in August 1974. Furthermore, the sweeping Democratic victories in the 1974 off-year election netted the Democrats a gain of 48 seats, giving the liberal northern Democrats a working majority throughout most of appointed-President Gerald Ford's twenty-nine-month stay in the White House.

Reagan and Bush

President Reagan's record of dealing with cross-party majorities has already been recounted. President Bush's success was mixed during his first year in office, but as he gained more experience in dealing with Congress—and aided by the Panamanian and Middle Eastern crises—he demonstrated more surefooted political leadership.

Because the Democrats held solid control of both houses of Congress during President Bush's first term, he found himself skirmishing frequently with the opposition and turning repeatedly to his veto. Since the Democrats lacked the necessary two-thirds majority in both Houses of Congress to override President Bush's vetoes (sixteen in the first eighteen months of the term), an executive–legislative gridlock persisted until the closing days of the One Hundred First Congress. Finally, President Bush's White House staff hammered out a historic budget-deficit reduction package with the opposition Democratic leaders. After several false starts and a House turndown of one package, President Bush and the congressional leadership agreed to a huge five-year, $490-billion deficit-reduction package.

Ironically, President Bush had to turn to the opposition party Democrats to rescue from the jaws of defeat the Budget Reconciliation Act of 1990—the most significant domestic legislation of the One Hundred First Congress (1989–1990). Passed by votes of 54 to 45 in the Senate and 228 to 200 in the House of Representatives, the historic deficit-reduction measure would have failed miserably in both chambers if President Bush had relied chiefly on his fellow Republicans. In the Senate the Democrats voted 35 to 20 to support the Bush administration–endorsed measure, while Republicans opposed their own president 25 to 19. In the House the Democrats voted 181 to 74 to support the Bush-endorsed deficit-reduction package, while Republicans opposed the measure 126 to 47.[28] Small wonder that presidents have often hesitated to use their heavy campaign artillery against incumbent opposition-party lawmakers, for they frequently need their votes to carry the day.

As a result of patient, skillful negotiation, President Bush and his White House aides won major concessions from the opposition Democratic leadership on the management of the national budget. Under the 1990 law, Congress ceded substantial power over spending decisions to the Bush Administration's Office of Management and Budget. Indeed, some Capitol Hill observers marveled at just how much power had been shifted from one end of Pennsylvania Avenue to the other on pinpointing deficit targets and spending cuts.[29] Still, the Bush administration's biggest cross-party coalition victory came in early January 1991 on the historic affirmative vote to authorize the president of the United States to go to war against Iraq if Saddam Hussein did not withdraw from Kuwait, the small, oil-rich country in the Persian Gulf. The affirmative vote on the measure, the Authorization for Use of Military Force Against Iraq Resolution, pursuant to the United Nations Security Council Resolution 678, removed the last political obstacle to an attack by United States-led forces against Iraqi troops occupying Kuwait.

By the close vote of 52 to 47, the United States Senate approved the use of military force. The cross-coalition majority consisted of 42 Republicans and 10 Democrats, mostly Southerners who were convinced that economic sanctions were insufficient to force Iraq out of Kuwait or who were unwilling to vote against the president. Two Republicans joined 45 Democrats in opposing military force in the Persian Gulf. Political analysts noted that a switch of just three "yes" votes to "no" would have reversed the outcome and might have led to a constitutional crisis if President Bush, as Commander in Chief, had chosen to disregard the Senate action.

In the House, the margin of the president's victory was more comfortable, 250 to 183. The bipartisan majority consisted of 164 Republicans and 86 Democrats, while 179 Democrats, 3 Republicans, and one independent opposed.[30]

Four days later, President Bush authorized the opening of hostilities against Iraq. The all-out air attack against Iraq, capped by the spectacular "100-hours" ground war victory in late February 1991 may have produced more future domestic cross-party victories for President Bush than any single action taken during his presidency. Indeed, some national observers concluded that his decisive handling of the Persian Gulf crisis had virtually assured his reelection in 1992. As presidents Lincoln, McKinley, and Franklin D. Roosevelt before him discovered, military victories can readily translate into future election triumphs.

THE PERSISTENT GOP–DIXIECRAT ALLIANCE

Presidents are not always the beneficiaries of cross-party majorities. From 1937 to the early 1960s, the alliance between southern Democrats and Republicans in Congress often spelled defeat for presidents Roosevelt, Truman, and Kennedy. Indeed, some analysts argue that we have had divided government in fact most of the time since the late 1930s. They point out that since before World War II the GOP–southern Democrat coalition has held the dominant votes on federal aid to education, social welfare, public housing, immigration, taxes, labor, antitrust, civil rights, and public works.[31] President John F. Kennedy, for example, soon collided with the southern Democrat–GOP coalition in the early months of his presidency, losing virtually every major vote on civil rights, federal aid to education, and social welfare.

This persistent conservative coalition in Congress continues to the present. Table 4.3 clearly shows the tenacity of this cross-party coalition of Republicans and southern Democrats. Only in the heyday of President Lyndon B. Johnson's "Great Society" programs (1965–1966) did LBJ's northern Democratic supporters manage to keep the conservative coalition at bay. By 1967, however, the conservative coalition had regained the upper hand; indeed, as Table 4.3 reveals, the proportion of "the successful" GOP–southern Democratic partnership vote has dropped below 55 percent only one year since then. Understandably, Democratic presidents frown whenever the term GOP–Dixiecrat coalition is mentioned. Republican presidents, on the other hand, usually smile at the mention of the conservative coalition because, although they invariably find themselves outnumbered by the Democrats in Congress, they know that their longstanding cross-party alliance can often avert a White House defeat.

Table 4.3
Conservative Coalition Votes and Victories, 1957–1988

Year	House		Senate	
	Votes	Victories(%)	Votes	Victories(%)
1957	16	81	11	100
1958	15	64	19	86
1959	13	91	19	65
1960	20	35	22	67
1961	30	74	32	48
1962	13	44	15	71
1963	13	67	17	47
1964	11	67	17	47
1965	25	25	24	39
1966	19	32	30	51
1967	22	73	18	54
1968	22	63	25	80
1969	25	71	28	67
1970	17	70	26	64
1971	31	79	28	86
1972	25	79	29	63
1973	25	67	21	54
1974	22	67	30	54
1975	28	52	28	48
1976	17	59	26	58
1977	22	60	29	74
1978	20	57	23	46
1979	21	73	18	65
1980	16	67	20	75
1981	21	88	21	95
1982	16	78	20	90
1983	18	71	12	89
1984	14	75	17	94
1985	13	84	15	93
1986	11	78	21	93
1987	9	88	8	100
1988	8	82	10	97

Source: Normal J. Ornstein, Thomas E. Mann, and Michael J. Malbin, *Vital Statistics on Congress 1989–1990* (Washington, DC: Congressional Quarterly Inc., 1990), p. 200.
Note: "Votes" is the percentage of all roll call votes on which a majority of voting southern Democrats and a majority of voting Republicans—the conservative coalition—opposed the stand taken by a majority of voting northern Democrats. "Victories" is the percentage of conservative coalition votes won.

Over the past decade, however, the GOP–Dixiecrat coalition seems to have lost some of its clout as more moderate southern Democrats have been sent to Congress. This conservative coalition—defined by the Washington-based *Congressional Quarterly* as a bloc consisting of a majority of Republicans and a majority of southern Democrats voting against a majority of northern Democrats—continues to win, but on a much smaller scale. In 1990, with only 11 percent of the congressional votes listed as test votes, the conservative coalition won 82 percent of the time. In the Senate the cross-coalition won on 95 percent of its votes, while in the House, where the alliance was not quite as solid, the coalition was successful 74 percent of the time.[32] Divided government may be another reason for the declining influence of the conservative coalition. With Republicans in control of the White House and Democrats running Congress, both parties are almost forced to come to the negotiating table to take care of the nation's business.

Overall, President Bush has not pushed a strong legislative agenda during his first two years in office. As a result, most of his major confrontations with the Democratic-controlled House and Senate have centered around his use of the veto.

A PRESIDENT'S TRUMP CARD—THE VETO

The veto power of the president of the United States has often been underestimated. President Andrew Jackson, who viewed himself as "the tribune of the people," first popularized the veto as a powerful political weapon and source of independent executive power. Because vetoes are so difficult to override, the veto power makes the president a "third branch of the legislature," declared an observant Woodrow Wilson almost three decades before he reached the White House.[33]

The potency of the veto power can be quickly measured by the small percentage of vetoes overridden—approximately 4 percent, or 102 out of 2,484, have been overridden in the two centuries between 1789 and 1990 (see Table 4.4). Even the threat of a veto can often win a victory or favorable compromise for a president. On more than one occasion, Franklin D. Roosevelt was heard to tell his aides, "Give me a bill I can veto," as an admonition to keep Congress in line on his main legislative goals. Indeed, as James L. Sundquist has observed: "It is the possession of the veto that makes the executive branch a full partner in the legislative process."[34]

Capitol Hill insiders fully appreciate the decisive trump card that the veto power gives to the president. To block a major legislative initiative, all that a president has to do is muster 146 votes out of 435 in the House or 34 out of 100 in the Senate. Even if the president operates in a divided government, his minority party colleagues will usually number 40 percent or more of each chamber. Therefore, he can usually count on them to uphold his veto.

If the president's party controls both houses of Congress, veto overrides usually occur less often than blue moons. All the president has to do is to retreat behind the White House ramparts and let his friends on Capitol Hill conduct trench warfare against the override. President Franklin D. Roosevelt, for example, had only nine of 372 vetoes overridden in his 12 years in the White House. President John F. Kennedy brandished

Table 4.4
Presidential Vetoes, 1789–1990

President	Regular vetoes	Pocket vetoes	Total vetoes	Vetoes overridden
Washington	2	---	2	---
Madison	5	2	7	---
Monroe	1	---	1	---
Jackson	5	7	12	---
Van Buren	---	1	1	---
Tyler	6	4	10	1
Polk	2	1	3	---
Pierce	9	---	9	5
Buchanan	4	3	7	---
Lincoln	2	5	7	---
A. Johnson	21	8	29	15
Grant	45	49	94	4
Hayes	12	1	13	1
Arthur	4	8	12	1
Cleveland	304	109	413	2
Harrison	19	25	44	1
Cleveland	43	127	170	5
McKinley	6	36	42	---
T. Roosevelt	42	40	82	1
Taft	30	9	39	1
Wilson	33	11	44	6
Harding	5	1	6	---
Coolidge	20	30	50	4
Hoover	21	16	37	3
F. Roosevelt	372	263	635	9
Truman	180	70	250	12
Eisenhower	73	108	181	2
Kennedy	12	9	21	---
L. Johnson	16	14	30	---
Nixon	24	19	43	7
Ford	48	18	66	12
Carter	13	18	31	2
Reagan	39	38	77	10
Bush (1989-1990)	15	6	21	---
Total	1,433	1,056	2,489	104

Source: Presidential Vetoes, 1789–1976, compiled by the Senate Library (Washington, DC: U.S. Government Printing Office, 1978), p. ix; *Congressional Quarterly Almanac* (Washington, DC: Congressional Quarterly, 1981), p. 7; figures for Reagan's two terms are from Roger H. Davidson and Carol Hardy, "Indicators of Congressional Workload and Activity," staff report, Congressional Research Service, Library of Congress, Washington, DC., 1989, cited in Norman J. Ornstein, Thomas E. Mann, and Michael J. Malbin, *Vital Statistics on Congress, 1989–1990* (Washington, DC: Congressional Quarterly, Inc., 1990), p. 162; figures for President Bush are from Congressional Reference Service and supplied to the author by Congressman Al Swift, 2nd District, Washington.

his veto a dozen times; none was overridden. Similarly, President Lyndon Johnson used his veto pen 16 times; none was overturned.

A popular president, even if his party is not in control on Capitol Hill, is seldom embarrassed by veto overrides. President Eisenhower, for example, vetoed seventy-three bills, and only two were overridden. President Reagan's veto record was not as formidable as Eisenhower's, but despite a split government throughout his two terms, Reagan saw only ten of his seventy-eight vetoes overridden.

President Bush's veto record was unblemished during his first two years in office; all 21 of his vetoes were sustained. President Bush appeared on the verge of losing a veto override when he rejected a Democratic-sponsored bill—the Chinese Emergency Immigration Act—that would have given Chinese students whose visas had expired four more years to apply for new visas or for permanent residence. President Bush, who considers himself "an old China hand" (in view of his diplomatic assignment in Beijing in the mid-1970s), considered the bill an infringement on his prerogative to make foreign policy. However, the House of Representatives voted overwhelmingly, 390 to 25, to override the president. So discouraged were Republican senators about protecting the president's veto that Senator Alan K. Simpson, the Senate minority whip, predicted two days before the Senate vote that a veto override "will pass like a dose of salts."[35] But the overconfident Senate Democrats turned the issue into the first major partisan battle of the session, and the White House argued that "the president knows best" and that he deserves the confidence of his party.

Over the next thirty-six hours, the White House pulled out all the stops to block the override. Secretary of State James Baker was sent to Capitol Hill to talk to wavering Republicans; President Bush phoned many of the same lawmakers. The administration even enlisted the support of former President Nixon, who had opened up diplomatic relations between China and Washington in 1972 after twenty-three years of nonrecognition, to help sway senators who had previously voted in favor of the bill. Republican Senator Alfonse M. D'Amato (New York), one of the last-minute switchers, said he changed his vote after telephone calls from White House Chief of Staff John Sununu and Mr. Bush himself.[36] When the roll call was finished, the Senate failed by four votes, 62 to 37, to override President Bush's veto. Eight Republicans joined by 54 Democrats voted to override, while 37 Republicans and no Democrats voted to sustain President Bush. Thus, even though only 62 of 535 members of the Senate and House—less than 12 percent of Congress—supported the president's position on the Chinese student bill, the president's 37 Republican senators were all he needed to block the override, demonstrating once again that the president can, when his back is to the wall, usually depend upon his party brethren on Capitol Hill to rescue him from an embarrassing legislative setback. Asked at a subsequent news conference whether the one-sided voted could be construed as a mandate for his China policy, the president said: "Yeah, because you've got to give disproportionate weight to how the executive branch feels. We're an equal branch. So you add to that the support on the Hill—we come out more than equal."[37] Few veteran Washington commentators shared this view of divided government doctrine.

Capitalizing on the successful conclusion of the Persian Gulf War, President Bush decided shortly after the halfway point in his first term to spend far more time in the months ahead trying to halt legislation he didn't want than signing legislation of his own.[38] This president's posture seemed to reinforce statements made earlier in the fall of 1990 by his White House Chief of Staff John Sununu, who had indicated that the Bush administration would be content if no new legislation emerged from the One Hundred and Second Congress (1991–1992). Unlike the contentious battles of 1990 with the Democrats over domestic policy issues, such as budget ceilings, deficit reduction, civil rights, and a capital gains tax cut, President Bush, in the glow of his Persian Gulf War victory, seemed perfectly satisfied with a status quo domestic agenda. Frequent use of the veto was considered his best weapon to keep the Democrats from imposing their activist domestic proposals upon the country.

Public works bills are the most likely candidates for a veto override. The reason is simple: These multibillion-dollar pork-barrel bills invariably contain a pet project for nearly every lawmaker—a rapid transit grant, a new federal courthouse, a rivers or harbor project, a research station, or something equally desirable. When it comes to a choice between supporting his president or voting for a public works project within his state or district, taking care of the home folks invariably prevails.

PRESIDENTIAL ROLE IN MID-TERM ELECTIONS

Active presidential involvement in mid-term or off-year elections began only in the Great Depression of the 1930s. Prior to this period, incumbent presidents seldom concerned themselves directly with Senate or House contests. In 1938, however, President Roosevelt, irritated by the conservative votes of more than a dozen House and Senate Democrats, mostly from the South, sought to purge them in the Democratic primary contests. But his attempt ended in near disaster. All but one of the legislators on his hit list won reelection, much to Roosevelt's embarrassment. Since then, presidents have generally shied away from meddling in intraparty nominating races. Since World War II, however, most presidents have taken an active role or used their vice presidents as surrogates to campaign in the mid-term general election for fellow party candidates for House and Senate seats.

In 1954, President Eisenhower sent Vice President Richard M. Nixon out on the hustings to campaign in more than twenty states; however, when September polls showed a dangerous shift to the Democrats, Eisenhower reluctantly agreed with his advisers that he too should enter the campaign. Thus, in the second half of October 1954, General Ike traveled over ten thousand miles and made nearly forty speeches.[39] He concentrated on states east of the Mississippi and stayed in states where moderate Republicans needed help. Still, Republicans lost eighteen seats in the House, but only one seat in the Senate. Four years later, in 1958, President Eisenhower decided to come to the aid of fellow Republican lawmakers and challengers again—to try to regain control of Congress—but with disappointing results. The Republicans lost forty-eight House seats and thirteen Senate seats—the largest loss of incumbent-party Senate seats in more than ninety years.[40]

In 1962, President John F. Kennedy decided early on to mount a vigorous off-year campaign to help Democrat incumbents retain and challengers win more seats in Congress. Kennedy left the White House in early October to barnstorm for his fellow Democrats. But Kennedy's foray in the Midwest was held short by the Cuban missile crisis, necessitating his sudden return to the nation's capital. Even so, the Democrats benefitted considerably from Kennedy's cross-country campaigning—the Democrats held their losses to four seats in the House—the second-lowest loss of incumbent party seats in more than ninety years. In the Senate, the Democrats actually picked up three seats.

In the 1966 off-year election, President Johnson indicated that he would go stumping for fellow Democrats after his return from a conference of Asian leaders in Manila. Indeed, reporters accompanying him to Asia were told that President Johnson planned a last-minute campaign "blitz" covering at least ten states with key Senate and House contests. But the rising crescendo of anti-war protests across the land persuaded President Johnson that his campaign efforts would not be fruitful. Instead, after his return from Southeast Asia, without mentioning any campaign plans, he announced that he would enter the hospital for some minor surgery. When the press reported that Johnson had cancelled his campaign plans, he angrily denied the plans had ever been drafted. The television network news programs carried not only his denial but also pictures of the dismantling of the stands that had been erected for his speeches in Chicago, Portland, and other cities.[41] The growing unpopularity of the Vietnam war cost the Democrats forty-seven House seats and four Senate seats.

In 1970, President Nixon dispatched Vice President Spiro Agnew on a cross-country swing to aid Republican House and Senate incumbents and challengers. Toward the last week of the campaign, Nixon decided that his help, too, was needed on the campaign trail. Nixon's appearance helped cut down GOP losses in the House to twelve seats and resulted in a gain of two in the Senate.

In 1978, President Carter found himself so unpopular in many conservative Democrat districts that incumbents deliberately avoided joint campaign appearances with him for fear of being identified too closely with an unpopular president. Democratic House losses numbered fifteen, but only three in the Senate.

In 1982, President Reagan made a determined effort to help Republicans in the off-year election. He made dozens of television and radio spots, plus several coordinated multistate radio broadcasts to help Republican House candidates seeking to unseat Democratic incumbents. Although the Republicans lost twenty-six seats in the House, they gained one Senate seat.

Presidents, it seems clear, are not of much value in helping members of Congress retain their seats in off-year elections. With the exception of 1934, the party in the White House has always lost seats. Presidents Wilson, Roosevelt, Johnson, Nixon, Ford, Reagan, and Bush have all discovered that their White House occupancy does not translate into off-year congressional victories for their party. President Bush's managers kept this political fact of life in mind as they prepared for the 1990 off-year congressional elections. An administration official announced in early January 1990 that the GOP hoped to use Mr. Bush primarily for "operational" support—raising money and boosting volunteers' morale.[42]

Starting with this modest goal in mind, President Bush, in 115 campaign stops, helped raise an estimated $80 million—the largest fundraising enterprise in history—for GOP congressional, senatorial, and gubernatorial candidates during the 1990 off-year election campaign.[43] Yet, despite Bush's almost nonstop electioneering in the final ten days of the race, the GOP still lost eight House seats, one Senate seat, and two governorships.

IMPACT OF THE TWENTY-SECOND AMENDMENT ON PRESIDENTIAL PARTY LEADERSHIP IN SECOND TERM

Until ratification of the Twenty-second Amendment in 1951, which imposed a two-term limit on the presidency, only four presidents since the Civil War—Grant, Cleveland, Wilson, and Franklin D. Roosevelt—had served two full terms or more. But during the Eightieth Congress (1946–1948) Republicans, who had regained control of both chambers, made it a top priority to prevent a repeat performance of four successive presidential victories by another candidate like Franklin D. Roosevelt. Ironically, the amendment first applied to a Republican president, Dwight D. Eisenhower, who was barred from running in 1960. If Eisenhower had been eligible to run and wanted to seek a third term, most political pundits agreed that he would have easily won renomination and reelection.

What has been the effect of the Twenty-second Amendment on presidential party leadership? Since we have had the experience of observing only presidents Eisenhower and Reagan through two full terms, it is not easy to generalize. The late Clinton Rossiter, a leading authority on the presidency, predicted more than thirty years ago that the amendment would permanently weaken the presidency: "Everything in our history tells us that a President who does not or cannot seek reelection loses much of his grip in his last couple of years, and we no longer can afford presidents who lose their grip."[44] But what does the record show?

In the case of President Eisenhower, historian Stephen Ambrose writes, "For Eisenhower, 1960 turned out to be a bad year, almost the worst of his Presidency."[45] General Ike's problems could probably be traced to a series of mistakes in dealing with Soviet leader Nikita Khrushchev, especially Eisenhower's original denial of United States involvement with an American U-2 spy plane shot down by the Soviets and the subsequent collapse of the Paris Summit meeting. On the home front, Eisenhower discovered that his influence in picking a successor was marginal. Eisenhower refused to endorse the party front-runner, Vice President Nixon, before the GOP convention, even though Nixon had, in effect, locked up the nomination soon after the New Hampshire primary. For a brief time, Eisenhower tried to encourage Treasury Secretary Robert Anderson to become a candidate; when that failed, he urged Secretary of Health, Education, and Welfare (now HHS) Oveta Culp Hobby to get the Texas Republicans to organize behind Anderson as a "favorite son." If that would not fly, Ike suggested that she run herself. Eisenhower also tried unsuccessfully to get his old chief of staff (and favorite bridge partner), General Alfred Gruenther, to run, with no luck. Ike's lack of understanding of insider presidential nominating politics was painfully evident. Clearly, Eisenhower's lame duck status weakened his party influence.

Once Nixon lost the close race to Kennedy, Republicans soon turned again to Eisenhower for endorsements, help in fundraising, and general publicity. In June 1961, he and Mrs. Eisenhower went to New York for a series of $100-a-plate Republican dinners. In the 1962 off-year election, Eisenhower visited twenty-one states, made twenty-eight speeches supporting Republican candidates, and attended more than two dozen fundraising dinners. During the summer of 1962, Eisenhower also tried indirectly to take the GOP leadership away from the old guard and the Republican National Committee by agreeing to serve as honorary chairman of a new group, the Republican Citizens.[46]

This attempt to liberalize and reform the Republican party, however, ultimately failed when congressional leaders, led by Republican Senate minority leader Everett M. Dirksen and House minority leader Charles Halleck, refused to participate. Soon after the 1962 election, the Republican Citizens project died. Eisenhower's choices for the 1964 GOP nomination included Robert Anderson again, Henry Cabot Lodge, Jr., and Pennsylvania Governor William Scranton. But none turned out to be a serious challenger to Senator Barry Goldwater of Arizona, the GOP nominee.

No president in the twentieth century, with the possible exception of Teddy Roosevelt, wielded more influence with his party after retirement than President Eisenhower. But like all his predecessors, General Ike learned that the political power of former presidents is fleeting.

Reagan

In late 1986, critics of President Reagan pointed out that he too was suffering from the same malady as all second-term presidents—"lame duckitus." And when reports of the Iran arms-for-hostages swap hit the headlines shortly after the 1986 November election, President Reagan's popularity ratings plunged more than fifteen points in the Gallup polls within weeks. Reagan's standing with Congress also continued to slide badly. In April 1987, for example, 102 of the 177 House Republicans and 13 of the 46 Senate Republicans voted to override his veto of a bill providing $88 billion in highway and mass transit funds.[47] In an effort to block the override of the highway bill, Reagan personally pleaded with all 13 GOP senators who voted to override for their support to sustain his veto.[48]

During a president's second term, legislators from both parties realize that their political survival may depend more upon asserting a certain degree of independence from the president than upon regularly backing the chief executive. This falloff in presidential support is especially marked among lawmakers who are members of the president's party. During his first year in office, Reagan could count on the near-unanimous support of congressional Republicans. But over the next four years, this partisan support became less dependable; and in his final two years in office, he often lost votes of Republican lawmakers on those issues that pitted legislators' constituency interests against their loyalty to Reagan. But later in 1987 the success of Reagan's negotiations with the Soviet officials at the Geneva nuclear arms reduction talks produced a remarkable switch for Reagan. When Soviet leader Mikhail Gorbachev arrived in Washington in early December 1987 for the INF Treaty signing ceremonies, Reagan was back at the top of his game. His Gallup poll ratings jumped back to the low fifties and remained there until the end of his term. Throughout the 1988 presidential campaign, Reagan was the top campaign draw for GOP candidate George Bush. Indeed, in his final months in office, the term "lame duck" and its symbolic implication of declining presidential influence seemed to have vanished as President Reagan jet-hopped in Air Force One from one campaign rally to the next.

On the basis of the Eisenhower and Reagan cases, the impact of the Twenty-second Amendment and its reputed weakening influence upon a president and his party show a mixed record.

EMERGENCE OF THE "INDEPENDENT" OR "SEPARATED" PRESIDENCY

Although the nation has been in the midst of the "independent" or "separated" presidency for more than two decades, academicians and the public alike have been slow to recognize its impact. Instead of a system of "separated institutions sharing power," in Richard Neustadt's felicitous phrase, we now have, in Charles O. Jones' words, "a government of separated institutions competing for shared power."[49] Under Neustadt's version of separate institutions sharing power, the president shared power in the legislative process through his signing or veto power; Congress, in turn, performed administrative-like functions with its authorization and dispensation of public funds. But in Jones' version, "The separation of powers interpreted as a competition for authority in addition finds each institution protecting and promoting itself through a broad interpretation of its constitutional and political status, even usurping the other's power when the opportunity presents itself."[50] Congressional foreign-policy making, such as the long battle over Contra aid in Nicaragua, budget one-upmanship, presidential impoundment of funds, the legislative veto (declared unconstitutional by the Supreme Court in 1983) all come to mind as evidence of a continuing power struggle between the two branches.

While James Madison and many of the other Framers expected that one branch would serve as a check upon the other, it seems doubtful that they could have anticipated the frequent deadlocks and near-paralysis that occur under the divided government. Traditionally, political parties have served to facilitate cooperation between the executive and legislative branches, but the president's party leadership role is seriously undermined in a divided government. Even though the president may have full control over the national party organization and enjoy excellent relations with his party leaders in Congress, this rapport does him little good if the opposition party controls Congress.

Except for President Reagan's brief legislative success in his first eight months in office, most recent presidents who have served in divided governments—Nixon, Ford, Reagan, and Bush—have spent most of their terms stalemated or deadlocked with the opposition Democrats in control of one or both houses of Congress. As a result, these White House incumbents have shifted their posture to become the "independent" or "separated" president. Thus, instead of negotiating or bargaining with opposition leaders over complex policy issues, the independent president "goes public" with a series of speeches to special-interest groups and heavily relies on numerous "photo opportunities" to make his case with the American public. In this connection Charles C. Euchner explains, "Media coverage of speeches reinforces the notion that speech is tantamount to substantive action."[51] But what actually happens is that the presidential address or photo opportunity diverts attention from the complicated process of policy making and implementation that is the essence of politics.

In commenting on the president's growing rhetorical role and his inability to deliver on many of his proposals, Theodore J. Lowi has noted, "Such are the president's channels of mass communication that he must simplify and dramatize his appeals, whether the communication deals with foreign policy, domestic policy or something else again. Almost every initiative is given a public relations name."[52] President Reagan, for example, has been a past master at coining clever names for his pet proposals—"peacekeeper," for MX intercontinental ballistic missiles; "freedom fighters," for the Contra rebels in Nicaragua, and so on. In other words, the president's role as party leader and policy maker becomes engulfed in a vast public relations enterprise. The White House occupant concentrates on his role as the independent president, battling the opposition party in Congress, hoping that he can pick up enough wavering opposition party members to carry the day.

DIVIDED GOVERNMENT—DOES IT MAKE A DIFFERENCE?

Since divided government has come to typify the federal government over the past quarter century—twenty out of the twenty-four years since 1968—the question can legitimately be raised: does divided government lead to policy paralysis and stalemate?

Political scientist David R. Mayhew, in the only careful empirical study of the policy consequences of divided government versus unified government since World War II, discovered that the presence or absence of unified party control of the national government has had surprisingly little effect on the legislative productivity of Congress. Mayhew identified 257 major pieces of legislation enacted between 1947 and 1988 and found, on average, that 12.8 laws were passed by each Congress during eighteen years of unified party government, while an average of 11.8 laws was enacted per Congress during twenty-four years of divided government.[53]

Nor did Mayhew find a strong temporal dimension to his data. With the systematic changes in American politics over the past four decades, especially the rise of divided government, the correlation between party composition of government and legislative productivity should have become progressively weaker over time, but Mayhew did not find this to be the case. From 1947 to 1959 Congress passed thirty-two major measures during eight years of divided government—an average of 4 per year. During six years of unified government, Congress passed twenty-seven major bills, for an average of 4.5 per year. More recently (1977–1988) an average of 5.5 major bills was enacted during the Carter administration's period of unified government, compared to an annual average of 4.6 during the Reagan years of divided government. In short, the general pattern for the two periods is remarkably similar. The only significant change in Mayhew's data occurred during the late 1960s and 1970s when there was a surge of legislative activity, but this encompassed periods of both unified and divided government (the Kennedy–Johnson and Nixon–Ford administrations).[54] Clearly, the executive and legislative branches have continued to churn out major pieces of legislation, despite divided control of the government. What accounts for this seeming aberration of party government?

Political scientist Timothy J. Conlan suggests that the dynamics of divided government, particularly interparty competition, may under some circumstances, depending upon an issue's strategic partisan potential and the degree to which existing partisan positions are firmly established, actually propel the enactment of major legislation rather than produce stalemate.[55] Indeed, if issue positions are not strongly identified, there may be considerable maneuvering space between the president and Congress for bipartisan accommodation and enactment.

In 1970, for example, President Nixon agreed with Democratic congressional leaders that amendments to the Clean Air Act were needed to reduce the ever-rising levels of air pollution across the country. With the enactment of the Clean Air Act amendments of 1970, President Nixon and the controlling congressional Democrats were both able to reap credit for this popular measure and to avoid blame for obstructing this needed reform. By joining hands in pushing through this legislation, each side also prevented the other from winning a lion's share of the credit for this major reform. In this case, divided government proved to be no insurmountable barrier to clean air legislation.

That mutual antagonism between the Nixon–Ford White House and the Democratic Congress did not stand in the way of other significant legislative enactments is clearly evident from a review of the record for the years 1969 through 1976. Major legislation included the National Environmental Policy Act of 1969, a comprehensive tax code revision, endangered species protection, a comprehensive organized crime bill, postal reorganization, urban mass transit and rail reorganization plans, the Occupational Safety and Health Act of 1970 (OSHA), the Consumer Product Safety Act, the Comprehensive Employment and Training Act (CETA), the Federal Election Campaign Act, coastal zone management, the trans-Alaska pipeline, the War Powers Resolution of 1973, and the Congressional Budget and Impoundment Control Act of 1974, as well as the Clean Air Act amendments.[56]

More recently, a Democratic House of Representatives and a Republican president and GOP-controlled Senate, deadlocked for months, finally reached an agreement in 1983 to eliminate a threatened multibillion-dollar social security fund deficit. Both sides recognized that a default in the social security program would have delayed the monthly benefit checks reaching more than twelve million senior citizens and other recipients—a disaster that both Democrats and Republicans wanted to avoid at all costs. Thus, when a bipartisan commission appointed by President Reagan and chaired by economist Alan Greenspan, currently chairman of the Federal Reserve Board, came up with a compromise solution, members from both sides of the aisle quickly accepted the proposal and President Reagan proudly signed the politically charged legislation.[57]

Similarly, in 1986—another period of divided government—major tax reform legislation was passed after more than a year of congressional bargaining and negotiation with President Reagan, with near unanimity in both chambers. To be sure, President Reagan was forced, in December 1985, to make a rare personal pilgrimage to Capitol Hill to plead with his own party's House delegation, which had voted almost unanimously against a Rules Committee resolution (requiring a two-thirds vote) to bring the tax reform bill to the floor late in the session, to reconsider their vote. Though Reagan found the bill deficient in several sections, he pleaded with his GOP brethren to reconsider their actions in order to "keep the process moving." He managed to persuade fifty-six Republican House members to switch their votes—not a majority of his own party but enough help to muster the needed two-thirds House vote to keep the tax bill alive.[58] Reagan and his White House staff then planned to have the GOP Senate majority in the second session of the Ninety-ninth Congress offer a variety of amendments compatible with Reagan's views on taxation. This strategy ultimately paid off in the passage and signing of the Tax Reform Act of 1986. Thus, both presidents Nixon and Reagan demonstrated how a chief executive, though operating within a divided government structure, can sometimes pull off major legislative coups.

Clearly, policy paralysis and stalemate need not always result from divided government. Institutional competition and "policy escalation" between the executive and legislative branches in a divided government may sometimes produce major policy reforms. In cases of the Clean Air Act amendments of 1970 and the Tax Reform Act of 1986, both the president and Congress staked out legitimate claims for responsible leadership in winning passage of the legislation. Nor did either side want to be blamed for failure to take action on these pressing issues. Beyond doubt, the competitive dynamics of separate parties controlling institutions offer presidents and lawmakers growing opportunities to tackle salient issues—subjects that can often generate broad public support and mutual political gains for the president and Congress alike, even in a divided government. Indeed, the separation of powers may spawn a system in which the president and Congress compete against one another to educate and impress an uninformed electorate on major policy matters and then arrive at the common goal—passage of the desired legislation.[59] Thus, Republican President Bush and the Democratic majorities in Congress have had conflicting views on taxes and spending, but because they had the common goal of reducing the huge federal deficit, they were able to reach a compromise on this critical national problem in late 1990. In this instance the frightful consequences of mutual intransigence on the nation's economy drove the two sides into a joint venture to reduce the deficit. Consequently, it seems fair to conclude that cooperative payoffs are more likely when the competing parties expect that the political benefits of cooperative policy change are substantial and the costs of recalcitrance and negativity are excessively high.[60] While this emerging system of bipartisan conflict resolution is not exactly what the Founding Fathers had in mind at Philadelphia in 1787, it seems fair to surmise that they would not have been completely unhappy with this governance process.

In view of the strong prospects for continued divided government for the remainder of the twentieth century—and perhaps longer—the American public may come to see far more of this bipartisan policy promotion than governmental stalemate in the years ahead.

SUMMARY

From the end of the Civil War through World War II, divided government was a near rarity. Only twice during this period did an incoming president confront either house of Congress under control of the opposition party. But the three most recently elected Republican presidents—Nixon, Reagan, and Bush—have all faced a divided government from the day they entered the White House. The American public, however, does not seem to be perturbed about a government with one party controlling the executive branch and the other controlling one or both houses of Congress. Public opinion polls show that a majority of the public feels more comfortable when the presidency and Congress are in the hands of opposite parties.

Recent presidents have developed several different strategies in dealing with a rival-party-controlled Congress. President Eisenhower, for example, was especially adept in courting leaders of the opposition Democrats. President Reagan was not far behind General Ike in building bridges with the opposition Democrats, though Reagan began to lose his touch when the Republicans lost control of the Senate in the 1986 off-year election. Clearly, party coalitions are the key to presidential success, but in the past few years the gap between the Republican president and a Democrat-controlled Congress has widened. The veto power gives the president a trump card that helps him maintain the power balance between the two branches. President Bush, for example, brandished his veto pen sixteen times during his first twenty months in office; none was overridden. The effect of the Twenty-second Amendment (the two-term limitation) on the political leadership of a second-term president is still an open question, since only two presidents—Eisenhower and Reagan— have served under this restrictive amendment.

Divided government has contributed to the mounting tension between the president and Congress. Some observers perceive a new type of independent or "separated" president who, in face of congressional recalcitrance, pursues a continuous public relations campaign with the American electorate—a tactic dangerously close to plebiscitarian leadership.

In recent years of divided government, partisan competition between the president and Congress over salient national issues and the resultant "policy escalation" has sometimes led to a new form of bipartisan accommodation, with each side sharing credit for their legislative accomplishments. Since the prospects for continued divided government show no signs of weakening, the nation may come to see a mounting trend toward more bipartisan accommodation.

If the president needs a special support group, especially during this era of divided government, he will not find a more dependable group than his national committee. This relationship between the president and his national committee is the subject of our next chapter.

NOTES

1. Donald L. Robinson, *Government for the Third American Century*, (Boulder, CO: Westview, 1989), p. 68.

2. James L. Sundquist, "Needed: A Political Theory for the New Era of Coalition Government in the United States," *Political Science Quarterly* 103 (Number 4, 1988), p. 613.

3. Morris P. Fiorina, "The Presidency and Congress: An Electoral Connection," in Michael Nelson, ed., *The Presidency and the Political System*, 3rd ed., (Washington, DC: Congressional Quarterly Press, 1990), p. 449.

4. David S. Broder, *The Party's Over* (New York: Harper and Row, 1971), p. 186.

5. David S. Broder, "Bush Gets Big Prize, But It's a Split Decision," *Washington Post National Weekly Edition*, November 14–20, 1988, p. 10.

6. *New York Times*/CBS News Poll surveys, cited in Gary C. Jacobson, *The Electoral Origins of Divided Government* (Boulder, CO: Westview, 1990), p. 121.

7. Gary C. Jacobson, "Congress a Singular Continuity," in Michael Nelson, ed., *The Elections of 1988* (Washington, DC: Congressional Quarterly Press, 1989), p. 144.

8. Ibid.

9. Ibid.

10. Ibid., p. 145.

11. Cabell Phillips, *The Truman Presidency* (Baltimore: Penguin, 1969), p. 187.

12. Susan M. Hartmann, *Truman and the 80th Congress* (Columbia: University of Missouri Press, 1971), p. 115.

13. Fred I. Greenstein, *The Hidden Hand Presidency* (New York: Basic Books, 1982), p. 78.

14. Fred I. Greenstein, "Eisenhower as an Activist President: A Look at New Evidence," *Political Science Quarterly* (Winter, 1979–1980), p. 579.

15. Rowland Evans, Jr., and Robert D. Novak, *Nixon in the White House* (New York: Random House, 1971), p. 106.

16. Richard E. Neustadt, *Presidential Power: The Politics of Leadership* (New York: Wiley, 1980), p. 67.

17. James W. Davis, *The American Presidency: A New Perspective* (New York: Harper and Row, 1987), p. 152.

18. Ibid., pp. 386–387.

19. *The New York Times*, May 28, 1988.

20. Roger H. Davidson and Walter J. Oleszek, *Congress and Its Members*, 3rd ed. (Washington, DC: Congressional Quarterly Press, 1990), p. 239.

21. Jacobson, "Congress a Singular Continuity," p. 147.

22. *The New York Times*, August 13, 1941. For a brief report on this crucial draft extension vote, see Ronald D. Elving, "The Context of a Century: Vote Stirs Old Questions," *Congressional Quarterly Weekly Report* 49 (April 6, 1991), pp. 869–872.

23. William E. Leuchtenburg, "Franklin D. Roosevelt: The First Modern President," in Fred I. Greenstein, ed., *Leadership in the Modern Presidency* (Cambridge, MA: Harvard University Press, 1988), p. 11.

24. Stephen E. Ambrose, *Eisenhower* (New York: Simon and Schuster, 1984), 2:234–235.

25. John F. Manley, "The Conservative Coalition in Congress," in Lawrence C. Dodd and Bruce I. Oppenheimer, eds., *Congress Reconsidered* (New York: Praeger, 1977), p. 89.

26. Ibid.

27. Ibid., pp. 89–90.

28. *Congressional Quarterly Weekly Report* 48 (November 3, 1990), pp. 3764 and 3769.

29. *The New York Times*, October 30, 1991.

30. Idem., January 13, 1991.

31. Representative Frank Thompson (D-N.J.), a leading member of the Democratic Study Group, cited by John F. Manley, "The Conservative Coalition in Congress," in Lawrence C. Dodd and Bruce I. Oppenheimer, eds., *Congress Reconsidered* p. 80.

32. "A Once Powerful Voting Bloc Loses Some of Its Punch," *Congressional Quarterly Weekly Report* 48 (December 22, 1990), p. 4192.

33. Woodrow Wilson, *Congressional Government* (Boston: Houghton Mifflin, 1885), p. 52.

34. James L. Sundquist, *Constitutional Reform and Effective Government* (Washington, DC: The Brookings Institution, 1986), p. 208.

35. *The New York Times*, January 24, 1990.

36. Ibid., January 26, 1990.

37. Ibid.

38. Ann Devroy, Los Angeles Times–Washington Post News Service dispatch, *The Oregonian*, March 13, 1991.

39. Ambrose, *Eisenhower*, 2:218.

40. Norman J. Ornstein, Thomas E. Mann, and Michael J. Malbin, *Vital Statistics on Congress 1989–1990* (Washington, DC: American Enterprise Institute, 1990), p. 51.

41. Broder, *The Party's Over*, p. 63.

42. *The New York Times*, January 14, 1990.

43. Walter R. Mears, Associated Press dispatch, *Bellingham* (Washington) *Herald*, November 7, 1990.

44. Letter to Representative Stewart L. Udall (D-AZ) in *Congressional Record* (March 25, 1957), cited by James L. Sundquist in *Constitutional Reform and Effective Government*, p. 48.

45. Ambrose, *Eisenhower*, 2:554.

46. Ibid., p. 644.

47. *Congressional Quarterly Weekly Report* 45 (April 4, 1987), pp. 604–606.

48. Ibid.

49. Charles O. Jones, "The Separated Presidency—Making It Work in Contemporary Politics," in Anthony King, ed., *The New Political System*, 2nd version, (Washington, DC: American Enterprise Institute, 1990), p. 3.

50. Ibid.

51. Charles C. Euchner, "Presidential Appearances," in *Presidents and the Public* (Washington, DC: Congressional Quarterly Press, 1990), p. 124.

52. Theodore J. Lowi, *The Personal President* (Ithaca, NY: Cornell University Press, 1985), p. 170.

53. David R. Mayhew, "Does It Make a Difference Whether Party Control of the American National Government Is Unified or Divided?" Paper prepared for delivery at the 1989 Annual Meeting of the American Political Science Association, Atlanta, Georgia, August 31–September 3, 1989, p. 5; see also David R. Mayhew, *Divided We Govern*, New Haven, CT: Yale University Press, 1991.

54. Ibid.

55. Timothy J. Conlan, "Competitive Government: Policy Escalation and Divided Party Control." Paper prepared for delivery at the 1990 Annual Meeting of the American Political Science Association, San Francisco, California, August 30–September 2, 1990, pp. 13–14.

56. Roger H. Davidson, "The Presidency and Three Eras of the Modern Congress," in James A. Thurber, ed., *Divided Democracy* (Washington, DC: Congressional Quarterly Press, 1991), p. 74.

57. Davis, *The American Presidency*, pp. 162–163.

58. *The New York Times*, December 17, 1985.

59. Conlan, "Competitive Government," p. 12; see also Timothy J. Conlan, Margaret T. Wrightson, and David R. Beam, *Taxing Choices: The Politics of Tax Reform* (Washington, DC: Congressional Quarterly Press, 1990), p. 237.

60. For further background on constructive conflict resolution, see Paul J. Quirk, "The Cooperative Resolution of Policy Conflict," *American Political Science Review* 83 (September 1989), pp. 905–921.

Chapter 5

The President and the National Committee

Since the rise of national nominating conventions in the 1840s, the president and the party's national committee have been partners in the task of winning control of the White House. In this chapter we focus on the changing relationship between the president and the national party, especially since establishment by both parties of permanent national headquarters during the late 1930s. Various presidential models for running the national committee will also be evaluated.

The shifting role and duties of national chairman during the present candidate-centered era of presidential campaigning is assessed, as well as the "professionalization" of the national committees and the impact of the frequent turnover of national party chairmen upon the national party organization.

Special attention is centered on the growing number of national party chairman in recent years who have figured prominently in the shaping of the party's presidential ticket. Since the Kennedy election in 1960, three former national party chairman have become nominees for vice president on the Republican ticket. More important, one former national party chair—George Bush—has become the first to be elected president of the United States. Finally, a discussion of the president's relations with state and local party chieftains—limited though these contacts may be—completes the chapter.

OFFICIAL HEAD OF THE NATIONAL COMMITTEE

The president is the official head of his or her national party—but only as long as he is president. Unlike British party leaders who continue in place whether their party is in power or in the opposition—Labour party leader Clement R. Attlee, for example, served for twenty years (1935–1955) both as opposition leader and as prime minister—the American president's party stewardship ends when he relinquishes office. Thus, when President Jimmy Carter lost his reelection bid in 1980, he, in effect, lost his party leadership position, though he was still considered "titular" leader until the selection of another presidential nominee. Many Democratic lawmakers and state organizational leaders breathed a sigh of relief that he would no longer be a "drag" on their future electoral campaigns.[1]

Earlier, President Truman found that once he left the White House, in 1953, he lost his political clout and ability to shape Democratic fortunes. In 1960, this political fact of life came home only too clearly in the Democratic nomination race when Truman opposed John F. Kennedy's candidacy (the former president favored Senator Stuart Symington of his home state of Missouri) but Kennedy nevertheless won the Democratic nomination.[2] More recently, retired President Ronald Reagan has been warmly welcomed in GOP circles and on the fundraising circuit, but his advice has not been openly solicited by his successor, President George Bush, or by the Republican national committee. In his first two years in office, President Bush held a number of perfunctory meetings with Reagan while on official trips to California, but nothing more.

The president's party leadership duties begin with his nomination. As soon as the national convention anoints him as the party's standard-bearer, he relays word to the national committee (which usually reconvenes the day after the convention) on his personal choice for national party chairman. The committee dutifully ratifies his choice. Furthermore, it is the president who determines the chairman's tenure. Some chairs may serve two or more years; FDR's first chairman, James A. Farley, served Roosevelt for eight years before breaking with him over the third-term issue. Since the national party chairman is the creature of the president, no national chairman—not even the famed Mark Hanna of the William McKinley–Teddy Roosevelt era—has ever been strong enough to undermine the president's party authority.

If the president is defeated for reelection, the party has no acknowledged leader, though the defeated chief executive may claim to be the party's "titular" leader. But in fact the party's center of influence and power will be found in the Senate, the House of Representatives, the national committee, or possibly among prospective future presidential contenders. The next officially recognized party leader, however, will not emerge until the next national convention four years down the road.

NINETEENTH-CENTURY RELATIONSHIP BETWEEN
THE PRESIDENT AND THE NATIONAL COMMITTEE

Presidents Thomas Jefferson and Andrew Jackson, the earliest strong party leaders, predate the national committee era. Lincoln ranks as the first strong party leader after the emergence of the national committee system in the 1840s; yet he is chiefly remembered as the commander in chief who preserved the Union, not as a party leader.

In the Gilded Age of the post–Civil-War era, presidents rarely exhibited strong party leadership. After Lincoln, Congress, in effect, took over the reins of government from President Andrew Johnson, overriding his vetoes, curtailing his appointment power, impeaching him, and coming within one vote of removing him from office. Anti-Johnson radical Republican leaders on Capitol Hill so distrusted the GOP national committee, however, that they organized a Republican congressional committee to direct the House election campaign. For the remainder of the century, the center of political gravity rested in Congress rather than in the presidency. Two decades later, President Grover Cleveland, formerly a strong governor from New York, lost his influence within the Democratic party when he was defeated after his first term. Indeed, his public career seemed to have reached a dead end. Prominent Democrats, such as Governor David B. Hill of New York and Senator Arthur P. Gorman of Maryland, spoke contemptuously of him to party insiders and believed that he had been eliminated, once and for all, from the national scene. "Cleveland in New York," one commentator remarked, "reminds one of a stone thrown into a river. There is a 'plunk,' a splash, and then silence."[3] When Cleveland bounced back four years later to recapture the White House and control the Democratic party, his divided party failed to respond to many of his initiatives. Near the end of his second term, it in effect disowned him at the 1896 Democratic convention. Nevertheless, the strong-minded Cleveland caused the public to focus their eyes on the White House, not Capitol Hill. Clearly, the concept of the president as a party leader was undergoing a transformation.

A CHANGED RELATIONSHIP IN THE TWENTIETH CENTURY

In the nineteenth century, the president and his national committee maintained a respectful social distance. National party chairmen were still picked by the national committee. In the twentieth century, the rise of the modern president as the recognized party leader has drastically shifted the power balance to the White House. President Teddy Roosevelt, who termed the presidency a "bully pulpit," used every means at his disposal—special messages to Congress, the distribution of political jobs, vetoes, and jingoistic foreign policy speeches—to enhance his position as leader of his country, his party, and the Republican national committee. Probably the most serious reelection challenge to an incumbent president by a party national chairman, however, occurred against Roosevelt shortly after the turn of the century. Roosevelt, who had been elevated to the presidency after McKinley's assassination in Buffalo, New York, in September 1901, still did not fully control his party during most of his first term. GOP national chairman Mark Hanna, who had headed McKinley's two highly successful presidential campaigns, continued to be a major rival in the Republican party, nor had he completely given up a lingering ambition to occupy the White House himself after McKinley's death.

Beyond question, the champion fundraiser for the Republican party during the first half of the twentieth century, Hanna served not only as national chairman but also as a powerful senator from Ohio. A member of the Senate's inner circle and multimillionaire owner of a big Cleveland steel company, Hanna had close ties with the captains of industry and finance throughout the East. The fact that TR was an "accidental president" who still had to face the voters for the first time in 1904 may have influenced Hanna's decision to withhold his endorsement of Roosevelt for a full term throughout 1902 and 1903—perhaps leaving the door ajar for his own nomination.[4] But because Hanna had failed to create a national political organization of loyal lieutenants across the country to oppose a popular president, his prospects of blocking Roosevelt's second term bid were more illusory than genuine. A serious Hanna threat—if it could be termed such—never materialized. The wealthy Ohioan died in mid-February 1904, shortly before the nominating season opened. Four months later, Roosevelt received a unanimous nomination at the Chicago convention.

President Woodrow Wilson dominated his national committee far more completely than did Roosevelt. Wilson's hand-picked national chairmen, William F. McCombs (1912–1916) and Vance McCormick (1916–1919) served as his emissaries at the Democratic national committee and followed his directives to the letter. Once the Democrats lost the White House in 1920, however, the Democratic committee fell once again under the wing of congressional leaders and wealthy benefactors.

Within the Republican party, President William Howard Taft found party leadership duties uncongenial, especially when it came time to referee disputes between the Stalwarts and the Progressives. When Taft lost his reelection bid in 1912, the Republican national committee reasserted itself within party circles and continued to make its voice heard even after Senator Warren G. Harding recaptured the White House in 1920. In accordance with custom, Harding had reason to assume that John T. Adams, his personal choice for GOP national party chairman in 1921, would follow the White House lead on policy questions. But when Harding advocated American membership in the Permanent Court of International Justice, Adams launched a venomous attack upon the leading European powers that had been allied with the United States in World War I. Adams was echoing the sentiments of many GOP senators and congressmen who had begun reverting toward isolationism and away from the international community. When the chairmen of the Republican congressional and senatorial campaign committees continued the attack against Harding's policies, Harding decided in the summer of

1923 to take his case over the heads of Congress to the people with a nationwide tour. His death in San Francisco while on this transcontinental tour left the divisive party issues unresolved.[5] But his successor, Calvin Coolidge, soon proved himself the master of his party. The recalcitrant Adams was replaced at GOP headquarters by William M. Butler, a Coolidge loyalist, who also managed his 1924 primary campaign. No more major GOP national committee uprisings have occurred since the flare-up in the 1920s. Party revolts at the Democratic national party headquarters against a Democratic president in the modern era are virtually unknown.

In 1940, however, Democratic national chairman James A. Farley, who had presidential aspirations himself, resigned the chairmanship when President Roosevelt refused to disavow all intentions of running for a third term. Farley's presidential bid in 1940 failed to get off the ground, and Roosevelt, of course, went on to win both a third and a fourth term.[6]

President Eisenhower, though he portrayed himself as a citizen-soldier, frequently used the prestige of the White House to advance the cause of the Republican party. Members of the GOP national committee were invited to his informal but regular "stag dinners" for business and party leaders.[7] President Eisenhower was the last president to take a personal interest in national committee members. Subsequent presidents—Democrats and Republicans alike—have kept national committee members at arm's length socially.

THE ESTABLISHMENT OF PERMANENT NATIONAL PARTY HEADQUARTERS

For many years, both parties and national committees lived like transients, renting quarters where price and convenience guided the choice. The Republican national committee was located in the nation's capital, unobtrusively in the Cafritz Building, 1625 I Street (the letter "I" is often spelled "Eye"). No plaque or sign marked the headquarters. In fact, the Republicans occupied the second floor, sharing office space with insurance offices, security brokers, lawyers, and office furniture firms. The Democratic national committee was usually located nearby, in similar rented upstairs quarters; Democratic staffers would often frequent the same restaurants and watering spots as the Republicans.[8] The author recalls visiting the Democratic national headquarters in the late 1950s while it was under the direction of Paul Butler. Located on the second floor of a building on Connecticut Avenue, the office looked like a small mail order firm, staffed by a handful of middle-aged ladies surrounded by old green file cabinets and a few typewriters. It scarcely seemed that the Democrats could ever win another presidential election, yet less than two years later, Senator John F. Kennedy captured the White House.

The most famous Democratic national headquarters was, of course, located in the Watergate complex near the Kennedy Center. In June 1972, a break-in there by a White House–directed team of burglars subsequently led to a full-scale congressional investigation that eventually toppled President Richard Nixon from office in August 1974.

In the mid-1960s, the Republicans, under some forceful prodding from a retired President Eisenhower, decided to build their own national headquarters within a few blocks of the Capitol. For the first time in the nation's history, a major party finally owned its own home. Neatly designed, the Eisenhower Center, as the headquarters is called, contains office space for more than two hundred employees. Equipped with the latest computers and data base, an excellent library, and a fine research staff, the GOP headquarters is a model of efficiency.

The Democratic national committee, strapped for cash, continued to rent space in downtown Washington for another fifteen years before party benefactors raised enough money to build a new headquarters. Completed in 1987, the DNC building is located on Capitol Hill a short distance from the Supreme Court. Equipped with the latest data processing and sophisticated communications equipment, the DNC can now, theoretically at least, go toe to toe against the GOP national committee in fundraising and information dissemination.

Both the GOP and Democratic national committee headquarters are, of course, a far cry from their temporary quarters in the late nineteenth and early twentieth centuries. Homelessness was a way of life during most of this earlier era. Both national committees established a national headquarters during presidential years, but as soon as the campaigns were over, the national committees usually closed up shop for three years until the next quadrennial presidential campaign cycle began again. During the 1920s and early 1930s, the offices of the Democratic national committee shifted back and forth between Washington and New York City for the convenience of its national chairman, or as party finances dictated. All three Democratic chairmen during this period—John Raskob, James A. Farley, and Edward J. Flynn—were New Yorkers with access to big party donors. Raskob, a multimillionaire himself, had a large financial interest in the newly constructed Empire State Building and reportedly made space available to the national committee at a fraction of its market cost—and sometimes without charge.[9] Neither party, however, established a full-time national headquarters until the mid-1930s. Since then, both parties have stayed open around the calendar.

THE HIGH TURNOVER OF NATIONAL PARTY CHAIRMEN

National party chairmen, especially those of the president's party, have uncertain tenure. As noted by Thomas E. Cronin: ''National party chairpersons come and go with embarrassing regularity and regular embarrassment."[10] Between 1967 and 1978, for example, there were eight Democratic and six Republican national chairpersons. The average tenure for national chairmen of the party controlling the White House since World War II has been about two years.

In 1982, President Ronald Reagan jettisoned his first national chairman, Richard Richards of Utah, reportedly for management inefficiency. But some party insiders said that Richards was too reform-minded in wanting to make the party more accountable to the rank and file.[11]

A variety of circumstances have led to the departure of party chairmen during the president's term. Some have resigned for personal reasons or to pursue other career interests. In several instances, presidents have created vacancies by appointing a national chairman to a high-level government post. Truman appointed J. Howard McGrath as his attorney general; Nixon picked Rogers Morton to be secretary of the interior; and Ford chose George Bush to head the liaison office in the People's Republic of China in 1975.[12]

Several chairmen have found it intolerable to continue their job when the White House placed a presidential agent at the national party headquarters, nominally subordinate to the chairman but with full-fledged decision-making authority. Even with the chairman's knowledge, this arrangement compromises the chairman's authority and his status with the White House and the state party organizations.

Formerly, a national party chairman served without pay. Either he was wealthy and needed no salary or held a position as senator, representative, or cabinet member and doubled as national party chairman. But the trend is toward a full-time, salaried chairman, and this development, coupled with the rise of independent candidate organizations, may cause a shift in the role of the national chairman.

NATIONAL PARTY CHAIRMAN DEMOTED FROM CABINET RANK

For the first half of the twentieth century, the national chairman of the party occupying the White House, generally the president's chief political adviser, usually held cabinet rank unless he also held elective office. Mark Hanna, one of the GOP's most famous national chairmen, was a senator from Ohio through most of his chairmanship (1896–1904), as mentioned earlier. President Franklin D. Roosevelt appointed his 1932 campaign manager, James A. Farley of New York, to serve as national chairman as well as postmaster general—a cabinet position until the postal service became a government corporation in 1970. Republican presidents have often preferred members of Congress to double as national chairmen. One of President Eisenhower's national chairmen was Senator Thruston Morton of Kentucky. Two of President Nixon's national chairmen were Representative Rogers Morton of Maryland (1969–1971), a brother of the former chairman, and Senator Robert Dole of Kansas (1971–1973).

No national party chairman of the incumbent party has simultaneously held cabinet rank since 1947, but this is not to imply that the chairman's status and influence declined immediately. President Eisenhower regarded one of his national chairmen, Leonard Hall of New York (1953–1957) as the "alter ego on party matters of the president."[13] General Ike also expected the chairman to be the in-house "political expert" in the presidential allocation of administrative responsibilities and advisory roles.

When John F. Kennedy moved into the White House, however, the political "clout" of the national chairman soon declined dramatically. Instead of Democratic national chairman John Bailey making the major decisions on patronage, the filling of political positions was handled by the White House staffer, Kenneth O'Donnell, one of the so-called "Massachusetts Mafia." This shift-over not only reflected the Kennedy style of operations but also the practice first started in the Truman years of designating a staff assistant as the president's personal liaison or contact with party officials and political leaders throughout the country, including national committee members. With the establishment of an assistant and an apparatus within the White House, the president was able to internalize the political tasks and functions once clearly associated with the national party organization. The net result was to strengthen the White House control over the national party organization and to weaken the influence of the national committee headquarters.[14]

Under this centralized White House direction, John F. Kennedy's national chairman John Bailey spent more of his time in a cheerleading role than as the chief executive officer at the national headquarters. The author recalls attending a Midwest Democratic conference in 1963 in Minneapolis, where Mr. Bailey was the chief speaker. No major personnel decisions were made at the meeting with the national chairman, since state party leaders were well aware that any major patronage decisions were handled by the White House staff, not by the national chairman. White House preemption of the national committee's political responsibilities has continued almost without interruption since the Kennedy years.

The Lyndon Johnson takeover of the Democratic national committee is chronicled in Chapter 4. President Richard Nixon shared Johnson's low opinion of the national committee and its chairman. A story recounted by former GOP national chairman Robert Dole best describes the relationship between the Nixon White House and the national chairman. Senator Dole recalled receiving a phone call late one afternoon from a White House staffer informing him that his longstanding request to see President Nixon was about to be granted; if he would tune his TV set to a network channel at 7 P.M., he could watch the president's scheduled address![15] In recent years, few party chairpersons of the president's party have enjoyed much influence. In the Watergate era, the Republicans had an ambitious national chairman by the name of George Bush. But little evidence has surfaced to suggest that he was anything more than a cheerleader in the high councils of the Republican party. Robert Strauss, former Democratic national chairman, summarized the White House–national chairman relationship this way: "If you're Democratic party chairman when a Democrat is president, you're a god-damn file clerk."[16]

Paradoxically, a national chairman possesses far more leadership clout when his or her party does not control the White House. Robert Strauss's performance in leading the Democratic party back to power in 1976, after eight years in the wilderness, is proof enough of this political maxim. Soon after Democratic President Jimmy Carter moved into the White House, Strauss resigned the party chairmanship to become Carter's special trade representative. Similarly, in the mid-1960s, GOP national chairman Ray Bliss's virtuoso performance had helped pave the way for a Republican return to the White House, but Nixon soon sacked him—allegedly for not being enough of a Nixon loyalist.[17]

It seems doubtful that national party chairmen of the president's party will ever regain the status they enjoyed in the Hanna or Farley eras, but President Reagan seemed to turn back the political clock in late 1982 when he made his longtime friend and close personal advisor, Senator Paul Laxalt of Nevada, "general chairman" of the GOP. Laxalt was, in effect, given carte blanche to operate the Republican party as he saw fit. Content to keep the national committee from straying too far on an independent course, Laxalt chose to delegate most day-to-day responsibilities to his protégé, Frank Fahrenkopf, a Nevada lawyer. When Laxalt declined to seek reelection in 1986 (in order to "test the presidential waters") and asked to be relieved of his chairmanship duties, Reagan elevated Fahrenkopf to a regular-status national chairmanship.

President George Bush, probably reflecting on his own brief tenure as national party chairman (1973–1974) during the Nixon years, decided soon after his election to shift GOP political operations from the White House back to the Republican national committee headquarters near the Capitol. This unexpected move clearly emphasized Bush's confidence in his new GOP national chairman Lee Atwater, the manager of his highly successful 1988 nominating campaign.

From the beginning of his chairmanship, the pugnacious Atwater viewed one of his most important assignments to be the party "hell-raiser." As described by Cotter and Hennessy, the leading authorities on the national committees, "Part of the accepted style of the national chairman is to be continuously, openly, and unremittingly partisan."[18] Atwater fit this qualification to the letter. Constantly punching and counterpunching the opposition Democrats, Atwater kept his adversaries off balance much of his time. Sometimes accused of gutter-style politics for his hard-edged attacks on the Democrats, Atwater rarely seemed to displease President Bush. But Atwater's political career came to an unfortunate detour in March 1990, when it was announced that he was suffering from a brain tumor. With Atwater no longer at the helm to handle the day-to-day GOP political operations, the political center of gravity again shifted back to the White House. For several months, party direction and strategy were handled by Bush's chief of staff, John H. Sununu, and his assistants in the Office of Political Affairs.[19]

Late in 1990 President Bush picked a new GOP national chairman, Clayton K. Yeutter, former secretary of agriculture—after retiring drug policy czar William J. Bennett first accepted and then turned down the job. But there has been no indication that national party direction will be removed again from the West Wing to the party headquarters. At the semiannual GOP national committee meeting, held in the nation's capital in January 1991, the once hard-driving Atwater was elected to the advisory position of general chairman, but he lost his bout with cancer less than three months after receiving this honor. Clearly, the unmistakable message contained in Bush's choice of Yeutter, an inexperienced political hand, was that centralized party decision making will once again reside in the White House.

PRESIDENTIAL MODELS FOR RUNNING THE NATIONAL PARTY ORGANIZATION

How can we evaluate the activities and attitudes of presidents in their party leadership role? To operationalize the concept of American presidential party leadership, we have borrowed from political scientist Ralph M. Goldman's model based on factional behavior.[20] As originally developed by Goldman, a longtime student of the presidency and the national committees, the typology included not only sitting presidents but also titular leaders of the out-of-power party since the rise of the first nominating conventions in 1832. Table 5.1 lists all presidents, including Washington, who served before the emergence of political parties. Leaders of the opposition party are not included. In Goldman's typology, the presidents fit into four basic models: nonpartisans, subpartisans, transpartisans, and partisans.[21]

Nonpartisans: These presidents were leaders with little or no party involvement who assumed a role "above" party and faction.

Subpartisans: These presidents behaved or were perceived as factional leaders before, during, and sometimes after leaving office. The factional identification frequently inhibited their efforts to unify the party.

Transpartisans: These presidents were those leaders whose party identification was weak or ambiguous to the degree of actually encouraging the formation of another party or shifting their allegiance to another party.

Partisans: These presidents have been explicit, articulate, and even unabashedly proud of their party affiliation, relatively active in the party's management, and willing to solicit and to campaign on behalf of the party.

Clearly, this typology does not encompass all phases of presidential party leadership, but several generalizations can be inferred from Table 5.1. First, a majority of presidents has been partisan, with twenty-two cases, while the other categories range between six and eight chief executives. Presidential partisanship will be found mostly in the post–Reconstruction era; moreover, this phenomenon reflects the relatively stable two-party system that developed by the 1880s.

Table 5.1
Factional Types of Presidential Partisanship
(Year of first inauguration indicated in parentheses)

Nonpartisan	Subpartisan	Transpartisan	Partisan
WASHINGTON (1789)	J. ADAMS (1797)	Tyler (1841)	JEFFERSON (1801)
J.Q. ADAMS (1825)	Pierce (1853)	Fillmore (1850)	MADISON (1801)
W.H. Harrison (1841)	Buchanan (1857)	Lincoln (1865)	MONROE (1817)
Taylor (1849)	Hayes (1877)	A. Johnson (1865)	Jackson (1829)
Grant (1869)	Arthur (1881)	Cleveland (1893)	Van Buren (1837)
Eisenhower (1953)	Taft (1909)	T. Roosevelt (1901)	Polk (1845)
	Harding (1921)		Lincoln (1861)
	CARTER (1977)		Garfield (1881)
			Cleveland (1885)
			B. Harrison (1889)
			McKinley (1897)
			Wilson (1913)
			Coolidge (1923)
			Hoover (1929)
			F.D. Roosevelt (1933)
			Truman (1945)
			Kennedy (1961)
			L.B. Johnson (1963)
			Nixon (1969)
			FORD (1974)
			REAGAN (1981)
			BUSH (1989)

Source: Reprinted by permission of Greenwood Publishing Group, Westport, CT, from Ralph M. Goldman, "The American President as Party Leader: A Synoptic History," in Robert Harmel, ed., *Presidents and Their Parties: Leadership or Neglect?* (New York: Praeger, 1984), p. 21. President Bush has been classified as "partisan" by the author.
Note: Presidents listed in capital letters are pre-1832 or post-1968 incumbents.

Second, five out of six of the nonpartisans were generals, objects of popular favor rather than partisan attachment. Generally, they preferred to maintain a posture "above" party, serving "all the people." Third, the transpartisans served during times of great instability in a party system marked by shifting coalitions. For example, John Tyler, a Democrat from Virginia, was put on the Whig ticket as a running-mate with General William Henry Harrison to attract Southern votes. Harrison's sudden death one month after his inauguration elevated Tyler to the presidency. Millard Fillmore, another vice president elevated to the presidency, was a Whig whose party disintegrated under pressure of the slavery controversy. In 1864, President Lincoln put Andrew Johnson, a War Democrat from Tennessee, on the Union ticket to help assure reelection in the midst of the Civil War. The year 1896, a realigning election year, found retiring President Grover Cleveland virtually disowned by the Silver Democrats; he supported a separate Gold Democratic ticket. Teddy Roosevelt, denied the GOP nomination in 1912 after having served over seven years previously (1901–1908), marched many of his supporters into the newly formed Progressive party.

Fourth, most of the partisans have been Democrats (but the Republicans are gaining ground) while most nonpartisans have been Federalists, Whigs, or Republicans. This coincides with the oft-made observation that the Democrats, more frequently the majority party, have been more heavily dependent upon party organization as their key to victory. As the minority party, the Republicans have had to down-play partisanship in order to attract disgruntled Democrats and independents. Generally, presidential behavior has mirrored these different party considerations.

NATIONAL PARTY CHAIRMEN—DECLINING POWER BUT RISING POLITICAL STATURE

Nineteenth-century party chairmen were powers to be reckoned with. Mark Hanna, McKinley's national chairman (and later Teddy Roosevelt's) immediately comes to mind. A champion fundraiser for McKinley in 1896 and 1900, Hanna commanded respect throughout Republican circles and the corporate business world. In 1904, he set a new record for corporate contributions—over $6 million (worth well over $100 million at 1990 price levels). Indeed, Hanna was so successful that Congress, responding to public outcries, banned all corporate contributions in the Tillman Act of 1907.[22]

James A. Farley, Roosevelt's campaign manager for nearly a decade and Democratic national chairman for Roosevelt's first two terms, was widely regarded as one of the strongest party chairmen in history. Meticulous in his organizational work and on excellent terms with state party leaders across the land, Farley reportedly could recall the first names of thousands of organizational Democrats.

President Eisenhower showed no hesitation in selecting two strong Republican national party chairmen—Arthur Summerfield of Michigan and later Leonard Hall of New York—and giving them broad authority to run the GOP national headquarters. Both Summerfield and Hall were longtime party professionals, and Eisenhower, who regarded himself as a novice in organizational politics, preferred to concentrate his duties on statecraft and streamlining federal government responsibilities.[23]

Since the Eisenhower presidency, national party chairmen of the incumbent party have seen their organizational influence decline. They have been eclipsed by White House staffers whom the president has assigned to oversee political appointments and other important party business.

This trend started under President John F. Kennedy, and with one possible exception, the downward slide has continued. President Lyndon B. Johnson saw little need for a national party chairman, since LBJ thought the national party headquarters could be run by one presidential assistant and a couple of secretaries. President Nixon held the GOP national committee and party chairman in such low esteem that he ordered his staffers to ignore the Republican national chairman. Prior to the 1972 election campaign, Nixon ordered his staff to form an independent reelection committee—the Committee to Re-Elect the President (CREEP)—to handle his bid for a second term. Organized completely outside party channels, CREEP developed a "dirty tricks" campaign strategy that, though successful in 1972, eventually came back to haunt the White House during the Watergate investigation.[24]

President Jimmy Carter had so little confidence in the Democratic party chairman, former Maine Governor Kenneth M. Curtis, that he installed several Carter insiders at the Democratic national headquarters to monitor closely every Curtis decision. After ten months of humiliation and over-the-shoulder management by the White House, Curtis resigned.

President Ronald Reagan, after a two-year experiment with a reform-minded GOP national party chairman, Richard Richards of Utah, sacked him in favor of a close friend and political ally, Senator Paul Laxalt of Nevada. To strengthen Laxalt's hand, Reagan gave him a broad-ranging portfolio that was reminiscent of strong party chairmen of yesteryear. In the Bush administration Secretary of State James Baker III, Bush's 1980 and 1988 presidential campaign manager and a longtime Texas friend, continues as his number one political adviser.[25]

NATIONAL CHAIRMEN AND THE PRESIDENTIAL TICKET

Traditionally, the national party chair has been more closely identified with organizational politics than with electoral politics. But since the 1960s, the incumbent party's national chairman has frequently been involved in the composition of the presidential ticket. This development has taken three forms: (1) the chairman has been available for the vice presidential nomination; (2) the chairmanship has been used as a consolation prize for the loser of the vice presidential sweepstakes; (3) former party chairs have been among the field of contenders for the party's presidential nomination.

In 1960, Democratic nominee John F. Kennedy passed over Senator Henry M. "Scoop" Jackson of Washington in favor of Senator Lyndon B. Johnson for the second spot on the presidential ticket.[26] But as a consolation prize, he selected Jackson to be the Democratic national chairman for the duration of the campaign.

Similarly, Vice President Nixon, the 1960 GOP nominee, left GOP national chairman Senator Thruston B. Morton of Kentucky on his "short list" of prospective running-mates. When Nixon chose Henry Cabot Lodge, Jr., for the number two spot on the ticket, Morton retained the chairmanship.

In 1964, GOP national chairman Representative William E. Miller of New York, was Senator Barry Goldwater's personal choice for running-mate—the first incumbent chairman ever named to a major party ticket.[27]

Richard M. Nixon, in his second bid for the presidency in 1968, seriously considered Representative Rogers B. Morton, younger brother of Thruston, as his vice presidential partner, before ultimately deciding on Maryland Governor Spiro T. Agnew for the number two spot. When a vacancy occurred in the chairmanship following Nixon's victory, however, Nixon asked the GOP national committee to select Morton for the post.

In 1972, former Democratic national chairman Larry O'Brien was among the prospective candidates for the vice presidential nomination on the Democratic ticket. Democratic presidential nominee, Senator George McGovern, however, finally settled on Senator Thomas Eagleton of Missouri, after receiving turndowns from Senators Ted Kennedy, Edmund Muskie, and Hubert Humphrey. But when Eagleton resigned the nomination two weeks later, after it was revealed that he had undergone electroshock treatment for depression, O'Brien was again mentioned as a possible choice. But McGovern passed over him in favor of R. Sargent Shriver, brother-in-law of President Kennedy.[28]

When Vice President Gerald R. Ford became president in August 1974, following President Nixon's resignation in face of impeachment charges, he seriously considered nominating GOP national chairman George Bush to be the new vice president. But at showdown time, Ford instead chose Governor Nelson Rockefeller of New York. Two years later, President Ford dumped Rockefeller from the 1976 Republican ticket and replaced him with another former GOP national chairman, Senator Robert Dole of Kansas.[29]

Four years later, the 1980 GOP nominating race included the candidacies of two former national party chairmen—Bush and Dole. Both lost their presidential bids to former California Governor Ronald Reagan, but Bush became Reagan's running-mate. The Reagan-Bush victory in November made Bush the first former national party chairman to be elected vice president.

With President Reagan barred from a third term in 1988, Bush and Dole once again resumed their presidential rivalry. For several months the Washington rumor mill also had retired Senator Paul Laxalt of Nevada, general chairman of the Republican party from 1982 to 1986, as another potential contender for president. But Laxalt eventually decided against entering the GOP race. Bush's subsequent nomination and election made him the first former national chairman to be elected president of the United States.

Clearly, national party chairmen have developed enough visibility and stature to be considered serious players in presidential nominating politics. But the decision of both major parties in the 1970s to make the national party chairmanship a full-time managerial position may in the future reduce the prospects of national party leaders to become active presidential contenders.

THE SHIFTING ROLES OF THE NATIONAL COMMITTEE AND ITS CHAIRMAN

The emergence of candidate-centered presidential campaigns has deprived the national committee and party chairman of one of their traditional responsibilities—running the general election campaign for the party nominee. Deprived of this major task, the national party chairman and the national committee headquarters have shifted into fundraising for congressional candidates and providing staff support, such as expertise in TV and radio campaign-commercial production, polling, and campaign organization. Amendments to the Federal Election Campaign Act of 1974 five years later have also opened the door for the national committees to become financially involved in congressional and state campaigns by permitting them to raise and spend approximately $7 million without this expenditure being charged against the presidential candidate's public-funded spending ceiling ($46.1 million in 1988). Under a 1979 federal statute, state parties can make unlimited expenditures in pres- idential election years for get-out-the-vote drives and other "party-building" activities. But these state contributions cannot be diverted to help presidential candidates unless they comply with the $25,000 federal lid on individual donations. However, both GOP and Democratic finance chieftains conceded that in 1988 they made no distinction between the use of private and public funds in their general election campaigns. The Federal Election Commission (FEC) completely ignored this seeming violation of the federal law. According to a *Washington Post* reporter, Charles Babcock, there were more individuals who contributed $100,000 in 1988 than in the Watergate year election of 1972.[30] In recent years the Republican national committee has developed "agency agreements" with its state and local counterparts, which allow the national party to spend both its share and the state's share in congressional campaigns. Federal law sets a $1,000 limit in each election for individual contributors. But in 1988, presidential candidates began soliciting large sums— "soft money"—from wealthy individuals for distribution to state parties to aid the presidential candidates with voter registration drives, computerized voting lists, and phone banks. To skirt the intent of the 1974 law, fundraising chairmen for both Vice President Bush and Governor Dukakis relied on a huge loophole, not previously used, to generate two huge campaign jackpots. Big contributors—"fat cats"—were urged to give $100,000 to the Republican or Democratic national committee "nonfederal accounts," which are not subject to the limitations of the 1971 and 1974 laws. Donations to such nonfederal accounts—which are administered by state and local party affiliates—do not violate federal law, according to the Federal Election Commission.[31] As a result, presidential fundraisers had a field day in 1988. Vice President Bush's fundraisers solicited approximately $22 million from individual contributors who gave upwards of $100,000 each. This figure does not include another $8.3 million spent by the GOP national committee in "coordinated expenditures." Dukakis's fundraising chairman raised approximately $23 million under the same ground rules.[32] The new technique works like this: Presidential fundraisers contact potential big donors about making a contribution. Instead of giving big sums directly to the presidential campaigns—which would be illegal—the soft-money contributors are encouraged to donate to state parties. Once collected, the money is put in the pipeline to the national committee for distribution to the state party organizations.[33] Understandably, national party committees are more than willing to funnel all this extra cash through their headquarters in order to have greater control over its use.

THE PROFESSIONALIZATION OF NATIONAL COMMITTEES

National committees today are a far cry from those of the 1930s when Franklin D. Roosevelt described the Democratic national committee headquarters as consisting of two middle-aged ladies operating an office the "size of a broom closet."

Direct mail operations have become the nerve center of both the Republican and Democratic committees. High speed printers, with patented hand signatures that give the appearance of personally addressed letters, can pump out thousands of fundraising letters every day. Television production studios enable the parties to turn out professional-quality political commercials. Satellite links can be rented to transmit messages from individual lawmakers to TV stations in their districts back home. Formerly, national committee staffs were cut sharply after presidential elections, but in this era of the "permanent campaign" the professional staff is utilized year round, especially for fundraising operations.

Both national party headquarters, located only blocks from the Capitol, are now in a much better position to coordinate their work with the House and Senate campaign committees. In the past, neither the Democrats nor the Republicans maintained close ties between their national committees and the Capitol Hill committees.

THE PRESIDENT'S RELATIONS WITH STATE AND LOCAL PARTIES

President Harry S. Truman had a standing appointment every Wednesday afternoon with the Democratic national chairman to discuss party politics.[34] Earlier presidents—Lincoln, Teddy Roosevelt, Woodrow Wilson, and FDR—also devoted hours to party matters, especially to patronage with the states.

Surprisingly, President Eisenhower devoted more time to state politics than was widely realized at the time. Ike was especially concerned to use patronage to strengthen Republican organizations in the southern states. Under White House prodding, the GOP national committee established a Southern Division by 1957 to handle all patronage to state parties south of the Mason–Dixon line.[35] More than another decade would pass, however, before the rich dividends from Eisenhower's strategy were harvested.

Most recent presidents, however, have not rolled up their sleeves as their predecessors did to deal with state and local party matters. Indeed, state party leaders and members of the national committee (who are, with few exceptions, chosen by the state parties) often feel neglected by the White House. In 1977, for example, members of the Democratic national committee became so incensed over President Carter's indifference that they unanimously passed a resolution rebuking the president for neglecting the state parties on patronage and appointments and for failing to help them with fundraising.[36]

Undoubtedly, the "nationalization" of politics, the emergence of TV as the ultimate campaign weapon, and the decline of political parties have reduced the importance of direct presidential concern about state and local party matters. Nor do presidents in this era of nuclear diplomacy and instantaneous international satellite communication have the time to devote to state and local politics. Negotiations on a Strategic Arms Reduction Treaty (START), a Middle Eastern military or hostage crisis, the breakup of the Eastern European Soviet bloc, and global economic questions place unceasing demands on the president's time. For the president of the United States, a federal judgeship appointment, a research station in a friendly senator's state, or an urban transit grant are all dwarfed by pressing international crises. The best that a president can do is to designate one of his White House staffers to look into patronage matters and find a solution.

This is not to say that the twentieth-century presidents ignore state politics. For example, President Bush, with one eye on the 1992 election and aware that California would gain as many as seven congressional seats (after the 1990 census reapportionment California will have more than 10 percent of all electoral college votes), twice visited the Golden State in a thirty-day period between mid-February and mid-March 1990. Ostensibly, Bush traveled to California to visit military installations and to defend his environmental policies; but Mr. Bush spent an equal amount of time campaigning for the 1990 GOP gubernatorial candidate, Senator Pete Wilson, and criticizing California Democrats' past gerrymandering of the state's congressional districts. Since the Democrats retained control of both houses of California's state legislature in Sacramento, Wilson's gubernatorial victory in November gave the Republicans an equal voice at the reapportionment bargaining table.

President John F. Kennedy set the pace for post–World War II presidents in working with state and local organizations. He spoke to eight Democratic fundraisers in his first year alone.[37] The Kennedy White House also began ambitious preparations for the 1962 off-year elections more than a year ahead. From the start, according to his chief aide, Ted Sorenson, "The President planned a mid-term campaign more vigorous than that of any president in history."[38] Kennedy kicked off his campaign activity in the fall of 1961 by stumping for gubernatorial candidate Richard Hughes in New Jersey and for House candidate Henry Gonzales in a Texas special election.[39] Both candidates won. From late July until mid-October 1962 (before the Cuban missile crisis forced him to halt campaigning), Kennedy had visited more than a dozen states.[40] Kennedy drew huge crowds at every stop. Contrary to conventional wisdom, the Democrats lost only four House seats—by far the best off-year election record for any party in power since the Democratic vintage political year of 1934.

Gerald Ford, the only appointed president in American history, worked assiduously, strengthening ties with GOP state and local party organizations. The former GOP House minority leader spoke proudly in 1975 of his success at raising money for Republican organizations at the national, state, and local levels. In noting that he had raised over $2 million at rallies and fundraising dinners, Ford said that he felt an "obligation to try to strengthen and rebuild the Republican Party organization."[41]

President Jimmy Carter's relationship with the Democratic national committee and state party organizations, even after two years in office, was at best lukewarm. Without strong party backing Carter failed to head off a primary challenge from Senator Ted Kennedy in the 1980 Democratic nominating race. Though he defeated Kennedy to win renomination, Carter was no match for former California Governor Ronald Reagan in the general election. In assessing Carter's relationship with his party, political scientist Bert A. Rockman has observed that Carter's "inability or unwillingness to be the flag carrier for his party's traditions" was a major failing. If there is one conclusion to be reached from the Carter presidency, Rockman continues, it is that "a President must have a strong base within his party."[42] Another political scientist, Stephen Skowronek, has echoed Rockman's comments on Carter's relationship with his party: "It was Jimmy Carter's peculiar genius to treat his remoteness from his party and its institutional power centers as a distinctive asset rather than his chief liability in his quest for a credible leadership posture."[43]

SUMMARY

Since the establishment of the Democratic national committee after the 1844 national convention, Democratic presidents and the national committee have been joint partners in the enterprise of winning and retaining control of the White House. The Republican party, which held its first convention in 1856, soon emulated the Democrats in establishing its own national committee with similar responsibilities.

For the first century after the founding of the national committees, the national party chairman of the incumbent party managed the general election campaign for the nominee and, if he was elected, also his reelection campaign. Mark Hanna, William E. McCombs, James A. Farley, and Leonard Hall are some of the best-remembered leaders of the national party. But all these chairmen served at the pleasure of the president.

Before the emergence of candidate-centered campaigns in the 1960s, national chairmen developed and implemented the grand strategy for winning the presidency. With the establishment of permanent national headquarters in the 1930s, the party chairman's duties expanded further. Skilled in organizational politics and fundraising, these chairmen were the masters of inside politics. But with the arrival of candidate-centered presidential campaigns, the national party chairman has been displaced by the candidate's veteran staff of personal advisers, long affiliated with him while he served as governor, or senator, or in some other public capacity. No longer the president's number one political adviser, the national chairman has in recent years performed mostly ceremonial duties and managed the national party headquarters under the watchful eye of White House operatives assigned to oversee party affairs.

Ironically, at the very time of the erosion of the chairman's authority, several GOP national chairmen have found themselves in the political limelight as potential vice presidential nominees. Three GOP chairmen or former chairmen—Representative William E. Miller (Goldwater),

Senator Bob Dole (Ford), and George Bush (Reagan)—were selected as presidential running mates, and several others in both parties were on nominees' "short lists" of prospective vice presidential running mates. George Bush, as we know, became vice president in 1980 and eight years later the first former party chairman to be elected president of the United States.

As official head of the national party, the president is expected to maintain ties with the state parties. But in view of the tight time constraints imposed on the president in this age of global diplomacy, highly charged domestic issues, and uncounted ceremonial duties, presidents have precious little time for dealing with mundane political matters affecting the state party organizations. Instead, these matters are usually turned over to the national party chairman to handle or, more likely, to a White House staff member who has the president's ear.

In recent decades the president has come to rely most heavily upon his staff in the White House and the Executive Office of the President—the quintessential presidentialists of his party—in his dealings with Congress and special interest groups. The next chapter is devoted to the growing importance of the presidential wing of his party.

NOTES

1. Charles E. Jacob, "The Congressional Elections," in Gerald M. Pomper, ed., *The Election of 1980* (Chatham, NJ: Chatham House, 1981), p. 126.

2. Theodore H. White, *The Making of the President 1960* (New York: Atheneum, 1961), p. 39.

3. Harry Thurston Peck, quoted in Howard R. Penniman, *Sait's American Parties and Elections*, 5th ed. (New York: Appleton Century Crofts, 1952), p. 313.

4. Lewis L. Gould, *The Presidency of Theodore Roosevelt* (Lawrence: University Press of Kansas, 1990), pp. 129–133.

5. Penniman, *Sait's American Parties and Elections*, p. 319.

6. Frank Freidel, *Franklin D. Roosevelt: A Rendezvous with Destiny* (Boston: Little, Brown, 1990), pp. 343–345.

7. Fred I. Greenstein, *The Hidden Hand Presidency* (New York: Basic Books, 1982), pp. 149–150.

8. Cornelius P. Cotter and Bernard Hennessy, *Politics without Power* (New York: Atherton, 1964), pp. 6–7.

9. Ibid.

10. Thomas E. Cronin, "The Presidency and the Parties," in Gerald M. Pomper, ed., *Party Renewal in America* (New York: Praeger, 1981), p. 171.

11. Harold F. Bass, "The President and the National Party Organization," in Robert Harmel, ed., *Presidents and Their Parties* (New York: Praeger, 1984), p. 76; Frank J. Sorauf and Paul Allen Beck, *Party Politics in America*, 6th ed. (Glenview, IL: Scott, Foresman, 1988), p. 137.

12. Bass, "The President and National Party Organization," p. 73.

13. Robert H. Ferrell, ed., *The Eisenhower Diaries* (New York: W. W. Norton, 1981), p. 357, quoted in Bass, "The President and the National Party Organization," p. 75.

14. Bass, "The President and the National Party Organization," pp. 76–78.

15. Theodore H. White, *The Making of the President 1972* (New York: Atheneum, 1973), p. 49.

16. Joseph A. Califano, Jr., *A Presidential Nation* (New York: W. W. Norton, 1976), p. 153.

17. Rowland Evans, Jr., and Robert D. Novak, *Nixon in the White House* (New York: Random House, 1971), pp. 30–33, 70–73.

18. Cotter and Hennessy, *Politics without Power*, p. 71.

19. Dom Bonafede, "The Ultimate Seduction," *National Journal*, May 18, 1991, p. 1205.

20. Ralph M. Goldman, "The American President as Party Leader: A Synoptic History," in Robert Harmel, ed., *Presidents and Their Parties*, pp. 20–23.

21. Ibid., p. 22.

22. Penniman, *Sait's American Parties and Elections*, p. 469.

23. Herbert S. Parmet, *Eisenhower and the American Crusade* (New York: Macmillan, 1972), pp. 210–214.

24. Richard M. Pious, "Richard M. Nixon," in Henry F. Graff, ed., *The Presidents: A Reference History* (New York: Scribner's, 1984), pp. 630–636.

25. Maureen Dowd and Thomas L. Friedman, "The Fabulous Bush and Baker Boys," *New York Times Magazine*, May 6, 1990, pp. 34–37, 58–67.

26. White, *The Making of the President 1960*, pp. 173–179.

27. White, *The Making of the President 1964* (New York: Atheneum, 1965), pp. 258–259.

28. White, *The Making of the President 1972*, pp. 209–210.

29. Jules Witcover, *Marathon* (New York: Viking, 1977), pp. 508–509.

30. David Ignatious, "The Fat Cats Are Back on the Prowl," *The Washington Post National Weekly Edition*, November 28–December 4, 1988, p. 25.

31. *The Christian Science Monitor*, August 24, 1988.

32. Herbert E. Alexander and Monica Bauer, *Financing the 1988 Election* (Boulder, CO: Westview, 1991), pp. 37–38.

33. Ibid.

34. Richard T. Johnson, *Managing the White House* (New York: Harper and Row, 1974), p. 52.

35. John D. Lees, "The President and His Party," in Malcolm Shaw, ed., *Roosevelt to Reagan: The Development of the Modern Presidency* (London: C. Hurst, 1987), p. 6.

36. Richard M. Pious, *The American Presidency* (New York: Basic Books, 1979), p. 138.

37. Roger G. Brown, "Presidents as Midterm Campaigners," in Robert Harmel, ed., *Presidents and Their Parties*, p. 141.

38. Theodore C. Sorenson, *Kennedy* (New York: Harper and Row, 1966), p. 396.

39. David S. Broder, *The Party's Over* (New York: Harper and Row, 1971), p. 34.

40. Brown, "Presidents as Midterm Campaigners," p. 135.

41. Gerald Ford, *Public Papers* (1976), quoted in Brown, "Presidents as Midterm Campaigners," p. 141.

42. Bert A. Rockman, ''The Style and Organization of the Reagan Presidency,'' in Charles O. Jones, ed., *The Reagan Legacy: Promise and Performance* (Chatham, NJ: Chatham House, 1988), p. 26.

43. Stephen Skowronek, ''Presidential Leadership in Political Time,'' in Michael Nelson, ed., *The Presidency and the Political System* (Washington, DC: Congressional Quarterly Press, 1984), p. 121.

Chapter 6

The Presidential Party

During the first quarter of the nineteenth century, presidential nominees in Jefferson's Democratic-Republican party (forerunner of the modern Democrats) were selected by the "congressional caucus," that is, by the Democratic-Republican members of Congress. Under this system, presidential nominees were in a sense captives of, or at least dependent upon, the legislative branch for their nomination. If this congressionally dominated system had continued, it is reasonable to conjecture that some form of parliamentary system could have emerged in this country. Early in the chapter it is noted that the sudden rise of the national nominating convention for selecting presidential nominees created a system completely divorced from congressional control. More than anything else, this development helped foster the idea of the president as an independent leader and the emergence of the presidential party.

Most historians credit President Andrew Jackson with combining the president's independent power base as leader of his party with his duties as chief executive to forge the president into a powerful national political leader. Indeed, Jackson has served as the model for most strong twentieth-century chief executives. As explained in this chapter, the growth of the presidential party in the twentieth century has operated in tandem with the president's expanded role in foreign affairs and national defense and as overseer of the economy. Not all presidents, it is noted, have welcomed the mantle of party leadership. Indeed, it is difficult to visualize presidents James Buchanan, Benjamin Harrison, Warren Harding, or Calvin Coolidge as forceful leaders of the presidential party. For long periods during the nineteenth century, the presidential party was completely overshadowed by the congressional party. But for most of the twentieth century the presidential party has generally held the upper hand over the congressional party. The final section of the chapter focuses on the continuity of membership in the presidential party that helps explain why the presidential party is a major source of strength to White House incumbents.

BACKGROUND

When the Framers constructed the separation-of-powers system at Philadelphia in 1787, they provided no mechanisms to make the system operate smoothly. To encourage interbranch cooperation, they established an elaborate system of separate institutions sharing power, each institution possessing the capacity to check the others and no branch capable of becoming predominant. In blending some powers, e.g., lawmaking, foreign policy, Senate confirmation of executive appointees, and the like, the Framers thought that the executive and legislative branches would be forced to cooperate with one another out of necessity. The Framers also believed that public-minded officials, despite their differences, could be reasonable and work out their conflicting goals. However, they left it to future generations to find the most practical means of transforming the new constitutional blueprint into a workable system. Fortunately, within a few years President Jefferson, long an advocate of a government of limited powers, concluded that only a strong president operating through his party leaders in Congress could bridge the gulf in the separation-of-powers system.

President Andrew Jackson carried the Jeffersonian leadership concept still another step further: He asserted that the president's link with the American people through his party gave him a popular mandate equal or superior to that of Congress. Accountable only to the electorate, Jackson proclaimed himself as the democratic tribune of the people. Further, Jackson asserted that the president was not simply the head of the executive branch but the leader of the government as well. The Constitution had not said anything about this dual role, but neither had it barred presidents from assuming it. Clearly, Jackson had used his presidential party leadership to reinforce his position as the nation's leader.

PRESIDENTIAL AND CONGRESSIONAL PARTIES

Since the early days of the Republic, each of the major parties has been divided into the "presidential" and "congressional" wings. Indeed, this bifurcation led political scientist James MacGregor Burns to describe this structure as a "four-party" system—the Democrats and Republicans each divided into presidential and congressional parties.[1]

The incipient stages of this division first became evident during the Washington and Adams administrations. The presidential parties—the Federalists and the Anti-Federalists—were essentially personal coalitions developed by Alexander Hamilton, a staunch Federalist, and Thomas Jefferson, leader of the Anti-Federalists, or as they came to be called, the "Democratic-Republicans." In this era of stagecoach communication, Hamilton and Jefferson relied heavily on personal correspondence to solicit electoral votes for the presidency. The Federalists, however, failed to remain competitive beyond 1808 and then slowly disintegrated under the powerful blows of the fast-growing Democratic-Republican party. Some Federalists eventually found a new home with John Quincy Adams's National Republicans and later with the Whigs.

JEFFERSON AND THE RISE OF THE PRESIDENTIAL PARTY

With his election in 1800, Jefferson, who had served as secretary of state during Washington's first term and vice president during Adams's single term, "took the machinery that the congressional Republicans had built up against Federalist Presidents and turned it to his own uses."[2] Some congressional Republicans complained bitterly about this presidential takeover, but they had little choice but to follow their new president. Jefferson, the apostle of limited government, had preached time and again about the sanctity of the separation of powers and of checks and balances while campaigning for president. But once he reached the White House, he discarded his campaign rhetoric. Jefferson quietly assumed the reins of power throughout the government. James MacGregor Burns has described Jefferson's actions as they unfolded:

Considering himself the national head of the party, close and constant leadership to his forces in Congress; he personally drafted bills and had them introduced into Congress; saw to it that the men he wanted took the leadership posts in Congress; induced men he favored to run for Congress by holding out promises of advancement; made the Speaker and the floor leader of the House his personal lieutenants; changed the leadership as he saw fit; used Ways and Means and other committees as instruments of presidential control; dominated the Republican caucus in the House.[3]

Thus, even in an anti–executive-party era, Jefferson stamped his firm imprint upon the presidency and the presidential party in a manner duplicated by only a handful of presidents over the next two centuries. Jefferson's leadership skills can be traced to his experience in the Continental Congress, the Virginia Assembly, and briefly as governor of Virginia during the American Revolution. His short tenure as governor of the Old Dominion (1779–1781) must especially have left its mark on Jefferson's views of leadership. Elected by the Assembly for a one-year term, Jefferson was responsible to it and had no executive veto over its legislation. His tenure as state chief executive, however, was not a glorious chapter in the life of the sage of Monticello. Jefferson left the governorship after two years, with the British Army under Lord Cornwallis occupying Richmond, the state capital, and Jefferson and remnants of the Virginia Assembly in flight across the Blue Ridge.[4]

Presidential candidates continued to be nominated by the congressional caucus until rivalry within the essentially one-party system led to the demise of "King Caucus" in 1824. Jackson was the first president to be nominated and elected without congressional involvement. Before he left office Jackson transformed his frontier farmer–urban labor coalition into a national political party and reinforced presidential independence from Congress. Furthermore, President Jackson insisted that his popular election conferred as much legitimacy on the executive's representativeness as on that of the legislative branch.

Jackson's independence from Congress, however, eventually led to the formation of the Whig party, a coalition of congressional leaders, including Clay, Calhoun, Webster, and others seeking to reassert legislative supremacy.[5] Nonetheless, the newly emergent role of the Jacksonian presidential party was the most significant development during the short interim between the demise of the congressional caucus and the rise of the national nominating convention.

Established in 1832, the national convention soon became the formal center of the modern presidential party. It remained the unchallenged decision-making agency of the presidential party until the era of party reform in the early 1970s, when the rapid spread of presidential primaries opened the door for White House candidates to appeal directly to the voters for their support. Most popularly elected delegates now run pledged to a specific presidential candidate. To win the presidential nomination, the successful candidate no longer bargains with state party leaders at the national convention; instead, he collects a majority of the pledged delegates in the primaries and caucuses to claim the nomination. Though the national convention still formally selects the party nominee, the winner of the primaries and caucuses, in effect, becomes the "popular choice," to be ratified pro forma by the national conclave.

From the start, national nominating conventions strengthened the hand of presidential nominees and their supporters, for they concentrated the electorate behind the nominees and divorced presidential nominations completely from congressional control. In short, the national conventions gave the successful presidential nominee a base of support independent of the legislative branch. Throughout the remainder of the nineteenth century, however, the presidential party, except during the Polk, Lincoln, and Cleveland administrations, was usually overshadowed by the congressional party. In the 1850s, for example, the Democratic congressional party, dominated by Southerners and armed with the two-thirds rule (which, until 1936, required the Democratic nominee to win two-thirds of the convention vote), twice denied Democratic presidents renomination at the national convention.

By contrast, the twentieth century, with a few exceptions in the Harding–Coolidge era, has been marked by the steady growth of the presidential party, at the expense of the congressionalists. Beginning with President Teddy Roosevelt, most presidents have taken over direct leadership of their parties. Without hesitation they have asserted that the president represents the nation as a whole while Congress represents it only as a collection of states and congressional districts. The late Clinton Rossiter, an avowed presidentialist, frequently called attention to "the sharp contrast between the traditions of the Presidency, which call for strength and action, and the rules and customs of Congress which place a high premium on caution and compromise."[6] Congressionalists, in turn, have continued to insist that the original constitutional formula of blended and coordinate powers is preferable to a strong presidential model in which Congress is relegated to a subordinate role in assenting to or confirming actions undertaken by the chief executive. The congressional party has sought to limit the power of the president. Even strong presidential party leaders—Wilson, both Roosevelts, Truman, Kennedy, Johnson, and Reagan—have all from time to time been hobbled by congressional leaders. Let us take a moment to assess the role of the congressional party in our governmental system before moving on to a discussion of the president as leader of the presidential party.

THE CONGRESSIONAL PARTY

The "congressional" wing of each party, based on Capitol Hill, also dates back to the earliest days of the Republic. Headed by such distinguished leaders as Henry Clay, Daniel Webster, Thomas B. Reed, Joseph Cannon, Nelson Aldrich, Sam Rayburn, Robert A. Taft, and Richard B. Russell, the congressional party has provided the counterbalance that maintains relative equilibrium in our separation-of-powers system. Republican members of the House of Representatives established their own congressional campaign committee in 1866 to help elect House members, since they feared that President Andrew Johnson might use the GOP national committee to "knife" radical Republicans who opposed Lincoln's successor. Democratic House members, supporting Johnson against efforts of his own party to remove him from office, also appointed a committee to manage their congressional campaign.[7]

Over the past two hundred years the congressional party of the Republic has proved to be as durable as the presidency, though its fortunes have waxed and waned as the tides of power have shifted between the White House and Capitol Hill. Based upon the seniority and noncompetitive congressional districts (less than 50 of the 435 congressional districts are competitive, that is, the vote is divided approximately between 52 percent and 48 percent), the congressional party reinforces the bulwark of the separation-of-powers system. The durability of the congressional party has thwarted more than one president. Indeed, presidents have often found that veteran congressional leaders are so entrenched in their committee chairmanships and protected by seniority that not even a bulldozer could remove them from the halls of Congress. Congressional leaders see presidents come and go. For example, Representative Jaime Whitten (D-Miss.), chairman of the House Appropriations Committee, first elected in 1941, has worked with every president since FDR—ten presidents in all. Representative Daniel Rostenkowski (D-Ill.), a product of the Chicago Democratic machine, first elected in 1958, has served with every president since Eisenhower. Such congressional leaders from "safe" districts are not going to be easily swayed by presidential rhetoric or power moves.

Members of the congressional party champion Congress as the more powerful branch. Congressionalists have never tired of pointing out that the Constitution makes certain that broad decisions regarding the major functions of government are entrusted to the legislative branch. But in the twentieth century, congressionalists have been less successful in delineating their role in national party leadership. Consequently, this has left the door open for the president to move into the driver's seat in party leadership. In a loosely confederated party system, the presidency serves as the unifying force to provide coherence in the fifty-state Republic. Without the president to act as party leader, the separation-of-powers system might well lead to endless deadlock, for there would be no powerful agent to negotiate the numerous compromises needed, especially during periods of divided government, to blend executive and legislative authority into a coherent government. Clearly, the president is ideally suited to represent the national interest. As leader of the presidential party, he can bridge the gap between the people and their government.[8]

LEADER OF THE PRESIDENTIAL PARTY

Since the rise of political parties in the nineteenth century, presidents have always had to attract a personal, organizational following in order to win high office; furthermore, they have had to maintain these organizations in order to gain reelection and to reinforce their political influence against competitive pressures from congressional leaders, within both their own party and the opposition. Most notably, charismatic-type presidents, such as Teddy Roosevelt, Woodrow Wilson, FDR, John F. Kennedy, and Ronald Reagan have all drawn a host of dynamic, able followers within their orbits.

The leader of the presidential party is, as the term signifies, the president. As head of the party, he sets its agenda, confirms its ideology, appoints White House staff members, and seeks public support for his policies, especially at reelection time. Just as the congressional party is organized around leading lawmakers, so is the presidential party organized around the chief executive. From the era of Jefferson and Jackson to the present, the man in the White House has served with varying degrees of success as party leader. The president, however, is not the sole head of the entire Republican or Democratic party. As political scientist Roger G. Brown has noted, "The notion of political party organizations as strictly responsible to the president is not, and never has been, a reality in the American system."[9] He shares power with the party's congressional wing and, to a lesser extent, with state party organizations. In some instances, however, the far left or far right sections of the party may not entirely accept the president as their true leader. Indeed, some sections of the party may openly rebel, as some southern Democrats did against FDR, Truman, and Kennedy, and as the wing of the GOP headed by Senator Joe McCarthy did against Eisenhower. Nevertheless, in that section of the whole party that is termed the presidential party, the president is the recognized leader. Furthermore, the president's power is, as James MacGregor Burns observed some years ago, "anchored in his presidential party rather than in the general party."[10] By contrast, the presidential party out of power is technically headed by the defeated presidential candidate and his partisans, but in fact it generally lies moribund within the "regular" national party until a new presidential nominee is selected nearly four years later.

From Inauguration Day onward, the White House serves as the command post for the presidential party. To run the national party, the president relies on his White House staff as well as the national party chairman. Cabinet members, top agency heads, and hundreds of subcabinet-level appointees serve as the officers and spear carriers for the presidential party. In the states and cities, dozens of federal attorneys, United States marshals, and other presidential appointees carry out the president's policies and protect the administration's local interests. At reelection time most of these officials participate directly or indirectly in helping the president retain office, since their continued employment depends upon his electoral success.

Who are the charter members of the presidential party? From Theodore Roosevelt's time, the leading members have been governors, senators, cabinet members, major publishers, investment bankers, and big-league lawyers who are interested almost exclusively in presidential politics and the White House incumbent. Especially for the Democratic presidential party, the top and middle-level leadership has also been drawn from universities, foundations, labor unions, and minority and ethnic group spokespersons. Members of the presidential party generally focus on national and international issues, rather than the parochial concerns of individual states and localities. The nationalization of American parties, the emergence of television, and the speedup of electronic communication and jet travel have all attracted additional members to the presidential party. Events in Topeka, Lansing, Madison, or Raleigh are of minor interest to the presidentialists. Instead their eyes are focused on Washington, New York, London, Moscow, Paris, Berlin, and Tokyo. Their concerns center on multinational corporations, labor–management problems, the environment, the New York stock market, the Pentagon, the Middle East, and superpower diplomacy. Understandably, the presidential party reaches its highest level of activity during a presidential campaign. Indeed, this challenge to win the White House is the ultimate test of the organization.

HOW A CANDIDATE-CENTERED NOMINATING
CAMPAIGN SPAWNS MEMBERSHIP GROWTH

With the emergence of candidate-centered campaigns in the 1950s and 1960s, membership in the presidential party has continued to grow. The term "party" here, borrowing a concept from Leon D. Epstein, refers to a following—or a "clan"—of activists rather than to larger numbers of voters.[11] The president's personal party, however, is not exactly a new phenomenon. James MacGregor Burns speaks of Theodore Roosevelt's "personal party," headed by the former presidential appointees and Progressive state party leaders whom he had gathered around himself in his administration and summoned back to political combat in 1912. More recently, the rapid proliferation of presidential primaries to more than thirty states and the passage of federal campaign finance legislation, which provides matching federal dollars to candidates, has generated a plethora of presidential candidates and their huge entourages of staffers and supporters—all members of the president's "personal" party.

Formerly, presidential contenders, such as Wilson and Franklin D. Roosevelt, relied upon a small cadre of lieutenants to develop contacts and "understandings" with governors, other state party leaders, and big-city mayors to carry them to victory at the national conventions and then on to the White House. Since these state party leaders usually held ironclad control over their state delegations (sometimes the governor handpicked them) at the national conventions, the key to winning the presidential nomination was to work through these state leaders and also to persuade the various "favorite son" candidates to drop out of the race and pledge their state delegations to the prospective nominee. If no candidate emerged as clearcut front-runner, the state bosses met in "smoke filled rooms" at the convention to "broker" the nomination. Generally, this meant picking a "safe" candidate who would run well in the big, competitive two-party states and offend the least number of voters.

Thus, in this earlier period a leading presidential contender needed only a few staffers and "drummers" and a handful of fundraisers to win the nomination. Throughout the nominating race, the prospective candidate rarely strayed far from home—for example, Governor Franklin D. Roosevelt in 1932 stayed in Albany, the state capital, throughout the entire preconvention period. Contrast this laid-back approach with the frantic activities of recent presidential contenders who conduct continuous preconvention campaigns for two years or more before the nomination. To win, the candidate must recruit a full staff of fundraisers, state organizers, media specialists, pollsters, advance men, and accountants long before the primaries start. The presidential candidate's national staff, consisting of his close advisors and media specialists, oversees a campaign that often closely resembles a huge military operation. Since the number of presidential contenders entering the nominating race has grown in this participatory democracy era, it follows that the membership in the presidential party has expanded commensurately. In 1976, for example, eleven contenders entered the Democratic nominating race; in 1980, eight major aspirants sought the Republican nomination. With the lure of more than $10 million in federal matching dollars now awaiting the well-organized candidate, the temptation to enter the race, despite the long odds, is almost irresistible for most prospective candidates. Such being the case, membership in the presidential party can be expected to grow.

That presidential parties are essentially personal organizations constructed around individual presidents suggests that they have an impermanent existence. This is, however, only partially true. Over the years distinct continuities have emerged within successive presidential parties. Political scientist Leon D. Epstein has commented that one can perceive a kind of continuous presidential "party" among adherents of previous presidents and party nominees—for example, FDR New Deal Democrats resurfaced in the Truman administration.[12] Some reappeared as Stevenson Democrats throughout the 1950s. Similarly, if one were to scratch below the surface of Reagan Republicans, one would most likely find many erstwhile Goldwater Republicans of the 1960s or even a few leftover Robert Taft Republicans from the late 1940s and 1950s. Political scientist John Kessel, among others, has found that party activists attracted to John F. Kennedy reappeared later working for George McGovern; Eisenhower backers resurfaced later supporting Nixon. This phenomenon led Kessel to conclude that "a presidential party at any time is a residue of its past campaigns."[13] Moreover, Leon D. Epstein has observed this membership "may sometimes be more highly personal than ideological or programmatic but it is focused on national purposes, electorally and governmentally."[14]

Several of the long-term presidentialists in the Bush administration are carryovers from the Ford administration, such as Secretary of Defense Richard Cheney, National Security Advisor Brent Scowcroft and President Bush himself. Secretary of State James A. Baker III, Secretary of Commerce Robert Mosbacher, and Secretary of the Treasury Nicholas F. Brady, however, have been Bush loyalists for more than two decades.

HOW THE PERSONAL PARTY DISPLACES
THE OLD PARTY ORGANIZATION

Displacement of old party professionals by the president's personal nominating campaign team is a relatively recent development. That the president should want to have his own campaign "team" in place, rather than old-line politicians, to operate the executive branch has been readily explained by political scientist Terry M. Moe:

Because the president can count on unequaled responsiveness from his own people, increases in White House organizational competence—for example, through greater size, division of labor, specialization, hierarchic coordination, formal linkages with outside organizations and constituencies—appear to him to have direct, undiluted payoffs for the pursuit of presidential interests.[15]

John F. Kennedy's takeover of the Democratic party after his presidential victory in 1960 marked the beginning of this new era of the personal party. The Kennedy "Mafia," consisting chiefly of his Massachusetts lieutenants, dominated the White House staff as well as subcabinet and independent agency positions. Old-line Democrats, waiting patiently for high-paying federal positions were, for the most part, left in the lurch. Clearly, Kennedy's "New Frontiersmen" had taken over the executive branch. When the Kennedy personal party lost its leader to an assassin's bullet in November 1963, many New Frontiersmen shifted their loyalty to Bobby Kennedy, the slain president's younger brother. Bobby remained briefly as attorney general in the Johnson administration, but he resigned in 1964 to run successfully for a Senate seat in New York. Some of the veteran New Frontiersmen reappeared in 1968 to help Bobby seek the Democratic nomination in the midst of the Vietnam War.[16]

When President Johnson announced in late March 1968 that he would not seek another term, the Democratic nominating battle became a three-cornered race among Kennedy, Vice President Humphrey, and Senator Eugene McCarthy of Minnesota. Although the assassination of the second Kennedy brother on the night of his major victory in the California primary stunned the nation, it did not end the Kennedy quest. Youngest brother Ted, the last of the four Kennedy sons, was urged by the New Frontier loyalists to pick up the family banner and run for president. Ted, senator from Massachusetts since 1962, declined the honor until his break with the Carter administration a decade later led him to challenge the incumbent Democratic president for the party nomination in 1980.

Once again, many of the New Frontiersmen, now well into their middle years, took up the Kennedy battle flag. But even the magic of the Kennedy name and the rallying cry to old New Frontiersmen could no longer rally enough Democratic supporters to take the nomination away from a sitting president.

California Governor Ronald Reagan also developed a formidable personal party organization long before he reached the White House. Many former staff members from Sacramento—Edwin Meese III, Michael K. Deaver, Casper W. Weinberger, Lyn Nofziger, and others—continued to aid his drive for the presidency, which did not succeed until he made his third try in 1980. Reagan had lost his initial bid for the White House to Richard M. Nixon in 1968, and he mounted a bold but unsuccessful challenge against President Gerald R. Ford in 1976. But the Californians who backed Reagan twice did not lose faith in the former movie actor. Their political skills, especially media management and fundraising, had been honed over a decade under actual battle conditions. Most of these West Coast operatives stayed with Reagan until he finally captured the GOP nomination and the presidency on his third try.[17] Along the road to the White House, Reagan also attracted many of 1964 GOP nominee Barry Goldwater's foot soldiers. These Goldwater "true believers," whose original hopes were dashed by President Johnson's landslide victory over Goldwater in 1964, found a new savior in Reagan. They joined forces with the Californians to become the janissaries of the Reagan campaign team. With the exception of John F. Kennedy, no recent president has been more successful than Reagan in rallying the troops to do battle against the opposition. Nor did this dedication to their chief falter once he reached the White House. As one veteran presidential watcher has commented on the "Reaganauts," "For sheer professionalism the Reagan White House's use of media specialists, legislative liaison experts, and the dedicated staff of writers . . . will be a model for future presidencies."[18]

President Reagan's establishment of the Office of Political Affairs reflects the continuing shift of political coalition building from the party to the White House and demonstrates how the impact of the post-1968 reforms of the presidential nominating process has affected the nature and functions of the White House staff. Establishment of a political affairs office is formal recognition of the need for a first-term president to maintain an experienced and professional campaign organization to cope with the demands of the new rules of the nomination game. With the rapid spread of presidential primaries, the choice of the party's presidential nominee is now beyond the control of party leaders. Moreover, with a nominating system so open that it sometimes encourages intraparty challenges, an incumbent president no longer enjoys the luxury of automatic renomination after four years. To protect his flanks, a president who desires a second term must now give far more continuous attention to electoral politics than in yesteryear. Nor have recent presidents been willing to leave their reelection chances in the hands of the parties' national committees. Instead, most chief executives now rely on an in-house political affairs unit, which can monitor a president's standings in the fifty states on a daily basis.

ELECTORAL COALITIONS AND GOVERNING COALITIONS

To win the White House, a modern president must blend together a combination of party enthusiasts and a host of regional, demographic, and ethnic coalitions within the fifty states that will produce the 270 electoral votes needed to claim the prize. Once elected, however, the president's electoral coalitions, especially in this era of divided government, do not necessarily translate into a viable governing coalition. Indeed, the governing coalition may have relatively little relation to the electoral coalition.[19] Since recent presidents have created an independent campaign organization separate and apart from the regular party organization, they no longer depend heavily on party regulars to carry them to victory. One consequence of this development is that presidents have taken most party affairs and coalition building out of the hands of the national chairmen and state party leaders and assigned them to White House staffers.

Over the past two decades, the White House office staff has averaged approximately five hundred members, and the Executive Office of the President has numbered about two thousand.[20] While it is difficult to determine exactly what portion of the White House is engaged regularly in activities that entail party affairs or involve media strategies, it has been estimated that at least 30 percent of the White House political staff members are engaged in promoting and publicizing the president and his policies.[21] Located in the nerve center of the executive branch, these loyal staff members are in a strategic spot to push the power levers to secure support for presidential policies. Thus, in a sense, the White House Office has become a "surrogate presidential party."[22]

The huge growth of single interest groups over the past several decades, which has occurred at the expense of political parties, has complicated the task of coalition building. Consequently, White House staffs maintain liaison with dozens of such mass-membership groups with the view of welding their support together to back presidentially sponsored measures. Once a measure has been enacted, the coalition-building process begins anew. White House staffers must seek to build another coalition, often with another distinct combination of interest groups, to advance another of the president's programs. As Seligman and Covington have noted, "Presidents are left with the difficult task of constructing a series of exclusive congressional coalitions from more peripheral sources of support, which are more issue specific and temporary in character."[23]

Beyond doubt, the tensions between winning the presidency and governing the nation put a premium on translating electoral support into governing support. Whether a president succeeds or fails often depends on his staff's coalition-building skills outside the party. Clearly, the presidential party takes on increasing importance as the decline of traditional party coalition building becomes more pervasive. No wonder Hugh Heclo commented more than a decade ago that presidents have created the "equivalent of a presidential party for governing."[24]

Especially in this era of divided government, the presidential party in the White House must demonstrate to Congress that the public backs the president on the key issues of the day. As a result, presidents have adopted a new campaigning strategy for building coalition support by turning to major interest groups across America.

Institutional structural changes in the White House reflect the campaigning strategy now employed by recent presidents to win public support from these mass membership interest groups. The establishment of a White House apparatus—the Office of Public Liaison (OPL)—has facilitated presidential communications with these interest groups. Established in the 1970s by President Ford, the Office of Public Liaison enables the president to activate these groups to generate support for his programs. Interest groups, which were founded originally to advance their own public agendas, now find themselves being "used" frequently by the White House Office of Public Liaison to communicate presidential policy positions to their memberships. During the first two and one-half years of its existence, for example, Ford's Office of Public Liaison organized 350 meetings or seminars and 24 conferences with leading officials of these special interest groups.[25] The number of participants varied from as few as 10 to as many as 250 members. Considering the "multiplier effect" generated by these participants carrying the presidential message back to their own mass-membership trade organizations, businesses, and finance groups, the impact of these White House sessions indirectly reached thousands of these issue-oriented influentials across the land. As Seligman and Covington have observed: "These communications serve the president's interests as opposed to catering to an interest group's preferences."[26] Most contacts tend to be initiated by the White House, with the flow of communication directed chiefly toward the interest group from the president rather than vice versa. By relying on the OPL, the president's staff can usually keep the initiative and organize the ad hoc coalitions of disparate interest groups to push the administration's programs before they bring out their own "wish list" at the White House. Whether the interest group's officials realize it or not, they have been coopted into the president's "governing coalition."[27]

Another dividend of the OPL–interest group cooperation can be cashed at reelection time. Indeed, linkages forged between the OPL officials and the mass-membership interest groups are especially handy at reelection time. The mutual benefits derived from working together with these mass-membership groups to push the president's policy agenda can be used again to help recreate the president's broad-based electoral coalitions. To strengthen the president's communications network with the public, the Office of Media Liaison was also established in the 1970s to concentrate on local news outlets across the country. This new office focused on circumventing the Washington press corps (distrusted by most presidents) to appeal more directly to local television stations and daily newspapers. This multipronged approach has enabled the president, when faced with congressional opposition, to go it alone in building coalitions and generating public support for his agenda. Without the ''White House presidential party'' working overtime to spread the word about the president's policies and programs across the land, the president would find himself vastly outnumbered in his frequent confrontations with Congress over public policy.

FUNDRAISER PAR EXCELLENCE

One of the most vital party functions performed by modern presidents is fundraising. Though the president's daily schedule is heavily loaded with appointments with foreign leaders, members of his cabinet, his national security staff, congressional leaders, and with ceremonial duties and various other meetings, the president usually can find time to fit in a fundraising dinner and speech. Since the 1960s, presidential fundraising has become big business. In his first twenty months in office, President Bush raised $73 million—an all-time record—in a series of campaign appearances for GOP congressional and gubernatorial candidates and Republican state parties.[28] None of these fundraising efforts, however, could match his star-studded performance at the 1990 annual President's Dinner, held on behalf of the GOP House and Senate campaign committees, which netted $6.9 million for the 1990 off-year elections. No other political figure can match the president of the United States as a money-raising draw to pull in the party faithful. More than four thousand Republicans, for example, attended the 1990 President's Dinner, which was conveniently scheduled on President Bush's 66th birthday.

Until Bush's arrival in the White House, President Ronald Reagan had been the champion presidential fundraiser. The former movie star, a one-time Democrat, brought all the enthusiasm of a political convert to Republican campaigning activities. Reagan was a tireless money raiser. In the 1986 off-year election, Reagan campaigned in over two dozen states, speaking on behalf of GOP senatorial incumbents and challengers. In the author's home state of Washington, a Reagan two-hour luncheon stopover in Seattle produced over $600 thousand for GOP Senator Slade

Gorton, locked in a tight race against former Secretary of Commerce Brock Adams.[29] Even though Adams won, Reagan's brief fundraising stopover was the most productive financial event of Gorton's entire campaign. For those party professionals who know how tough the money-raising business is, these six-figure events are the lifeblood of a statewide campaign. From the president's view, if his senatorial candidate wins, the president can almost always count upon his vote in future showdown battles on Capitol Hill.

Presidential involvement in party fundraising is chiefly the product of the TV age. Before the arrival of the electronic screen in the early 1950s, most fundraising for the presidential party was handled by the party's national chairman and national committeepersons in the big states. To be sure, President Franklin D. Roosevelt appeared at a handful of Jefferson–Jackson Day fundraising dinners in the 1930s, and President Truman made an occasional appearance at fundraising dinners, but the practice of major-scale presidential money-raising activities dates but from the Eisenhower–Kennedy era.

The quantum leap in the cost of campaigning—national, state, and local—between 1952 and 1972 triggered more direct involvement of presidents in campaign fundraising activities. Before passage of the Federal Election Campaign Act of 1974—which provides full public funding of presidential election campaigns, major underwriting of the two national conventions, and matching funds for presidential nominating campaigns—fundraising was a major function of political parties. Before the advent of television, political campaigns were also much less expensive. The combined cost of presidential campaigns for both parties before 1952 exceeded $10 million only twice in the period 1912–1948 (see Table 6.1). The price tag for Senate races during this period averaged slightly over $1 million. Most House races averaged less than $100,000 per candidate. Granted, the cost-of-living index was much lower, but so were the cash outlays.

The age of television, however, profoundly changed the rules of the game. Television advertising costs, especially those for thirty-second spot ads, skyrocketed. Money, not campaign workers, became the most important commodity of campaigns. To win the presidential nomination, contenders had to develop a large fundraising operation. Especially since the passage of the 1974 reform act, which limits individual contributions to $1,000 per candidate per federal election, presidential contenders have organized huge direct-mail operations. Most presidential contenders devote several hours a day working the phones to collect the cash needed for the primary races. Once in the White House, the president can use this same fundraising machinery to identify and solicit contributors for other party candidates, until the second-term renomination campaign gets under way. Since the Watergate era (1973–1974), presidential can-

didates and their staffs, knowing that their general election bills will be
paid by Uncle Sam, have been able to lend a helping financial hand to
House and Senate incumbents seeking reelection or to less affluent candidates on the state level.

Table 6.1
Direct Campaign Expenditures by Presidential and National Party Committees,
General Elections, 1912–1988

Year	Millions
1912	$ 2.9[a]
1916	4.7
1920	6.9
1924	5.4[a]
1928	11.6
1932	5.1
1936	14.1
1940	6.2
1944	5.0
1948	6.2[a]
1952	11.6
1956	12.9
1960	19.9
1964	24.8
1968	44.2[a]
1972	103.7
1976	88.7
1980	142.9[a]
1984	90.4
1988	108.8

Source: Citizen's Research Foundation. Reprinted from Herbert E. Alexander, *Financing
the 1980 Election* (Lexington, Mass.: D.C. Heath and Company, 1983), p. 110. Data for 1984
and 1988 furnished by Herbert E. Alexander, Director, Citizens Research Foundation.
Note: Data for 1912–1944 include transfers to states. Total for 1948 includes only the direct
expenditures of the national-party committees. For 1952–1968, data do not include transfers to states but do include the national senatorial and congressional committees of both
parties. For 1972, for comparative purposes, data do not include state- and local-level
information, except for the presidential candidates. The Nixon component includes all
spending for his reelection. For 1976, amounts decreased due to public financing and
expenditure limitations.
[a] Totals include minor-party and independent-candidate spending, notably John Anderson
in 1980.

As Table 6.2 shows, the total cost of presidential spending doubled from $30 million in 1960 to $60 million in 1964—reflecting the rapidly escalating costs of campaigning in the age of television. By 1972—the last presidential election before major campaign finance reform—the total cost of presidential spending had more than doubled again from 1964. To be sure, the cost-of-living index had risen substantially, but even with this adjustment, presidential campaign spending increased more than threefold between 1960 and 1972. Since passage of the 1974 Federal Election Campaign Act, federal underwriting and matching subsidies seem to have reduced the pressure on presidential incumbents to raise huge piles of money. Still, the escalating costs of campaigning at all levels show no sign of abating, so the money chase continues. Presidents also know that the best insurance policy for helping to elect or reelect their party brethren to House and Senate seats is to assist them to raise money at joint campaign appearances. Presidents Reagan and Bush, as indicated earlier, both developed this art into a science. President Jimmy Carter, on the other hand, found himself so unpopular in 1980 that many Senate and House incumbents and Democratic House challengers chose not to ask for his fundraising assistance.

Table 6.2
Presidential Spending: 1960–1988 (Adjusted for inflation, 1960 = 100)

Year	Actual Spending[a]	CPI (1960 Base)	Adjusted Spending[a]
1960	30.0	100.0	30.0
1964	60.0	104.7	57.3
1968	100.0	117.5	85.1
1972	138.0	141.2	97.7
1976	160.0	192.2	83.2
1980	275.0	278.1	98.9
1984	325.0	346.8	93.7
1988	500.0	385.4	126.5

Source: Citizens' Research Foundation. Reprinted from Herbert E. Alexander and Brian A. Haggerty, *Financing the 1984 Election* (Lexington, Mass: D. C. Heath Company, 1987), p. 84. Revised 1984 figures and 1988 data furnished by Herbert E. Alexander, Director, Citizen Research Foundation.
[a] All spending figures are in millions of dollars and include prenomination, convention, and general election costs.

HOW THE WHITE HOUSE PERFORMS BEHIND-THE-SCENES MANAGEMENT OF REELECTION CAMPAIGNS

The 1956 Eisenhower reelection campaign was the last one to be managed by the party's national committee. President Eisenhower had full confidence in GOP national chairman Leonard Hall's ability to direct the campaign in every respect.[30] And Eisenhower's landslide reelection victory over Adlai E. Stevenson was convincing proof that his confidence had been justified. President Lyndon B. Johnson, seeking a full term in 1964, used a two-pronged approach against GOP challenger Barry Goldwater. He relied partly on the Democratic national committee, but he also used an independent committee, Citizens for Johnson and Humphrey, in his successful drive to retain the White House. President Johnson's campaign managers also joined the trend started by the Eisenhower strategists of hiring a New York advertising agency to handle all television campaign advertising.

Since the Nixon years, the national party organization has taken a back seat to the president's White House–directed reelection committee. In 1972, the White House assumed full control of the Nixon reelection campaign by organizing a completely independent agency to run the campaign—the Committee to Re-Elect the President (CREEP). Established nearly a year before the 1972 election, CREEP mounted one of the most expensive reelection drives in American history. Funded by huge sums from individual Republican "fat cats" and illegal corporate contributors, CREEP spent over $62 million to overwhelm the hapless George McGovern. Indeed, CREEP had such a huge excess of campaign funds that, in trying to disrupt the Democratic nominating campaign, they used a variety of "dirty tricks" to embarrass leading Democratic Senators Hubert H. Humphrey and Edmund Muskie.[31] While successful in the short run, revelations of CREEP's underhanded activities during the course of the Watergate investigation, severely damaged Republican electoral prospects in 1974 and 1976.

Federal legislation, which now provides full funding for presidential election campaigns, virtually assures that the White House will handle the management of the incumbent president's general election campaign. Under the 1974 Federal Election Campaign Act, Uncle Sam gives each of the major candidates a lump sum ($46.1 million in 1988) to run the general election campaign, provided that the candidate agrees not to accept private contributions. So far, no candidate has refused the federal dollars in the general election campaign. Only one presidential contender— former Secretary of the Treasury John Connally—has declined to accept federal matching funds during the nominating campaign. In 1980, Connally raised over $12.4 million in private funds, but despite this huge financial outlay and months of campaigning, he garnered only one delegate (from Arkansas)—the most expensive national convention delegate in American history.[32]

Because the candidate or the incumbent receives the money directly from the Federal Election Commission, the national party organization is effectively cut out of any meaningful role in the presidential campaign. Originally, after passage of the 1974 law, the national committee could not legally spend its own funds on behalf of the presidential candidate because these expenditures would violate the federally imposed limit ($46.1 million in 1988). National committees, however, have been permitted under a 1979 amendment to the federal campaign law to expend $8.3 million in "party coordinated expenditures" within the states for lawn signs, bumper stickers, and local headquarters staffing—and to raise "soft money." These funds, raised and spent outside the constraints of federal law, are regulated by state laws, many of which are less stringent. Sanctioned by the 1979 amendments to the Federal Election Campaign Act, soft money was solicited in low-key fashion in 1980 and 1984, but four years later, soft-money fundraising suddenly became a big business. In 1988, both the Republican and the Democratic candidates, their staffs, and the two national committees became heavily involved in collecting huge sums of soft money from individual contributors to be channeled directly to state parties to help the Bush and Dukakis general election campaigns.

The Bush prenomination campaign finance managers collected $22 million and the Dukakis prenomination money managers collected $23 million in soft money. These funds were raised at a frantic pace—frequently as much as $100,000 each from individual contributors—as if no public funding and expenditure limits existed. This money, in turn, was ploughed back into the state party organizations for voter registration drives, operating state headquarters, and paying staff members.[33]

As a result of this legal loophole, both presidential candidates were able to use the soft money to free up more of the $46.1 million in public funds awarded to them for advertising, travel, and other expenditures directly associated with the presidential general election campaigns.[34]

By early spring 1991, White House officials were already taking steps to prepare for President George Bush's reelection bid in 1992. White House Chief of Staff John H. Sununu indicated the Bush White House would roughly follow the model of President Reagan's insider 1984 reelection campaign, leaving the Republican National Committee with only token chores. Under this plan, President Bush would make major decisions on the structure and staffing of his campaign organization in the fall of 1991—approximately one year before the 1992 presidential election.[35] Like President Reagan four years earlier, Bush would formally announce his reelection bid in the late fall or in early January 1992. With this type of schedule, the White House incumbent can appear mainly presidential—rather than political—until the 1992 nominating sweepstakes are well under way.

SUMMARY

Once political parties emerged in the John Adams administration, the rise of a presidential party as well as a congressional party was almost inevitable in our separation-of-powers system. President Thomas Jefferson was the first chief executive to recognize the need for a cadre of party loyalists in the executive and legislative branches to move the levers of government. By frequent meetings, including dinners, with his loyal followers in Congress, Jefferson used his "carrot and stick" leadership approach to achieve most of his legislative goals. Not until Andrew Jackson's election did the country see another chief executive who recruited his own cadre of congressional partisans to strengthen his presidential hand in dealing with Congress. For the remainder of the ninteenth century, however, the presidential party was, except during the Polk, Lincoln, and Cleveland presidencies, overshadowed by the congressional party. Congress set the agenda, approved the legislation, and, for the most part, determined the nation's priorities. Clearly, the era of the "postage-stamp" presidencies was not a period of strong executive party leadership.

Presidents Teddy Roosevelt and Woodrow Wilson injected new life into the presidential party and demonstrated to the nation that a chief executive, backed by solid party majorities, can change the nation's direction. Most presidents since then have endeavored to follow the Roosevelt–Wilson model of building strength in the presidential party in order to withstand congressional resistance to their leadership.

Continuity of membership has been one of the most notable characteristics of the presidential party. Old Wilsonians surfaced again in Franklin D. Roosevelt's administration. Similarly, veteran New Dealers could be found in the Truman administration. Eisenhower Republicans reappeared in the Nixon and Ford administrations, and Goldwater Republicans found a new home in the Reagan administration.

Since the 1960s, all presidential campaigns have been run directly from the candidate's headquarters or from the White House, if the president is seeking a second term. Clearly the nerve center of the presidential party is now the candidate's headquarters, not the party's national committee. Federal funding of national elections has almost guaranteed that campaigns will be run from the presidential candidates' headquarters because Uncle Sam's funds are transmitted directly to the candidates, not their parties. Once elected, recent presidents have assigned to their White House staffers most of the patronage functions formerly handled at the national committee headquarters. More important, the White House has assigned its political staff the task of developing close ties with mass-membership interest groups to build public support for presidential programs. In a sense, the White House has become a "surrogate presidential party," focused on constructing governing coalitions, especially in this era of divided government. Finally, over the past three decades the president has also become the party's leading fundraiser, collecting huge sums at campaign dinners for the party's senatorial, congressional, and gubernatorial incumbents or challengers.

Faced frequently with a divided government and the decline of political parties, presidents have concluded in recent years that their governing success depends more upon their ability to influence and persuade the public than the leaders on Capitol Hill. This heavy reliance on "going public" is the subject of Chapter 7.

NOTES

1. James MacGregor Burns, *The Deadlock of Democracy* (Englewood Cliffs, NJ: Prentice-Hall, 1963).

2. Ibid., p. 36.

3. Ibid.

4. John S. Pancake, *Thomas Jefferson and Alexander Hamilton* (Woodbury, NY: Barron's Educational Series, 1974), pp. 66–86.

5. Ralph M. Goldman, *Search for Consensus: The Story of the Democratic Party* (Philadelphia: Temple University Press, 1979), p. 33.

6. Clinton Rossiter, "President and Congress in the 1960s," in Marion Irish, ed., *Continuing Crisis in American Politics* (Englewood Cliffs, NJ: Prentice-Hall, 1963), pp. 104–105.

7. Hugh A. Bone, *Party Committees and National Politics* (Seattle: University of Washington Press, 1958), pp. 127–128.

8. Roger G. Brown, "The Presidency and Political Parties," in Michael Nelson, ed., *The Presidency and the Political System* (Washington, DC: Congressional Quarterly Press, 1984), pp. 331–332.

9. Brown, "The Presidency and the Political Parties," p. 315.

10. James MacGregor Burns, *Presidential Government* (Boston: Houghton Mifflin, 1966), p. 190. This discussion of the presidential party draws heavily on this text, especially pp. 155–191.

11. Leon D. Epstein, *Political Parties in the American Mold* (Madison: University of Wisconsin Press, 1986), p. 85.

12. Ibid.

13. John H. Kessel, *Presidential Parties* (Homewood, IL: Dorsey, 1984), p. 322.

14. Epstein, *Political Parties in the American Mold*, p. 85.

15. Terry M. Moe, "The Politicized Presidency," in John E. Chubb and Paul E. Peterson, eds., *The New Direction in American Politics* (Washington, DC: The Brookings Institution, 1985), p. 244.

16. Theodore H. White, *The Making of the President 1968* (New York: Atheneum, 1969), pp. 167–168.

17. Lou Cannon, *Reagan* (New York: Putnam, 1982), pp. 98–226.

18. Fred I. Greenstein, "Nine Presidents in Search of a Modern Presidency," in Fred I. Greenstein, ed., *Leadership in the Modern Presidency* (Cambridge, MA: Harvard University Press, 1988), p. 343.

19. Samuel Huntington, "The Democratic Distemper," *The Public Interest* 41 (1975), p. 27.

20. United States, House of Representatives, Committee on Post Office and Civil Service, 1978, quoted by Lester G. Seligman and Cary R. Covington, *The Coalition Presidency* (Chicago: Dorsey, 1989), p. 64.

21. Michael Baruch Grossman and Martha Joynt Kumar, *Portraying the President* (Baltimore: The Johns Hopkins University Press, 1981), pp. 83–84.

22. Seligman and Covington, *The Coalition Presidency*, p. 64.

23. Ibid., p. 71.

24. Hugh Heclo, "The Changing Presidential Office," in Arnold J. Meltsner, ed., *Politics and the Oval Office* (San Francisco: Institute for Contemporary Studies, 1981), p. 169.

25. Grossman and Kumar, *Portraying the President*, pp. 113–115.

26. Seligman and Covington, *The Coalition Presidency*, p. 105.

27. Joseph Pika, "The President and Interest Groups," in Edward N. Kerney, ed., *Dimensions of the Modern Presidency* (St. Louis: Forum Press, 1981), p. 70.

28. *The New York Times*, September 28, 1990; see also Chuck Alston, "Bush Ladles Gravy for GOP Mashed-Potato Circuit," *CQ Guide to Current American Government, Spring 1991*, Washington, DC: Congressional Quarterly, Inc., 1991, pp. 94–96.

29. *Seattle Times*, December 13, 1985.

30. Bone, *Party Committees and National Politics*, p. 31.

31. Theodore H. White, *Breach of Faith: The Fall of Richard Nixon* (New York: Atheneum, 1975), pp. 151–187.

32. Herbert E. Alexander, *Financing the 1980 Election* (Lexington, MA: Heath, 1983), pp. 192–199.

33. Herbert E. Alexander and Monica Bauer, *Financing the 1988 Election* (Boulder, CO: Westview, 1991), pp. 37–40.

34. Ibid.

35. Ann Devroy and Dan Balz, "An Unofficial Announcement," *Washington Post National Weekly Edition*, February 11–17, 1991, p. 14.

Chapter 7

The Public President Overshadows the Party President

Modern presidential communication has been given a new name in recent years: ''the public presidency.'' As the governing process has become more an extension of the election campaign, presidential speech-making has in turn become one of the chief executive's most valuable assets for setting the agenda and influencing the American electorate in the age of television and the era of divided government. Between April 16, 1945 and December 31, 1985, according to communications specialist Roderick P. Hart, American presidents spoke in public on 9,969 occasions.[1] During this period, presidents spoke in public an average of twenty times a month—approximately one speech per working day. President Eisenhower spoke least often, averaging ten speeches a month, while President Ford spoke most frequently, averaging forty-three speeches a month during his brief tenure in the White House.

With the decline of political parties, fragmented leadership in Congress, and the persistence of divided government, presidents have found that public speeches, especially ''nonpartisan'' nationwide TV addresses, have become the most effective means of swaying public opinion and winning popular support for White House–sponsored programs. As Lester G. Seligman and Cary R. Covington have commented, ''The president enlists the public's support for the presidential legislative agenda in the same way as when the president gained their votes as a candidate.''[2]

In this chapter major attention will be focused on how the president appeals to the general public, rather than partisans, speaking in the interest ''of all the people.'' As another aspect of this development, it will be noted that presidential travel has increased in tandem with presidential speech-making. In the age of jet travel, a president can speak to business, trade, fraternal, or political groups in several states in one day. As is noted throughout the chapter, the president can use his speaking schedule to set the national agenda and also counteract, if not control, the treatment he receives from the mass media. Has the public presidency so eroded the president's role as party leader that it is no longer a major factor in presidential decision-making? The final section of the chapter seeks to answer this perplexing question.

THE RISE OF THE RHETORICAL PRESIDENT

The twentieth century marks the rise of the "public" or rhetorical presidency. This political phenomenon has been described as follows:

Popular or mass rhetoric which presidents once employed only rarely, now serves as one of their principal tools in attempting to govern the nation. Whatever doubts Americans may now entertain about the limitations of presidential leadership, they do not consider it unfitting or inappropriate for presidents to attempt to "move" the public by programmatic speeches that exhort and set forth grand and ennobling views.[3]

Quite simply, in the age of the public presidency, the spoken word and the TV image have replaced the written word. President Woodrow Wilson did not invent the public presidency, but his decision in 1913 to deliver the State of the Union Address to Congress in person, rather than forwarding the speech to the House and Senate clerks to be read to the lawmakers, can serve as the dividing line between the traditional mode of handling presidential business and "going public." This term, coined by Samuel Kernell, "is a class of activities in which presidents engage as they promote themselves and their policies before the American public."[4] Wilson's three Republican successors—Harding, Coolidge, and Hoover—failed to grasp the full significance of change in modern communication, especially the emergence of radio in the 1920s, but the arrival of Franklin D. Roosevelt in 1933 heralded the beginning of the public presidency era.

Franklin D. Roosevelt's famous "fireside chats" delivered to the nation via the three major radio networks (TV did not come until after World War II) was his mode of "going public." Even before the age of television, FDR's fireside chats averaged an audience of sixty million listeners. Roosevelt, however, used these chats sparingly—only once or twice a year. But the nation, in the throes of the Great Depression, listened intently beside their radios, as they received reassurance from the ever-confident president that the nation was heading in the correct direction and that with patience, all would be right with America.

Franklin D. Roosevelt operated in an era when parties were still formidable agents for implementing the president's agenda; hence, he did not rely so heavily on going public as have our recent TV-age presidents. But FDR, always sensitive to public opinion, would have fully understood our recent presidents' tactics on going public whenever they encounter heavy resistance from Congress.

Going public is such a common occurrence in this era of divided government that the American public has come to accept it as a way of life for our presidents. A trip to China, a televised news conference, a speech before a business convention on the West Coast, a prime-time address to the nation, or a mini-summit meeting in Malta with Soviet leader Mikhail Gorbachev, all these events are intended principally to place the president and his message before the American people in a way that raises his public opinion ratings and thus enhances his chances of success in Washington. As Samuel Kernell writes, "the ultimate object of the president's designs is not the American voter, but fellow politicians in Washington."[5] By going public, the president seeks to transfer approval of his performance to support for his policies. To rally national public opinion is, therefore, the keystone of this new style of presidential leadership. In Samuel Kernell's words, "Going public represents little more than an extension of the process that placed the outsider in the White House."[6]

Over the past half-century, the frequency with which presidents have communicated with the American public has risen steadily—the more recent the president, the more likely that he went public. Table 7.1 shows the record of television time utilized by presidents from Kennedy to Reagan during their first nineteen months in office. Most recently, President Bush has set new highs in going public. In his first year in office, he visited 87 cities, held 33 full-blown press conferences and 15 informal press gatherings, gave 54 interviews, and delivered 320 speeches (an estimated total of three million words).[7]

In recent years, the most notable growth in presidential appearances has occurred in the class of minor addresses. Nixon, Carter, and Reagan have on average spoken five times more frequently than Hoover, Roosevelt, or Truman. Both Carter and Reagan averaged one speech a day. President Reagan, for example, made some twenty-five appearances around the country in 1983, promoting his views on "excellence in education" (chiefly merit pay for teachers and the need for tighter classroom discipline) after polls showed a two-to-one public disapproval of his cuts in the education budget.[8]

THE ADVANTAGES OF "GOING PUBLIC"

With the steady decline of political parties and party discipline and the frequency of divided government, the president can no longer simply implore his fellow partisans on Capitol Hill to support his program. Furthermore, the fragmentation of Congress, especially the "subcommit-

Table 7.1
Presidential Television from Kennedy to Reagan;
First Nineteen Months in Office

President	Number of Appearances in Prime Time	Time on Air in Prime Time (hours)	Total Number of Appearances	Total Time on Air (hours)
Kennedy	4	1.9	50	30.4
Johnson	7	3.3	33	12.5
Nixon	14	7.1	37	13.5
Carter	8	5.1	45	32.2
Reagan	12	8.9	39	26.5

Sources: For Kennedy, Johnson, and Nixon, data were supplied by the White House Press Office, quoted in *New York Times,* August 3, 1970. For Carter and Reagan, data are from program logs at CBS News, New York. Data are for speeches (including inauguration) and press conferences broadcast live by the national television networks. Reprinted from Samuel Kernell, *Going Public* (Washington, DC: Congressional Quarterly Press, 1986), p. 91.
Note: Gerald Ford has been omitted from analysis since his first nineteen months in office cross into the reelection period.

teeization" of the House, has made it far more difficult for the president and his staff to negotiate agreements with committee and subcommittee chairs and the various special issue-related caucuses. It is much easier for a president to go public and seek support nationwide for his programs by appealing to a variety of interest groups. Going public helps the president indirectly build coalition support, even if it is for only one major vote in Congress. Coalition-building in this age of the mass media, however, has become much more difficult because senators and representatives operate more as independent contractors and less as team players. As Thomas E. Mann has explained, "Senators and representatives are in business for themselves." "Consequently," Mann continues, "they are all more likely to view themselves first and foremost as individuals, not as members of a party or as part of the president's team."[9]

By going public, the president can often avoid having to bargain with 535 individuals on Capitol Hill. Also, by going public, the president can sometimes gain the upper hand with Congress because its members do not want to risk being viewed by their constituents as being uncooperative with a popular president or being on the wrong side of an issue that may damage them in a future reelection campaign. On a cost-benefits analysis of going public or choosing to bargain privately with congressional leaders, modern technology—especially television—has made the president's public approach increasingly attractive.

Televised nationwide speeches may enable presidents to create or modify public opinion at critical points during their terms. By appealing to mass audiences, the president can often gain more public support for White House policy proposals. Generally, the president's popular approval ratings increase significantly with the delivery of a major address. Presidential speeches may also enhance his reelection efforts. While these addresses are no guarantee of reelection, they can serve throughout his first term as an excellent opportunity to "run for office while in office."[10]

Going public, however, will not always rescue the president's chestnuts. In the late spring of 1974, for example, as the Watergate investigation closed in on him, President Nixon endeavored to go public to demonstrate that he was "still in charge" by traveling to the Soviet Union to talk with Soviet leader Leonid Brezhnev. On his return trip, he also stopped off in the Middle East to talk with Israeli leaders. But the net effect of Nixon's international trip was zero. With the Watergate special prosecutor Leon Jaworski moving ever closer to the Oval Office and with the national press in hot pursuit of the Watergate story, Nixon's diversionary trip flopped. Within two months, he resigned rather than face impending impeachment—the first president ever to be forced out of office.

President Jimmy Carter's public speeches often fell flat and, in the case of his well-publicized "malaise" speech in July 1979, seriously undermined public confidence in his presidential stewardship. Scheduled to give a nationwide address shortly after his return from an economic summit conference in Japan, Carter abruptly cancelled his speech on his new energy conservation program less than twenty-four hours before telecast time. Instead, he invited more than 125 of the nation's top leaders to consult with him at Camp David over a ten-day period to discuss pressing national issues and his administration's failure to communicate adequately with the American public.

Armed with these private briefings, Carter rescheduled his cancelled speech for the following Sunday evening. Separating himself from the government, as he had done throughout his successful presidential campaign, Carter described the American system as incapable of action, marked by "paralysis and stagnation and greed." Moreover, he continued, "The gap between our citizens and our government has never been so wide."[11] Carter also found fault with the American people who were too concerned with self, too filled with despair. He pledged that he would provide the kind of moral leadership that the people need to end the nation's malaise and restore national confidence.

Three days after his speech, Carter fired several members of his cabinet. Unfortunately for President Carter, the nation's negative reaction to his national address and the cabinet firings drove his low poll ratings even lower. Indeed, some commentators later observed that this "crisis in confidence" speech and the cabinet purge probably sealed Carter's fate as a one-term president.

TELEVISION AND MOBILIZING PUBLIC SUPPORT

The public president conducts his office as if he were still campaigning for it. President Reagan, for example, made extensive use of television—even running a few Republican party–paid commercials—during non-election periods. Before each major televised address by President Reagan to win support for budget cuts, his staff spent hours of preparatory work. They used a multipronged approach: polls were taken; data from these surveys were incorporated into the preliminary draft; the Washington media were briefed, either in the White House newsroom or via selective leaks. To sway undecided members of Congress, the president traveled to a number of states, addressing various business forums. In addition, grass roots lobbying campaigns were launched, initiated and directed by the White House staff and aided by the Republican National Committee and sympathetic business organizations.

To influence and mold public opinion, modern presidents must, of course, become "great explainers."[12] Invariably, they turn to national television, since no other medium routinely gives them instant access to such a huge audience. But as George C. Edwards III has noted: "The public's lack of interest in politics constrains the president's leadership of public opinion in the long run as well as a given day."[13] Indeed, the president has to wait until the issues he wants to discuss are on their minds, which occurs only when an issue in question is personally affecting their lives. Thus, although the president can use television to reach his multimillion-member audience, the president cannot turn to the American people every time an important issue crosses his mind. If he does, his television rhetoric will become commonplace and lose much of its drama and impact.

THE TRAVELING PRESIDENT

President George Bush is well on his way to becoming the most traveled chief executive in history. During his first year in office, Bush traveled 185,000 miles.[14] His journeys included three summits (on Malta with Gorbachev, in Brussels with NATO leaders, and in Paris on economics with Western leaders). Most of the domestic trips involved statecraft, but Bush also found time to campaign for GOP gubernatorial candidates in New Jersey and Virginia (they both lost) and to attend several major fundraising dinners. Early in year two of his first term, Bush also used a tried and tested joint-travel venture that combined presidential duties and party service. Twice he traveled to California, the first time to review United States troops and military installations and to speak to a huge $1,000-a-plate GOP dinner on behalf of the Republican gubernatorial candidate, Senator Pete Wilson. On his return trip, he stopped off at a Strategic Air Command (SAC) base in Nebraska to check out the readiness of the nation's B-1 bomber fleet, and he also found time to attend a GOP fundraising dinner to help raise money for Governor Kay Orr, seeking a second term. By combining presidential and party duties, the president could pro-rate the cost of the trip and charge the California and Nebraska candidates only for that percentage of the trip related to party business. Opposition Democrats could fume that Bush was using the taxpayers' money and jet aircraft to gain an advantage for his fellow Republicans, but the White House could easily brush aside the charge, declaring that President Bush was merely adhering to a practice long ago established by FDR, Eisenhower, and Kennedy to share costs for these trips.

That President Bush would continue to use heavy foreign travel as a means of maintaining his high post–Persian Gulf War popularity and keeping the opposition Democrats off balance throughout the remainder of his first term was evident soon after he gave a nationally televised gulf war report to a joint session of Congress in early March 1991. In his address, he also called upon lawmakers to approve his new crime control and transportation proposals within one hundred days (neither house of Congress met this deadline). The message to the controlling Democrats was crystal clear: if the United States government could win a ground war in one hundred hours, certainly it could enact a tough crime control law and an expanded transportation bill in one hundred days.

But instead of following up these initiatives with personal meetings with congressional leaders, President Bush launched into another series of top-level international meetings with several allied leaders of the Persian Gulf coalition. Within a five-day period Bush met with Canadian Prime Minister Brian Mulroney in Ottawa, French President François Mitterand in the West Indian island of Martinique, and British Prime Minister John Majors in Bermuda—almost a repeat performance of his 1990 summer itinerary. Over the following weekend, President Bush used *Air Force One* to hop to southern California for a top-level rendezvous with Japanese Prime Minister Toshiki Kaifu. Two days later, he winged to Houston to discuss free trade with Mexican President Carlos Salinas. Bush's nonstop traveling prompted one columnist to describe him as ''the Flying Dutchman of diplomacy.'' White House officials have indicated that President Bush, who holds the modern one-year record for presidential travel, plans to make up this year for the travel time lost because of the Persian Gulf War. His planned junkets included a tour of Kuwait and other Middle Eastern countries, a postponed trip to the Soviet Union, and another trip to Western Europe. By keeping in almost constant motion, President Bush found it relatively easy to maintain his agenda-setting dominance over opposition Democrats in Congress. As explained by one Bush aide, "When we are in Washington, we end up playing on the Congressional playing field. But when we get outside Washington, we have a better opportunity to convey our message to the public, and we are not forced to follow the Congressional agenda."[15]

President Woodrow Wilson was the first chief executive to travel abroad when he attended the Versailles Peace Conference in 1919. The first international airplane flight by a president occurred in 1943 when President Franklin D. Roosevelt secretly journeyed to North Africa (Casablanca, Morocco) to meet Prime Minister Winston Churchill to map war strategy. The straight-line distance to Casablanca is less than four thousand miles, and a modern *Air Force One* could make the trip in less than seven hours. In the pre-jet age, given the limited range and slower speed of piston-driven aircraft, and the lack of sophisticated navigational aids in the Boeing 314 and Douglas C-54, President Roosevelt's wartime journey required four legs of flying, three stopovers, a change of planes, and more than three days' travel time each way. As FDR hopscotched across the Atlantic and back, he touched on three continents, crossed the equator four times, and spent approximately ninety hours in the air. By the time Roosevelt had returned to the White House, he had covered seventeen thousand miles.[16]

As late as 1948, a train was the president's standard mode of travel. But since a round trip across the country and back took at least seven days, the president and his schedulers usually tried to combine presidential duties with politics. The leisurely train travel enabled the president to make several speeches along the way, visit with governors and state party leaders, invite them to travel across their states in the president's special observation car, and then dedicate a federal project or two. FDR, who enjoyed train travel, used this approach successfully on several occasions, and of course President Harry Truman's 1948 cross-country campaign special was tailor-made for his uphill reelection bid.

President Eisenhower was the first chief executive to travel extensively by air around the country. With the arrival of the jet age, presidential international travel, which also increased perceptibly in the 1960s, has continued to grow. President Eisenhower's 1959 "goodwill" global tour is generally considered to have been the first international junket conducted primarily to produce favorable publicity both at home and abroad for the president. Since then, presidents have become far more personally involved in public relations. By the late 1960s, live satellite communications brought the president to TV screens instantaneously in millions of American homes, no matter where he might be on the globe. With these remarkable inventions at their fingertips, presidents seldom pass up an opportunity to go public—whether it is an election year or not. The classic example of presidential travel being used with devastating effectiveness during an election year occurred in March 1972. President Nixon timed his arrival on Capitol Hill for a special report to Congress on his historic mission to Communist China to overshadow the announcement of the early returns from the hotly contested New Hampshire Democratic presidential primary.

President Ronald Reagan was also a foremost practitioner of the "Marco Polo" approach to presidential politics. His frequent foreign excursions offered him a priceless opportunity to combine statecraft and practical politics on foreign shores. Few voters would forget President and Mrs. Reagan's visit in the spring of 1984 to the Normandy Beach cemetery to commemorate the fortieth anniversary of the D-Day landings; nor did the White House staff overlook the unmatched photo opportunities this ceremony presented during the early phase of the 1984 presidential campaign. Another memorable episode on this same European trip was the Reagans' visit to Ballyporeen, the small Irish village of his ancestors in Tipperary. In this picturesque setting the 1,800-member traveling TV and print media contingent accompanying the Reagans clearly outnumbered the 350 villagers who turned out to greet the American president by more than five to one.[17]

Can there be any doubt that incumbent presidents have found a time-tested strategy of carefully planned foreign travel to dominate the news, eclipse their political adversaries, and keep the national agenda in their court, leaving many intractable domestic problems behind them at home?

THE CORRELATION BETWEEN A PRESIDENT'S POPULARITY AND HIS ABILITY TO INFLUENCE PEOPLE

Over two decades ago, presidential scholar Richard E. Neustadt, in his seminal study *Presidential Power*, argued that the key to presidential effectiveness can be measured most directly by the chief executive's standing with the public and the president's ability to persuade Congress to support his programs.[18] In other words, the level of public support is both a result and a determinant of the president's effectiveness. Recently, several political scientists have echoed Neustadt's reciprocal-relationship thesis. As put by one team of scholars: "The president's standing in the polls has become the most important determinant of his power to persuade. In fact, presidential politics has become a kind of perpetual election with the public assessing the president's performance each month and the politicians watching the results."[19]

Political scientists Charles W. Ostrom, Jr., and Dennis M. Simon, in their study of the monthly Gallup poll on the president's overall performance, have pointed out the average number of these presidential performance polls has grown from twelve per year during the Eisenhower administration to roughly twenty-four per year during the Carter administration. It is significant that since the election of Eisenhower occupants of the Oval Office have been subject to almost continuous evaluation via the Gallup opinion poll. Between 1953 and 1980, for example, the Gallup organization posed the following general performance question to cross-sections of the American public 538 times: "Do you approve or disapprove of the ways [name of the incumbent] is handling his job as president?"[20] This Gallup poll question, in effect, serves as a continuous referendum on the president and heavily influences his current power situation. Throughout the past thirty years, the Gallup poll data show that the issues—peace, prosperity, and domestic tranquility—have dominated the public's agenda. It is on these three issues that presidential performance is most closely judged.

Recent studies show that presidents have been most effective when their standing with the public has been above 55 percent in the Gallup poll. For example, President Reagan, with his popularity riding above 55 percent, was able to push his tax reform, budget cuts, and military buildup program through Congress with ease during his first year in the White House. Most post-Roosevelt presidents have experienced similar legislative success when their popularity ratings were above 55 percent, even if—as in the case of Eisenhower—the opposition party controlled both houses of Congress for six years. President Johnson was able to move his ambitious Great Society program through Congress during his first eighteen months in the White House, partly because he was the beneficiary of a huge outpouring of good will and public support that followed the Kennedy assassination (see Table 7.2). But his legislative program came to a near standstill after mid-1965 when his policy of escalating United States involvement in the Vietnam War drove his popularity ratings down to 50 percent and below. Low levels of public support tend to immobilize a chief executive. Furthermore, declining public approval generally translates into a declining probability of success for subsequent decisions and actions.[21]

President Carter saw his popularity ratings plummet to 38 percent in the second year after he failed to obtain congressional passage of a comprehensive energy program. Not until he successfully negotiated the Camp David accord between Israel and Egypt in September 1978, which generated a surge of popular support, did Carter obtain congressional approval of his energy package. But then Carter's ratings began to slide again, and even after the Iranian hostage crisis temporarily boosted his ratings, his last two years in the White House were widely regarded as a period of presidential ineffectiveness. In each instance, when a president

Table 7.2
Public Support for Modern Presidents: A Summary

| Administration | Average Approval Rating | | | |
	Year 1	Year 2	Year 3	Year 4
Truman 1949-1952	58.5	41.0	28.3	29.6
Eisenhower 1953-1956	69.3	65.4	71.3	73.3
Eisenhower 1957-1960	65.0	54.6	63.3	61.1
Kennedy 1961-1963	76.0	71.6	63.5	--
Johnson 1964-1968	66.4	51.2	44.0	41.5
Nixon 1969-1972	61.4	56.9	49.9	56.4
Ford 1974-1976	--	53.9	43.1	48.1
Carter 1977-1980	62.4	45.5	38.1	39.5
Reagan 1981-1984	57.0	43.7	44.6	54.3
Reagan 1984-1988	60.5	61.5	47.6	52.0
Bush 1989-1990	65.0	66.0	--	--

Sources: Gallup Report, No. 182, October–November 1980; *Gallup Report*, No. 219, December 1983; *Gallup Report*, No. 225, June 1984. Reprinted from John H. Aldrich, Gary J. Miller, Charles W. Ostrom, Jr., and David W. Rohde, *American Government: People, Institutions, and Policies* (Boston: Houghton Mifflin, 1986), p. 490. Figures for 1988, 1989, and 1990 supplied by Gallup Poll News Service; reprinted with permission.

has kept his popularity rating high, he has been able to translate this popularity into political power and win most of his legislative battles with Congress. As one team of scholars has recently noted: ''Presidential power is an ephemeral commodity. It cannot be stored in a bank like money, and it cannot be withdrawn when needed. It depends on the president's popularity.''[22]

PRESIDENTIAL POPULARITY AND PUBLIC CONFIDENCE

Several studies suggest that the impact of public support of the president extends far beyond specific policy issues. The electorate's confidence in the president and their trust in government rises when a president's popularity is high. Indeed, the importance of public support to the president is nowhere more evident than its impact on reelection prospects. As Table 7.3 shows, the four post-Truman presidents whose popularity ratings were 55 percent or above in the last year of their first term—Eisenhower, Johnson, Nixon, and Reagan—easily won reelection. On the other hand, no president has been reelected whose standing in the Gallup poll for June of the year in which he was eligible for reelection was below 55 percent. Presidents Truman and Johnson, influenced in part by their low standings in the Gallup polls, declined to seek reelection. Presidents Ford and Carter tried and failed.

Recent research has confirmed the conventional view that a president's legislative performance and his actions toward the Soviet Union are important determinants of public support. Until the recent end of the Cold War, public support for the president appeared to rise whenever the United States became involved in a diplomatic confrontation with the Soviet Union.[23] Also, presidential handling of the economy weighs heavily

Table 7.3
Presidential Popularity and Presidential Elections

Year	Popularity in June	Election Result
1952	32%	Truman declines to run.
1956	69	Eisenhower is reelected.
1960	57	Eisenhower is not eligible.
1964	74	Johnson is elected.
1968	40	Johnson declines to seek reelection.
1972	55	Nixon is reelected.
1976	45	Ford is defeated.
1980	31	Carter is defeated.
1984	55	Reagan is reelected.
1988	51	Reagan is not eligible

Sources: Gallup Report, No. 182, October–November 1980; *Gallup Report,* No. 219, December 1983; *Gallup Report,* No. 225, June 1984. Reprinted from John H. Aldrich, Gary J. Miller, Charles W. Ostrom, Jr., and David W. Rohde, *American Government: People, Institutions, and Policies* (Boston: Houghton Mifflin, 1986), p. 487. Figure for 1988 is from *The Gallup Poll Monthly Report,* No. 277, August 1988, p. 26.

in the public's assessment of the White House occupant. A president's public support will usually be above 50 percent if the nation's "misery index" (the combined rate of inflation and unemployment) is low.[24] Conversely, when the misery index rises over a period of months, presidential popularity will drop noticeably.

In the wake of 10.8 percent unemployment in 1982, President Reagan's popularity level dropped to 35 percent by January 1983—from its previous all-time high of 68 percent in May 1981, shortly after the near fatal attempt on his life. But by December 1983, his rating had rebounded to 55 percent. Three major factors seemed to account for President Reagan's resurging popularity. First, between March and December 1983 the misery index declined from 15.4 in June to 11.8 in December. Second, not only was the adverse impact of the economy neutralized by declining unemployment and inflation rates, but there was a marked shift of public attention away from domestic matters. Between March and December 1983, the percentage of the public citing inflation and unemployment as "the most important problem" the country faced dropped from 79 to 43 percent, whereas the percentage of the public identifying foreign affairs as the nation's number one problem rose from 6 to 37 percent. Third, the Soviet downing of a Korean Air Lines Boeing 747 with the loss of 263 lives, including 69 Americans; the terrorist bombing of the United States Marine barracks at the Beirut airport that killed 241 American troops; and the American military action in the Caribbean island of Grenada triggered a rapid upswing in public support of President Reagan.

This favorable reversal of public opinion was noteworthy for two reasons: First, no post-Eisenhower president had earned a higher approval rating after three years in office (President Kennedy had a higher rating but served less than three years). Second, President Reagan was the first chief executive in the history of the Gallup poll to drop below 40 percent and then rebound to sustain a level above 50 percent. President Reagan's approval ratings continued to climb gradually—they reached 64 percent in January 1986. Indeed, his popularity ratings were more reminiscent of the Eisenhower–Kennedy years than of the "revolving door" presidencies era of the late 1960s and 1970s.

Foreign policy issues dominated the Eisenhower–Kennedy years. Both these presidents benefitted from approval-enhancing events—summit meetings, the Formosa Straits resolution of 1955 against Communist China, General Eisenhower's "open skies" nuclear test-inspection proposal, the Cuban missile crisis, the Kennedy-sponsored limited test ban treaty signed in record time in 1963, and the Washington–Moscow telephone "hot line." These events, it should be noted, not only helped the Eisenhower–Kennedy popularity ratings but also diverted attention from the economy and divisive domestic problems. By contrast, the 1964–1980 period was marked by the prolonged, unpopular Vietnam War, the

Watergate scandal, and a period of spiraling inflation, escalating unemployment, and skyrocketing oil prices. As a result, public attention shifted from consensual issues to a set of divisive issues. Dissatisfaction and cynicism replaced public approbation of national leadership. Presidents failed to live up to public expectations. White House occupants seemed unable to extricate themselves from a vicious spiral of high public expectations and low job-performance ratings.

Since then, President Reagan's success with Congress has coincided with high popularity ratings. Conversely, when his popularity dropped after the surfacing of the "guns for hostages" swap report from Beirut in late 1986, after his public refusal to negotiate with the hostage-takers, and the beginning Iran-Contra hearings, he lost two major veto overrides to Congress in early 1987 on public works and highway construction measures. But then a breakthrough in the stalled negotiations with the Soviet Union on a treaty to ban Intermediate Nuclear Forces (INF) and the historic signing that treaty in Washington, D.C., shortly before the 1987 Christmas holidays led to a resurgence of Reagan support in the polls. Throughout his final year in office, President Reagan's Gallup poll ratings consistently stood above 50 percent. In his final monthly Gallup approval rating, Reagan finished in a blaze of glory at 63 percent—the highest approval rating of any president since Franklin Delano Roosevelt's 66 percent.[25]

In the midst of the Persian Gulf War, at the halfway point in his first term, President Bush saw his Gallup poll approval ratings suddenly leap from 58 percent to a record-breaking 89 percent a few days after the air war began in mid-January, 1991. Bush's high approval ratings exceeded those of President Franklin D. Roosevelt on the all-time high approval charts started by the Gallup poll in 1938.

Will these stunning numbers translate into a series of successful presidential initiatives on the domestic front and keep him in the driver's seat in his relations with the Democratic-controlled Congress? More to the point, will these sky-high poll ratings virtually assure his reelection in 1992? It is, of course, too early to know the answer to these questions. If presidential popularity is the key to presidential effectiveness with Congress, as Richard E. Neustadt and others insist, the answer to these questions should be in the affirmative. Some political handicappers, however, suggest that President Bush cannot hope to maintain these inordinately high approval ratings for the remainder of his first term. Nevertheless, he could drop 20 points or more in the polls over the next year and still be a heavy favorite to win reelection in 1992 as a "foreign policy" president. (After the United States invasion of Panama in late December 1989, Bush's overall Gallup approval rating jumped to 80 percent favorable, but by May 1990, it dropped to 60 percent.) Other cautious observers recall that President Reagan's approval rating stood at 68 percent in the wake of an assassination attempt in late March 1981. By the start of 1983, however, the nation's unemployment rate had jumped to 10.8 percent, while Mr. Reagan's poll ratings plummeted to an alarming 35 percent.[26] Inasmuch as Mr. Bush's approval ratings for handling the economy have consistently been 40 points lower than his Persian Gulf War rating, political prognosticators have been somewhat hesitant to award him a second term more than 12 months before the 1992 election.

Meanwhile, President Bush, whose Republican party is outnumbered by the Democrats 56 seats to 44 in the Senate and 263 seats to 172 in the House of Representatives, faces the prodigious task, as a minority party president, of winning majority support for his legislative agenda. Clearly, his test of political leadership and coalition building in a divided government will be put to a severe test over this same twelve-month period.

LEADER OF ALL THE PEOPLE

No president, at least in his first term, has been more successful than Woodrow Wilson in portraying himself as "leader of all the people." Even before he reached the White House, Wilson observed, "the president is the only national voice in affairs." In contrast, Wilson noted, "There is no one in Congress to speak for the nation. Congress is a conglomeration of unharmonious elements." Speaking of the president's role as legislative leader, Wilson asserted: "He is the representative of no constituency, but of the whole of the people."[27]

One of Wilson's most eloquent statements on his national leadership role came in the wake of a filibuster by a dozen noninterventionist senators opposed to the arming of American merchant ships to combat German submarine warfare shortly before the United States' entry into World War I. When the Sixty-fourth Congress (1915–1916) adjourned without approving Wilson's anti–U-boat measure, he indignantly declared: "A little group of willful men, representing no opinion but their own, have rendered the great Government of the United States helpless and contemptible."[28]

President Franklin D. Roosevelt, who served as Assistant Secretary of the Navy during the Wilson administration, was undoubtedly one of the most partisan chief executives in the history of our country, but few will ever match the unforgettable lines in his 1936 acceptance speech for his second nomination:

Governments can err, presidents do make mistakes, but the immortal Dante tells us that divine justice weighs the sins of the cold-blooded and the sins of the warmhearted in different scales. Better the occasional faults of a government that lives in a spirit of charity than the constant omission of a government frozen in the ice of its own indifference.[29]

Though delivered at a Democratic national convention, Roosevelt's memorable words rose above mere partisanship and touched the hearts of millions, while the nation still struggled to emerge from the depths of the Great Depression.

President Eisenhower, with his congenial manner and the immense good will that his credentials as the victorious supreme Allied commander in World War II brought to the presidency, played the "leader of all the people" role to perfection. As Eisenhower scholar Fred Greenstein has commented on General Ike's political adeptness, "Rather than allowing the presidential roles as nonpolitical chief of state and political leader to undermine each other, he enabled them to coincide."[30] By maintaining an impression of distance from the contentiousness of politics, despite his behind-the-scenes political machinations, Eisenhower's ecumenical appeal to all Americans produced continuously high positive-approval ratings—the highest of any president between Truman and Reagan. Other writers, notably Murray Kempton and Garry Wills, have also commented on Eisenhower's ability to convey the impression that he was a political amateur while he was in fact involved in shrewd maneuvering to achieve his policy objectives. Indeed, it seems fair to say, as Greenstein has put it, that "a covert preoccupation with getting political results while appearing publicly nonpolitical was central to Eisenhower's leadership style."[31]

President John F. Kennedy seldom cloaked his partisanship during his brief thousand days in the White House, but most of the American public did not seem to view him as an extremely partisan chief executive but rather as a president of all the people. Carl M. Brauer reminds us, Kennedy "inspired idealism about the importance of trying to achieve great things as a whole." "Beyond question," Brauer continues, "he ennobled politics and public service."[32]

President Lyndon B. Johnson is often remembered as one of our most partisan presidents; indeed, his decision to withdraw from the 1968 presidential nominating race was heavily influenced by the deep split between the pro-war and anti-war factions—"hawks" and "doves"— within the Democratic party. Yet President Johnson's most fundamental and distinctive concept that he brought to the presidency was his idea of "consensus politics."[33] A product of Texas one-party politics, Johnson sought to attract all shades of Democratic supporters—liberals, conservatives, middle-of-the-roaders. Johnson often spoke of the Democratic party as "a great party tent," capable of making room for everybody. (Recently, President George Bush has used the same concept, borrowed from his former GOP national chairman Lee Atwater, to make room for both pro-life and pro-choice forces within the Republican party.) President Johnson told a crowd that included the present writer, in Minneapolis in 1964, that "by uniting our people, by bringing our capital and our management and our labor and our farmers all under one great Democratic tent, and saying to them all, 'Contribute your part, do your share, and you will share in the fruits that are ours.'"[34] As David S. Broder observed, Johnson deliberately tried "to obscure even the vaguest notions of party ideology, party program or party loyalty—anything that might be a barrier to keeping everyone inside the fold."[35] Sometimes on Johnson's campaign trips, Broder recalls, it was hard to tell which party he supported. He had effusive words of praise for Democrats and Republicans alike. To Johnson's way of thinking, partisanship was the enemy of consensus.

Despite a Herculean effort, especially his civil rights record and the huge outpouring of Great Society domestic programs, Johnson's unrelenting drive to build consensus and serve as president of all the people failed miserably in the end. His inability to resolve the Vietnam War, especially the animosity that it produced on the home front, destroyed consensus politics and the Johnson presidency.

President Richard Nixon, the most partisan-oriented modern president, never quite fit the role of president of all the people, but it was not for want of trying. The first president in 120 years to begin his White House tenure with an opposition-controlled Congress, Nixon faced an uphill climb to win widespread bipartisan support for his programs. At one point, he introduced the concept of "the silent majority," which he identified as the broad, mainstream American electorate that had rallied behind his leadership. Although his attempts to convert conservative southern Democrats, blue-collar workers, and new suburbanites produced two electoral-college victories, it failed to generate a broad mandate for Nixon's New Federalism programs; David S. Broder's assessment of "Nixon's mangled mandate" is close to the mark:

Richard Nixon got to be President of the United States by being more durable than any of his political rivals—not by being brighter, more attractive, wittier, or more eloquent. He is not the best-loved politician of his time, only the most familiar.[36]

For all of the above reasons, Nixon was never really able to master the role of president of all the people.

President Gerald R. Ford, our first unelected chief executive, began his tenure under the most trying circumstances since Harry S. Truman's sudden elevation to the presidency after FDR's death in April 1945 during the late stages of World War II. Ford came into the presidency when President Nixon, threatened with an impeachment trial in the midst of the Watergate investigation, resigned in August 1974. The nation, in a state of shock, welcomed Ford's assurances that "our long national nightmare is over." Ford's candor and conciliatory speech to the nation, seeking continuity and stability, was an auspicious and confidence-building start. But within four weeks Ford's performance as president of all the people was shattered by a single act: his unconditional pardon of former President Nixon. This decision was made less than ten days after the new president had publicly announced that he would make no decision on a pardon until the "legal processes" of the indictment and the trial had been completed. Much of the good will that he had acquired within his first thirty days in office vanished overnight. The "openness and candor" that Ford had projected in his first days in the White House was destroyed by his sudden action, taken without consulting his cabinet or close aides. The obvious conclusion that many people drew was that Ford had struck a deal with Nixon to gain the presidency and that he had agreed, before assuming office, to pardon Nixon if he would step aside. Instead of enjoying his early popularity as president of all the people, Ford discovered that many voters suddenly concluded that "he was just another politician."[37] Ford's Gallup poll popularity ratings plummeted 22 points within a three-week period—the sharpest drop in the poll's history. From that point on, Ford could no longer utilize his initial reservoir of good will to lead the country. When he sought a mandate to continue his White House tenure in the 1976 election, the American voters rejected him by a narrow margin, in favor of former Georgia Governor Jimmy Carter.

Few presidents have worked harder at serving as president of all the people than Jimmy Carter, and fewer have been accorded less appreciation for their efforts. The role seemed to come easily to Carter. Even before he reached the White House, one Carter watcher has noted, "Carter developed the idea that the proper responsibility of the elected official was to be the voice of the unorganized citizen and all the citizens who made up the general public."[38] Unlike most of his predecessors, Carter concentrated on developing "comprehensive solutions" to the nation's major problems. Carter eschewed the standard practice of building political coalitions behind proposals and instead espoused the gospel of "public goods."[39] As a noncoalition builder, Carter did not view Congress as an institution or its members, with their numerous special constituencies, as "trustees" capable of serving the public interest. Rather, Carter considered himself, as president, the guardian of the public interest.[40] Carter's public philosophy, however, was not sheer altruism; he expected to be rewarded politically for his achievements at reelection time. But the American public viewed his "comprehensive solution" and worship of competence in a less favorable light. Indeed, most voters perceived him as a weak leader whose priorities were unclear and whose direction was uncertain. When voters reassessed his inability to deal with a high rate of inflation, high interest rates, and the Iranian hostage crisis in the 1980 election campaign, they decided not to continue his stewardship. Instead, they turned to the former governor of California, Ronald Reagan, to be the nation's new leader.

President Reagan often succeeded in establishing himself as champion of the people and portraying his political opponents as tools of the "special interests." Reagan did not specifically identify the special interests, a pejorative phrase that traditionally had meant the powerful and privileged, but he often pointed to big labor, liberals, and Washington bureaucrats as operating against the public interest.

All presidents thrive on being the "representative of all the people," and President George Bush was merely following the strategy of his illustrious predecessors when he announced, for the public interest, in late June 1990 that he was abandoning his "read my lips, no new taxes" pledge of his 1988 presidential campaign. Faced with a mounting federal deficit of an estimated $225 billion for fiscal year 1991 that threatened the nation's economy, Bush defended his policy reversal by painting a bleak economic picture, saying he trusted Americans to understand why he was prepared to accept higher taxes.

Repeatedly, Mr. Bush turned to the legacy of Abraham Lincoln, who in 1862 spoke of the need to leave old dogmas behind in troubled times. In Lincoln's words, the president declared, "I'll think anew."[41] The historical reference was not to taxes, of course, but to how the Great Emancipator should deal with the Southern secession. When the president has a great problem, Bush continued, "I think the president owes the people his—his judgement at the moment he has to address that problem. . . . I've got to do what I think is right, and then I'll ask the people for support."[42] Bush cited the need for "responsible government," appealed for bipartisan support, and defended his announcement on the need for "tax revenue increases" to reduce the huge federal deficit as an act of national leadership. Critics noted at the time (before the Iraqi invasion of Kuwait) that probably the only major obstacle to his reelection in 1992 would be a sour economy two years down the road so that sound statesmanship now was also good reelection politics.

THE PRESIDENT APPEALS TO THE GENERAL PUBLIC RATHER THAN PARTISANS TO WIN SUPPORT FOR KEY DOMESTIC AND FOREIGN POLICIES

Especially in this era of divided government, presidents often direct their appeals to the general public rather than their party supporters to win support for their administrations' programs. Before the age of radio and television, however, presidents lacked the means to communicate directly with millions of American voters. To be sure, the small White House press corps offered an avenue to the public via the growing number of mass circulation daily newspapers. But unless the president had a major policy decision to announce, the reporters were unlikely to send copy to their editors. Unlike the present era, in which more than 1,200 print journalists and network TV and radio reporters send out a continuous stream of news and comment from the White House and their national press offices detailing every activity of the president, the McKinley White House had only a handful of wire service reporters covering the president.

Still, in early years of the twentieth century, presidents went to the people to generate support for the priority items on their legislative agendas. President Teddy Roosevelt often sought to reconcile the deeply split progressive and conservative wings of the Republican party to gain support for his antitrust legislation, but he sometimes found it easier to appeal to the country than to bring the two wings of his own party together. To demonstrate his deep concern in protecting the public from the predatory trusts, Teddy released documents demonstrating that the Rockefellers opposed the measure. This tactic helped speed Roosevelt's program to completion.[43] Since Teddy Roosevelt's era, presidents have frequently gravitated toward issues that endow them with the strongest claim to represent the "public interest."

Even before Woodrow Wilson became president, he had been impressed by President Teddy Roosevelt's frequent use of the presidency as a "bully pulpit" (Teddy's own words) to present his case to the American people and arouse public opinion. President-elect Wilson began following Teddy's footsteps even before he was inaugurated. In a series of bold speeches during the four-month preinaugural transition period (before passage of the Twentieth Amendment in 1933, the new president was not inaugurated until March fourth), Wilson spelled out the broad goals of his "New Freedom" program. Moreover, he warned the masters of capital not to use their massive power to obstruct the fulfillment of this program. Wilson repeatedly stated that he did not believe that the leaders of the business world would use their power to block the enactment of this reform program.[44]

A strong believer in party government, Wilson preferred to work through and with his party in Congress, rather than to govern by a coalition of progressive Democrats and Republicans, as he might have done. Nevertheless, his messages to Congress were couched in such broad, sweeping rhetoric that they were addressed to the American public as much as to the lawmakers on Capitol Hill. But Wilson's most ambitious project—his proposed ratification of the Versailles Treaty ending World War I, which would have provided for United States membership in the League of Nations—ended in failure. Faced with a recalcitrant group of senators, Wilson decided to take the peace treaty issue directly to the American people with a cross-country speaking tour. On this strenuous trip Wilson suffered a serious stroke that left him incapacitated and a semiinvalid for the remainder of his second term. When the ratification vote finally came up in the Senate, the treaty failed to receive the necessary two-thirds majority by a vote of 49 yeas and 34 nays.[45]

In recent years the growing importance of foreign policy has eroded the president's relationship to his party. For a president to assert that he represents the entire nation, not just his party, is a compelling argument to downplay his party ties in favor of the "national interest." Thus, our contemporary presidents take special pains to stay above partisan conflict to win bipartisan support for their foreign policies.

THE STEADY GROWTH OF INDEPENDENT AND SPLIT-TICKET VOTERS MAKES THE PRESIDENT'S ABOVE-POLITICS STRATEGY MORE ATTRACTIVE

In recent decades, the general trend of voters away from allegiance to either party, especially among the Democrats, has made a president's above-politics strategy increasingly attractive. As Table 7.4 indicates, the percentage of citizens identifying themselves as Democrats has declined from 47.2 percent in 1952 to 35.2 percent in 1988; the percentage of Republicans has remained relatively stationary, 27.2 percent in 1952 and 27.5 in 1988. But during the same period the number of persons declaring themselves "Independents" has jumped from 22.6 to 35.7 percent of the electorate. For the first time in presidential election history, the number of Independents exceeded the number of Democrats in 1988.[46] Data show that this trend toward independence has been especially notable among younger voters. Approximately 45 percent of potential voters under thirty now claim independent status, compared with 27 percent of those over fifty. Furthermore, the number of new voters professing partisan independence from the outset has almost doubled—from 26 percent in 1952 to 49 percent of those who cast their first ballots in 1980.[47]

Moreover, the trend away from partisan voting in the late 1960s and 1970s has been coupled with widespread split-ticket voting (see Table 7.5). In the early 1960s more than 60 percent of the electorate cast "straight" ballots (supporting the entire ticket of candidates of one party for all offices), but by 1972 approximately 53 percent cast "split" ballots (dividing their votes among candidates of both parties for president, senator, or representative).[48] With the decline of partisanship presidential candidates, especially Republicans, have generally made it standard operating procedure to tone down their partisan rhetoric and focus more of their political appeals on such nonpartisan or bipartisan issues as patriotism, the environment, health, land conservation, child care, education, and anticrime measures in order to win over more independents. With so much attention focused on the style and personal attributes of the president, his party ties often fade into the landscape. Consequently, the

Table 7.4
Party Identification, 1952–1988

	1952	1956	1960	1964	1968	1972	1976	1980	1984	1988
Democrats	47.2	43.6	45.3	51.7	45.4	40.4	39.7	40.8	37.0	35.2
Independents	22.6	23.4	22.8	22.8	29.1	34.7	36.1	34.5	34.2	35.7
Republicans	27.2	29.1	29.4	24.5	24.2	23.4	23.2	22.4	27.1	27.5
Apoliticals	3.1	3.8	2.5	0.9	1.4	1.4	0.9	2.2	1.7	1.6
Democratic plurality	20.0	14.5	15.9	27.2	21.2	17.0	16.5	18.4	9.9	7.7
Democrats plus Democratic leaners	56.8	49.9	51.6	61.0	55.2	51.5	51.5	52.3	47.8	47.0
Pure Independents	5.8	8.8	9.8	7.8	10.5	13.1	14.6	12.9	11.0	10.6
Republicans plus Republican leaners	34.3	37.4	36.1	30.2	32.9	33.9	32.9	32.6	39.5	40.8
Apoliticals	3.1	3.8	2.5	0.9	1.4	1.4	0.9	2.2	1.7	1.6
Democratic plurality	22.5	12.5	15.5	31.1	22.3	17.6	18.6	19.7	8.3	6.2

Source: SRC/CPS National Election Studies. Reprinted by permission of the publishers from *The Decline of American Political Parties, 1952–1988* by Martin P. Wattenberg, Cambridge: Harvard University Press, Copyright © 1991 by the President and Fellows of Harvard College.

president, the nation's principal lawmaker, can tailor his messages to appeal to the broad spectrum of American voters rather than just loyal partisans. Moreover, network television, rated as the most believable news source by a wide margin since the early 1970s, can be used by the president to reach the public without the intermediate intervention of the party apparatus. Thanks to his dominance of television, the president can focus on issues that will generate maximum support from the general public, not just his own partisans.

FIGHTING THE "SPECIAL INTERESTS"

One sure-fire way for a president to win public support is to fight the "special interests." Indeed, the president's legitimacy in going to the people to defend the public interest from private greed has been a popular tactic since the rise of the modern presidency at the turn of the century. President Theodore Roosevelt, one of the most colorful and dynamic chief executives in the nation's history, scored a grand slam with the public during his campaign in 1903 to regulate the trusts (huge monopolistic business or industrial combinations, now illegal). His promise to eliminate the "malefactors of great wealth" and his victories against the Northern Securities Company and the "beef trust" soon earned him the sobriquet "Teddy the Trustbuster."

President Woodrow Wilson's successful campaign against the lobbyists opposing the Underwood tariff reduction bill of 1913 early in his first administration, according to historian Arthur S. Link, quickly established Wilson's dominance in the Democratic party.[49] Opponents of the Underwood bill descended on Washington in droves to block the tariff reform package. Wool and sugar lobbyists, joined by the spokesmen of the cotton manufacturers, citrus fruit growers, and others, swarmed in the halls of the Capitol, bombarding lawmakers with resolutions, petitions, and appeals. The nation's capital was so full of the representatives of special interests, Wilson said that "a brick couldn't be thrown without hitting one of them." In a dramatic move to capture the nation's attention, Wilson struck back at the lobbyists and issued a public statement denouncing the "industrious and insidious lobby. . . . It is of serious interest to the country [he declared] that the people at large should have no lobby and be voiceless in these matters, while great bodies of astute men seek to create an artificial opinion and to overcome the interests of the public for their private profit."[50] Though the opposition Republicans talked tariff all summer, their resistance finally wilted. The House approved the final version of the tariff reform bill on September 30; the Senate followed suit on October 2. President Wilson happily signed the Underwood act a day later.[51]

Table 7.5
Trends in Split-ticket and Party-line Voting, 1952–1988

Split-Ticket Voting

	1952	1956	1960	1964	1968	1972	1976	1980	1984	1988
President-House	12	16	14	15	26	30	25	34	25	25
Senate-House	9	10	9	18	22	23	23	31	20	27
Local	27	30	27	41	48	56	NA	59	52	NA

Source: SRC/CPS National Election Studies. Reprinted in Martin P. Wattenberg, *The Decline of American Political Parties 1952–1988* (Cambridge: Harvard University Press, 1990), p. 165.

No president was more distrusted by the business community than Franklin D. Roosevelt, who launched a series of New Deal measures— the Security and Exchange Commission, the Public Utility Holding Company Act, the Federal Communications Act, the National Labor Relations Act, and others—that transformed the way business has been conducted in America since then. The barrage of criticism against Franklin D. Roosevelt from the National Association of Manufacturers, the American Liberty League, the public utilities industry, and other business groups never ceased. Yet Roosevelt always delivered more blows than he received. FDR took special pride in having "earned the hatred of entrenched greed." During the 1936 campaign, he lashed out at the "economic royalists" who took "other people's money" to impose a "new industrial dictatorship."[52] At the closing rally of his 1936 campaign in Madison Square Garden, Roosevelt taunted the special interests. "The forces of organized money," he told the roaring crowd, "are unanimous in their hatred of me—and I welcome their hatred."[53]

President Truman's favorite special-interest target was the "Do Nothing Eightieth Congress" (1947–1948) that he lambasted throughout his hard hitting, successful election campaign of 1948. Mr. Truman covered more than 20,000 miles by train and gave more than 250 speeches. He excoriated the "gluttons of privilege" in the Republican party who, said the scrappy president, were men "with a calculating machine where the heart ought to be."[54] At a Sacramento, California, rally Truman talked about the control of the Republican party by "eastern mossbacks," and he told the West Coast crowd: "This is a crusade of the people against the special interests, a crusade to keep the country from going to the dogs. You back me up and we'll win that crusade."[55] In his come-from-behind victory, Truman carried California, thought to be safely in the Republican column, by fewer than 18,000 votes.

President Dwight D. Eisenhower preferred to take the "high road" both on the campaign trail and in dealing with Congress. In his 1956 election campaign tour, for example, he talked about the accomplishments of his first administration—ending the Korean War, reducing inflation, maintaining prosperity, and so on. Meanwhile, he assigned the job of attacking the opposition Democrats to Vice President Nixon, a veteran of bare-knuckled campaigning in California.

President John F. Kennedy seldom resorted to attacks on the "special interests"; but when he did, his words were laden with dynamite. His tongue-lashing of the chairperson of the United States Steel Company, Roger Blough, has seldom been equaled. Big Steel suddenly announced a $6-a-ton increase in 1962, after the young president had seemingly been assured that no price increase would take place as part of the recent wage settlement between the company and the United Steel Workers

Union. Few public figures have ever received the kind of blistering verbal attack John F. Kennedy directed against Blough:

The simultaneous and identical actions . . . constitute a wholly unjustifiable and irresponsible defiance of the public interest. In this serious hour in our nation's history, with grave crises in Berlin and Southeast Asia when . . . restraints and sacrifice are being asked of every citizen, the American people will find it hard, as I do, to accept a situation in which a tiny handful of steel executives, whose pursuit of private power and profit exceeds their sense of public responsibility, can show such utter contempt for the interest of 184 million Americans.[56]

Within three days, the chairperson of United States Steel backed down and announced that the 3.5 percent price increase had been rescinded.[57]

Soon after his election, President Jimmy Carter began a series of prime-time network television addresses on behalf of his comprehensive energy-saving program, then before Congress. He wasted no time in conjuring up the threat of rapacious special interest: "We can be sure that all the special interest groups in the country will attack . . . this plan. . . . If they succeed with this approach, then the burden on the ordinary citizen, who is not organized into an interest group, would be crushing. There should be only one test for this plan—whether it will help our country."[58] Despite Carter's four network addresses, however, Congress took over a year to pass a watered-down version of his energy-saving program.

President Ronald Reagan seldom failed to cloak his major legislative proposals in the public interest. Unlike the Progressives of the early twentieth century, who envisaged a responsive federal government led by an energetic chief executive vigorously promoting the general political and economic welfare of the country over sectional or economic interests, Reagan advocated a scaling-back of federal responsibilities to provide social services and encouraged the deregulation of industry. To expand public support for his streamlined tax reform proposal, Reagan turned the old Progressive doctrine on its head. He portrayed the special interests as being entrenched in the federal bureaucracy that never tired of handing out our government funds from the "puzzle palaces on the Potomac" or issuing indecipherable regulations that strangle business initiative.[59] An excerpt from his tax reform message to a nationwide television audience in May 1985 typifies the standard Reagan theme:

The proposal I am putting forth tonight for America's future will free us from the grip of special interests and create a binding commitment to the only special interest that counts, you, the people who pay America's bills. It will create millions of new jobs for working people and it will replace the politics of envy with a spirit of partnership.[60]

Though given little chance of passage at the time, the tax reform proposal, pushed by the president at every turn, was finally passed late in the second session of the Ninety-ninth Congress and signed by President Reagan in November 1986—the first major overhaul of the tax code in forty years.

CAN THE PRESIDENT OPERATE EFFECTIVELY WITHOUT PARTIES?

The office of President of the United States was designed by the Framers without parties in mind. Indeed, as mentioned earlier, political parties did not exist in this country at the time of the founding of the Constitution. The Founders, who spent more time deciding how the president should be selected than outlining the powers of his office, had in mind a president of limited powers. He would serve as an armchair chief executive most of the time—signing or vetoing an occasional legislative measure, overseeing the administration of a federal government that consisted of only a few hundred employees, and conducting foreign policy in an international community of less than two dozen nations. Only in times of national emergency would the president's duties as commander-in-chief assume major importance. Under these circumstances, the Founders could envisage no function for political parties or a similar instrumentality for conducting the business of government.

By the time of President Thomas Jefferson's election in 1800, however, parties had become an important agency for operating the government. And they have remained so to the present day. But from time to time a few critics have raised the question: Does the president really need parties to operate the federal government effectively? The answer, in short, is an unequivocal yes. To be sure, modern presidents use independent campaign organizations, management consultants, federal funds, and network television to win office and largely ignore their parties in the quest for the White House. But once they reach the Oval Office, they discover that they must work with party members in Congress if they expect to transform their campaign blueprints into constructive programs.

As political scientists Lester G. Seligman and Cary R. Covington have commented, "the White House is not an adequate substitute for strong partisan links to the public and Congress as a basis for creating a stable governing coalition."[61] In the field of foreign policy, however, presidents since World War II have increasingly moved in the direction of an imperial or plebiscitary presidency. As defined by Arthur M. Schlesinger, Jr., and Theodore Lowi, these terms connote "the president's power and responsibility to do whatever he judges necessary to maintain the sovereignty of the state and its ability to keep public order, both domestic and international."[62] Lowi continues: "The imperial presidency turns out on inspection, therefore, to be nothing more nor less than the discretionary presidency grounded in national security rather than domestic government."[63] Fortunately, the self-correcting mechanisms of the American governmental system—the separation of powers, the checks and balances, and the political parties—saved the nation in the 1970s from an imperial presidency takeover. Presidents Johnson and Nixon, despite their intense suspicion and distrust of political parties, learned to their everlasting regret that they could not function effectively without these constraining instruments of popular authority.

President Ronald Reagan, though faced with a House of Representatives controlled by the opposition Democrats, found that by working closely with his Republican cohorts in the House (the GOP gained control of the Senate in 1980 for the first time since 1954) and by winning over more than forty conservative Southern "boll weevil" House Democrats to his cause, he was able to implement his tax and budget cuts during his first year in office. But his magic touch with the controlling Democrats in the House was much less evident in subsequent years.

President George Bush, operating in a divided government, with both houses of Congress in Democratic hands, has relied upon his minority party Republicans in one or both houses to sustain his vetoes of the minimum wage bill, a budget measure for the District of Columbia to fund abortions, a bill to allow Communist Chinese students to remain in the United States, a high-cost child care measure, and others. In his first twenty months in office, Bush had sixteen vetoes sustained by Congress without a single override.[64] Without the support of the minority Republicans to uphold his vetoes, Bush's agenda would have been in shambles.

The president who operated most effectively without his party, in this writer's view, was Abraham Lincoln. Following the fall of Fort Sumter in mid-April 1861, Lincoln decided to prepare for an all-out attack on the Southern secessionists without consulting his party in Congress. During the first eleven weeks of the Civil War, Lincoln drafted nearly 100,000 soldier recruits, purchased millions of dollars of munitions and military supplies, and imposed a naval blockade on Southern ports. Not until July 4, 1861, did he call Congress back into special session to ratify his actions.[65] Despite sharp complaints from congressional Republican leaders, they nevertheless quickly approved his actions, for as Lincoln said, the very survival of the nation was at stake.

Several presidents since then have privately expressed the wish to operate selectively in the policy arena, especially foreign affairs, without working through their parties, but they have usually kept these statements off the record.

SUMMARY

Especially in this era of divided government, the public presidency has overshadowed the party presidency. In other words, presidents have resorted increasingly to public speech-making, frequently on nationwide television, rather than party coalition-building to overcome congressional opposition to their policies.

Since World War II, presidents have delivered nearly ten thousand speeches, averaging more than twenty per month. Many of these speeches present "photo opportunities," often recaptured on the TV networks' evening news programs, that can be utilized to help persuade millions of viewers on the soundness of the president's policies and course of action. Faced most of the time with a Congress controlled by the opposition party, a president is likely to board *Air Force One* several times a month to carry his case to the American people, far away from the fractious debate on Capitol Hill. During his first year in office, President Bush visited eighty-seven cities and delivered a total of 320 speeches across America. By "going public" the president can use the mass media regularly to help avoid having to bargain with 535 members of Congress each time a vote comes up on Capitol Hill. Clearly, the public presidency enables the president to keep the pressure constantly on Congress and to control the public agenda.

Public speech-making also offers the president repeated opportunities to mask his partisanship under the cloak of speaking "for all Americans." With approximately one-third of the American electorate listing themselves publicly as "independent" voters, presidential public appeals can be made in the name of nonpartisanship without fear of alienating large segments of the electorate. Or, if the president wants to shift gears, he can use the nation's podium to flail the "special interests" who are seeking to block his policies "aimed at helping all Americans."

Can the president operate effectively without parties? Superficially, the president can turn repeatedly to the "going public" approach to help solicit public support from various interest groups across the land. But when it comes to decision time on Capitol Hill, most presidents have found that their party is a far more reliable ally in a showdown legislative battle than the numerous interest groups, who are often at odds with one another on the major issues surrounding the debate.

Frequent gridlock and stalemate—usually the result of divided government—have marked the recent history of presidential–congressional relations. To overcome this recurring deadlock in our separation-of-powers system, several close students of the presidency have offered a number of institutional reforms to help parties overcome this seemingly intractable problem—the subject of our next chapter.

NOTES

1. Roderick P. Hart, *The Sound of Leadership* (Chicago: University of Chicago Press, 1987), p. xix.

2. Lester G. Seligman and Cary R. Covington, *The Coalitional Presidency* (Chicago: Dorsey, 1989), p. 101.

3. James W. Ceaser, Glen E. Thurow, Jeffrey Tulis, and Joseph M. Besette, ''The Rise of the Rhetorical Presidency,'' *Presidential Studies Quarterly* 11 (Spring, 1981), p. 159; see also Jeffrey K. Tulis, *The Rhetorical Presidency* (Princeton, NJ: Princeton University Press, 1987).

4. Samuel Kernell, *Going Public: New Strategies of Presidential Leadership* (Washington, DC: Congressional Quarterly Press, 1986), p. viii.

5. Ibid.

6. Samuel Kernell, ''Campaigning, Governing, and the Presidency,'' in John E. Chubb and Paul E. Peterson, eds., *The New Direction in American Politics* (Washington, DC: The Brookings Institution, 1985), p. 139.

7. Hugh Sidey, ''Totaling Up Year One,'' *Time* 135 (February 5, 1990), p. 23.

8. Kernell, *Going Public*, p. 93.

9. Thomas E. Mann, ''Elections and Change in Congress,'' in Thomas E. Mann and Norman J. Ornstein, eds., *The New Congress* (Washington, DC: American Enterprise Institute, 1981), p. 53.

10. Lyn Ragsdale, ''The Politics of Presidential Speechmaking, 1949–1980,'' *American Political Science Review* 78 (December 1984), p. 972.

11. Betty Glad, *Jimmy Carter in the Search of the Great White House* (New York: W. W. Norton, 1980), p. 446.

12. Michael Baruch Grossman and Martha Joynt Kumar, *Portraying the President* (Baltimore: The Johns Hopkins University Press, 1981), pp. 314–315.

13. George C. Edwards III, *The Public Presidency* (New York: St. Martin's, 1983), p. 41.

14. Sidey, ''Totaling Up Year One,'' p. 23.

15. *The New York Times*, September 21, 1991.

16. J. F. terHorst and Col. Ralph Albertazzie, *The Flying White House* (New York: Coward, McCann and Geoghegan, 1979), p. 33, quoted in Samuel Kernell, *Going Public*, pp. 98–99.

17. Hugh Sidey, ''The New Style of Exposé,'' *Time* 123 (June 18, 1984), p. 37.

18. Richard Neustadt, *Presidential Power: The Politics of Leadership* (New York: Wiley, 1960).

19. John H. Aldrich, Gary J. Miller, Charles W. Ostrom, Jr., and David W. Rohde, *American Government: People, Institutions, and Policies* (Boston: Houghton Mifflin, 1986), p. 486.

20. Charles W. Ostrom, Jr., and Dennis M. Simon, ''Promise and Performance: A Dynamic Model of Presidential Popularity,'' *American Political Science Review* 79 (June 1985), p. 334.

21. Charles W. Ostrom, Jr. and Dennis M. Simon, ''Managing Popular Support: The Presidential Dilemma,'' *Policy Studies Journal* 12 (1984), pp. 677–690.

22. Aldrich et al., *American Government*, p. 487.

23. Ostrom and Simon, ''Promise and Performance,'' pp. 355–356.

24. See D. A. Hibbs, Jr., ''On the Demand for Economic Outcomes: Macroeconomic Performances and Mass Political Support in the United States,'' *Journal of Politics* 44 (May 1982), pp. 426–462.

25. *The Gallup Poll Monthly* No. 280 (January 1989), p. 12.

26. Ibid.

27. Woodrow Wilson, *Constitutional Government in the United States* (New York: Columbia University Press, 1908), p. 68.

28. *The New York Times*, March 5, 1917, quoted in Arthur S. Link, *Woodrow Wilson and the Progressive Era 1910–1917* (New York: Harper and Row, 1954), pp. 273–274.

29. William E. Leuchtenburg, *Franklin D. Roosevelt and the New Deal, 1932–1940* (New York: Harper and Row, 1963), p. 333.

30. Fred Greenstein, "Leadership Theorist in the White House" in Fred I. Greenstein, ed., *Leadership in the Modern Presidency* (Cambridge, MA: Harvard University Press, 1988), p. 106.

31. Murray Kempton, "The Underestimation of Dwight D. Eisenhower," *Esquire* (September 1967), pp. 108 ff; Garry Wills, *Nixon Agonistes: The Crisis of the Self-Made Man* (Boston: Houghton Mifflin, 1969); and Greenstein, "Leadership Theorist in the White House," p. 78.

32. Carl M. Brauer, "John F. Kennedy: The Endurance of Inspirational Leadership," in Greenstein, ed., *Leadership in the Modern Presidency*, p. 109.

33. David S. Broder, *The Party's Over* (New York: Harper and Row, 1971), p. 67.

34. Ibid., p. 66.

35. Ibid.

36. Ibid., p. 79.

37. Jules Witcover, *Marathon* (New York: Viking, 1977), pp. 43–44.

38. Erwin C. Hargrove, "Jimmy Carter: The Politics of Public Goods," in Fred I. Greenstein, ed., *Leadership in the Modern Presidency*, p. 230.

39. Ibid.

40. Ibid.

41. *The New York Times*, June 30, 1990.

42. Ibid.

43. John Morton Blum, *The Republican Roosevelt* (Cambridge, MA: Harvard University Press, 1954), p. 58.

44. Ibid., p. 33.

45. Thomas A. Bailey, *A Diplomatic History of the American People*, 10th ed., (Englewood Cliffs, NJ: Prentice-Hall, 1980), p. 622.

46. Martin P. Wattenberg, *The Decline of American Political Parties 1952–1988* (Cambridge, MA: Harvard University Press, 1990), p. 139.

47. Center for Political Studies, University of Michigan, cited by David E. Price, *Bringing Back the Parties* (Washington, DC: Congressional Quarterly Press, 1984), pp. 11–12.

48. Martin P. Wattenberg, *Decline of American Political Parties*, pp. 162–165; see also Walter DeVries and V. Lance Tarrance, *The Split-Ticket Voter* (Grand Rapids, MI: Eerdmans, 1972).

49. Arthur S. Link, *Woodrow Wilson and the Progressive Era* (New York: Harper and Row, 1954), p. 43.

50. Ibid., p. 41.

51. Ibid.

52. Leuchtenburg, *Franklin D. Roosevelt and the New Deal*, pp. 183–184.

53. Ibid., p. 184.

54. Cabell Phillips, *The Truman Presidency* (Baltimore: Penguin, 1969), p. 232.

55. Ibid., p. 240.

56. Cited in Hobart Rowan, "The Big Steel Crisis: Kennedy vs. Blough," in Earl Latham, ed., *J. F. Kennedy and Presidential Power* (Lexington, MA: D. C. Heath Company, 1972), p. 95.

57. Ibid., p. 110.

58. Jimmy Carter, "The Energy Problem" (address to the nation April 18, 1977), *Public Papers of the Presidents of the United States*, (Washington, DC: 1978), pp. 661–662, quoted in Kernell, *Going Public*, p. 226.

59. Kernell, *Going Public*, p. 226.

60. "Text of Speech by President on Overhauling the Tax System," *The New York Times*, October 19, 1985, quoted in Kernell, *Going Public*, p. 226.

61. Seligman and Covington, *The Coalition Presidency*, p. 68.

62. Theodore J. Lowi, *The Personal President* (Ithaca, NY: Cornell University Press, 1985), p. 180.

63. Ibid.

64. *The New York Times*, October 25, 1990.

65. E. S. Corwin, *The President: Office and Powers, 1787–1984*, 5th rev. ed., by Randall W. Bland, Theodore T. Hindson, and Jack W. Peltason (New York: New York University Press, 1984), p. 264.

Chapter 8

Proposed Institutional Reforms to Strengthen the President's Hand

Proposals to reform the presidency are nearly as old as the Constitution itself and number in the hundreds. That proposed presidential reforms have appeared frequently throughout our history should occasion no surprise, since the Founding Fathers deliberated longer and debated more vigorously over the power and structure of the presidency—as well as the selection process—than over any other part of the nation's fundamental document.

In this chapter we examine and evaluate a variety of institutional reforms of the presidency proposed over the years—parliamentary government, plural executive, the no-confidence vote in the president amendment, the six-year, nonrenewable-term plan, the direct election of the president, and modification of the electoral college system—and then assess the prospects for and desirability of presidential reform.

RESPONSIBLE PARTIES MODEL

Members of the responsible parties school argue not only that parties should assume collective responsibility for government policy-making but also that presidential leadership should be an integral part of the plan.[1] For most members of this school, as Leon D. Epstein has pointed out, "the president is important as the leader of a team, but he is responsible to others on that leadership team as well as to the voters."[2] But the nature of the presidential–party relationship is not the same for all advocates of responsible party government. President Woodrow Wilson, one of the early proponents of responsible parties, put so much emphasis on a president's own popular mandate, derived from the electorate, that it could be argued that his concept of responsible parties departs altogether from the standard doctrine. For most members, "party government implies collective rather than strictly personal leadership."[3]

In other words, stronger parties should be developed "to secure effective government without a too powerful president governing independently of party or other intermediaries between himself and the people."[4] Clearly, for the responsible party advocates the president is important as the team leader, but he is responsible also to others on the leadership team as well as to the electorate. Briefly, then, this plan would help provide a deterrent to the rise of a plebiscitary president.

Among the leading advocates of responsible parties, James MacGregor Burns emphasizes the need for both a strong party and a strong party leader, each complementing the other.[5] Burns has in mind a leader capable of mobilizing a party majority, not simply a personal, independent, or bipartisan majority. Burns's goal is to find a presidential party able to lead a congressional majority. According to Burns, "Each presidential party must convert its congressional party into a party wing exerting a proper, but not controlling or crippling, hold on party policy."[6] Most of Burns's hopes for party policy-making are based on innovative leadership and would require party members to campaign to elect congressional candidates committed to the program of the president's party.

Burns's presidential leadership version, like some other proposals for responsible government, appears to be an attempt "to achieve the results of British parliamentary government by American constitutional means."[7] Though the British model is not specifically cited, it seems clear that Burns is trying to build a national party whose elected members would regularly unite behind the president and his cabinet in the manner of the British parliamentary party.

Before assessing the prospects of a responsible parties system in the United States, let us briefly review the proposal to establish parliamentary government in this country.

PARLIAMENTARY GOVERNMENT

Parliamentary government, according to its supporters, is just the cure for divided government and the inability of the president most of the time to win majority support for his programs in Congress. To overcome this frequent deadlock, advocates of parliamentary government (which fuses executive and legislative powers under the leadership of a prime minister and cabinet) claim that an American parliamentary system would achieve democratic responsibility and accountability and thereby improve the linkage between public opinion and public policy. Supporters of parliamentary government insist that there is steady pressure inherent in the British system for members to vote so as to furnish the solid majority needed to maintain their leaders in power.

Beyond doubt, a parliamentary system would reduce the direct ties of the president and executive branch to the national electorate and would most likely serve as a counterforce to the candidate-centered politics that has characterized American presidential elections in the past two decades.

Critics of the existing system argue that the separation of powers prevents the development of responsible party government; in other words, voters have no assurance when they elect a president that he can implement a specific legislative program, since the legislative branch may be controlled by the opposition party, or control of the two houses of Congress may be divided between the two major parties. Under these circumstances, the president finds himself, in effect, a prisoner of the separation of powers and nearly powerless to act. Even if the president's party controls both houses of Congress, opponents of the presidential system point out that members of his party may defy party discipline and vote with impunity against the president's legislative program.

HARDIN'S PARTY GOVERNMENT PLAN

One interesting variation of the parliamentary system is the plan for party government developed by political scientist Charles M. Hardin more than a decade ago. According to Hardin: "The foremost requirement of a great power is strong executive leadership."[8] But this executive must not be allowed to escape the political controls needed to maintain constitutional—that is, limited—government. The problem is further complicated by the danger that restraints may seriously weaken the effectiveness of the president.

Hardin's solution is "presidential leadership and party government." To achieve this goal, Hardin proposes a fundamental constitutional change in the American separation-of-powers system. This is how this new plan would be established:

1. Presidents, senators, and congressmen would all be elected for four-year terms. The election date would be fixed at four years from the date of the inauguration of the last government, but a provision would allow the government to change the date and call a special election.

2. The House of Representatives would continue to be elected from single-member districts, but an additional 150 members would be elected at large. To assure a majority in the House, each party would nominate 100 at-large candidates; the party winning the presidency would elect its entire at-large slate. The losing party would elect a maximum of at-large candidates, diminished by whatever number would be required to give the winning party a majority of five in the House. At-large candidates would be nominated by committees of 41 in each party. The winning party's committee would be composed of the president, the 10 cabinet members, and 30 congressmen for single-member districts. The opposition party's nominating committee would be composed of the opposi-

tion party leader, the "shadow" cabinet (the opposition party leadership), and 30 congressmen. In both parties, the 41-member nominating committee would have the right to reject local nominees if they had refused to accept party discipline.

3. Presidential candidates would be nominated by party committees composed of all house members from single-member districts as well as all candidates for election in such districts. In the event of either physical or political presidential disability, the nominating committee of his party would be empowered to suspend him temporarily or to remove him, but in any case it would be required to replace him. The office of vice president would be abolished.

4. The Senate would be deprived of its power to approve treaties and presidential nominations. Bills would continue to be considered in the Senate, but if the Senate rejected a bill that had passed the House twice in the same form (sixty days would have to elapse between the first and second passage), the bill would go to the president.

5. The presidential veto would be retained, but it could be overridden by an adverse majority vote in the House. The Senate could require the House to reconsider, but it could be overridden by the House after sixty days.

6. Article I. Section 6, Clause 2 of the Constitution, which prevents members of Congress from serving in other offices of the United States, would be repealed, but the similar office-holding ban for the judiciary would be retained.

7. The loser in the presidential election would be designated the leader of the opposition and given a seat in the House with privileged membership on all committees and privileged access to the floor. The opposition leader would have an official residence and adequate funds for office staff, travel, and other items essential for the vigorous operation of his office. Like the president, the opposition leader could be removed by his party's presidential nominating committee.

8. Presidential elections would be by national ticket. The winning party would be required to secure a national plurality of votes.

9. All parts of the Constitution which are presently in conflict with the foregoing proposals would be repealed or modified to conform to them. The 22nd Amendment (which limits the president to two terms) would also be repealed.[9]

To the critics' charge that his plan is unrealistic and unworkable, Hardin's reply is that the existing system cannot cope with a politically disabled president who operates under a system of fixed calendar elections. To those opponents apprehensive of change, Hardin points out that all other major Western democracies have undergone constitutional change in the past century. He reminds us: "Only the United States persists with constitutional forms essentially as they were devised nearly 200 years ago."[10] Hardin argues that the party government system, which could provide party accountability and a smooth transition of presidential leadership, is preferable to the crippled system we now have.

The case against parliamentary government for America, however, seems stronger. Hardin's party government would reduce the direct accountability of the president and the executive branch to the national electorate and substantially undermine constitutional checks and balances. The merger of executive and legislative leadership does not guarantee governmental effectiveness. As Norman C. Thomas has commented: "In all probability . . . an American parliamentary system would be characterized by a multiplicity of political parties, given our social pluralism, and hence it might encourage chronic instability like that of the French Fourth Republic or the current Italian Republic."[11]

Nor is Hardin's proposal that the winner of the presidential election be given a majority of the House of Representatives by awarding his party "bonus" seats to assure a partisan majority likely to generate much support in the House. This proposal would dilute the power of members, and it would create more competition for committee assignments and subcommittee chairpersonships. Furthermore, congressional leaders might find that such a plan would endanger their influence and lead to possible presidential domination of the legislative party. Just how easily this plan would function in our persistently divided government system, Hardin does not say.

PRESIDENTIAL–CONGRESSIONAL CONSTITUTIONAL RELATIONSHIPS

Several reformers of the national government have proposed other presidential–congressional constitutional arrangements. Generally, these reforms aim to strengthen the capacity of the presidency for leadership, not through the selection of strong, competent leaders, but through constitutional revisions in the rules of government so that the lawmakers on Capitol Hill will have more inducements to cooperate with the chief executive.

Bingham–Cutler Plan. Lloyd N. Cutler, a White House adviser in the Carter administration, for example, has recommended adoption of Congressman Jonathan Bingham's plan, which would require in presidential election years that voters in each congressional district vote for a trio of candidates as a team—president, vice president, and House of Representatives member. Under this plan, the political fortunes of the party's presidential and congressional candidates would be tied to one another and provide some incentive for sticking together after they are elected. Furthermore, Cutler and Bingham would extend the term of House members to four years to foster greater teamwork and to provide House members with greater protection against the pressures of single-interest groups. Actually, Cutler would prefer to move a step further and elect two senators to four-year terms, along with the candidates for president, vice president, and the House of Representatives."[12] Thus, members of Congress would come into office as part of a presidential team.

Another proposal Cutler has put on the table for consideration would permit or require the president to select 50 percent of his cabinet from among the members of his party in the Senate or House; they would retain their seats while serving in the cabinet. This plan, which helps bridge the separation of powers, would require a change in Article 1, Section 6, which provides that "no person holding any office under the United States shall be a member of either house during his continuance in office."

Still another proposal that Cutler has offered for consideration would provide the president with the power—to be exercised not more than once in a term—to dissolve Congress and call for new congressional elections. Cutler believes this plan would provide the opportunity that does not now exist to break an executive–legislative deadlock and permit the public to decide whether or not it wants to elect senators and members of Congress who support the president's legislative program. This plan, Cutler admits, would require a number of constitutional changes both to the timing and conduct of the election and to the staggering of senatorial terms, but Cutler believes his reform "would significantly enhance the president's power to form a Government."[13] Experience over the past several decades suggests, however, that a new election would be no guarantee that the president would gain legislative support; in fact, loss of congressional seats in the president's party in the mid-term election has been the normal pattern.

Cutler has also suggested another variant of his special election plan: empower a majority of two-thirds of both Houses to call for new presidential elections. This plan, too, would require amending the Constitution.

Cutler's proposals, which are reactions to the weakness of the Carter presidency, aim to reinforce the hand of a beleaguered president. Unfortunately, as Erwin Hargrove and Michael Nelson have cogently noted: "Reforms of this kind would not strengthen such presidents because they seek to substitute rules for politics, and this cannot be done effectively."[14] The reason is simple: "New rules will not cause legislators to follow presidents."[15]

The Robinson Plan. Presidential scholar Donald L. Robinson has also offered a package of four proposals for constitutional reform, less drastic than Cutler's modified form of cabinet government, that would "remove features which serve primarily as a deterrent to coherent political action and accountability [and] provide a way to resolve deadlocks between the branches."[16] The Robinson plan includes the following: (1) allow members of Congress to serve in administrative offices; (2) provide four-year terms for members of Congress and eight-year terms for senators, with the election of all House members and half the senators at each presidential election; (3) allow the president to call new elections during his term (provided at least one-third of the House and Senate concur) and give Congress the same power by majority vote in each chamber; and (4) establish a "federal council" consisting of "100 notable persons" chosen for life by the president who, in turn, would select one of their number to serve as "chief of state" for a term of two years, an officer who would be empowered to initiate dissolution.[17]

How members of Congress, who are primarily legislators and constituent intermediaries, would enhance the performance of administrative offices in the executive branch is unclear. Robinson insists that eliminating the constitutional provision that prevents legislators from serving in the executive branch would encourage "the integration of legislative and administrative approaches to policy."[18]

Robinson's proposal of four-year and eight-year legislative terms is designed to maximize presidential coattails. But in view of the current high rate of incumbency, especially in the House, reinforced by political action committee contributions and effective constituency service records by most incumbents, it is not clear how this reform would give the president party majorities. With incumbency rates running as high as 96 to 98 percent (1986 and 1988) for House members, and with generally over fifty House seats uncontested by the opposition party, the president would be hard-pressed to collect legislative majorities. Even if the president were successful, what would assure the chief executive a party government? Weak legislative discipline and the Madisonian checks and balances—"ambition counteracting ambition"—often frustrate presidents with solid legislative majorities. One need look no further than President Jimmy Carter. Though he enjoyed sizable majorities in both houses of Congress, Carter failed to obtain action on most of his legislative agenda. Even President Lyndon Johnson, the most skilled legislative strategist since FDR, found that by the 1966 mid-term election the United States involvement in the Vietnam War had so badly eroded his congressional party support that his Great Society legislation dried up.

Our constitutional tradition of fixed terms of office would be a Himalayan-sized barrier to the dissolution power. Nor is there any guarantee that the new election would yield a working majority for the president.

Robinson's proposal for a "federal council" is somewhat reminiscent of the Framers' intent to have the electoral college consist of the most gifted citizenry who would choose the "best-qualified" person to serve as the nation's chief magistrate. Selected by the president, the members would most likely be retired or defeated members of the House and Senate, former cabinet members, and presidential staffers. It is difficult to see how these partisans, especially the "chief of state," would generate widespread respect. If the same party retained control of the White House for most of two decades, the council would be so overpopulated with partisan appointees that its legitimacy as the overseer of the dissolution process would be seriously undermined. A statutory commission with bipartisan membership seems preferable. In any event, the Robinson plan, like the Cutler plan, would require wholesale constitutional amendments. The prospects for such an overhaul of the Constitution do not seem bright.

Corwin's Legislative Cabinet. Almost four decades ago, a leading authority on the presidency, Edward S. Corwin, suggested that more harmonious party relations would develop between president and Congress if the president would choose part of his cabinet from among leading members of Congress. The restructured cabinet would be selected by the president from both houses of Congress. Added to this group would be as many executive department heads as required by the nature of the activity.[19]

Corwin's proposal of a legislative cabinet to replace the presidential cabinet, however, takes little account of the political facts of life governing the American separation-of-powers system. The idea is an attempt to change the recognized ineffective advisory role of the cabinet as it is presently constituted. But the possibility of developing a viable advisory relationship between a president and cabinet composed of independently elected senators and representatives who are firmly entrenched in a seniority system is extremely remote. Not only would this proposal weaken congressional political leadership, it would also undercut the president's independent sources of political authority.

As the chief magistrate, the president can now go over the heads of Congress and appeal directly to the people for support of his programs. By adroitly playing competing interest groups against each other and by appealing to the ''national interest,'' the president can frequently achieve his goals despite congressional footdragging. To force the president to surrender his initiative in both domestic and foreign affairs and to limit his goals to what he can sell to a legislative cabinet of senior members of the two houses would leave him at the mercy of a congressional cabal. In addition, the legislative cabinet idea gives the president no more support or clout than he can secure at present by direct negotiation with party leaders on Capitol Hill.[20]

Direct Election of the President. Direct popular election of the president is a reform proposal that would probably have the most far-reaching impact—and undoubtedly a number of unanticipated consequences—on the presidency and the American party system. Andrew Jackson, a losing candidate in the 1824 electoral college deadlock, won the presidency four years later. In his first annual message to Congress, Jackson proposed that the electoral college be abolished and the president chosen by popular vote, with a run-off election between the two high candidates if no one received a majority in the initial ballot.[21] Senator Birch Bayh (D-Ind.), the main sponsor of the 25th Amendment, which deals with presidential disability, proposed an amendment whereby presidents would be elected directly by the voters just as governors are. In addition, the Bayh plan contained a provision that called for a national run-off election between the two top vote-getters in the event that no candidate received 40 percent of all votes cast.[22] After more than a decade of debate and parliamentary skirmishing, the proposed amendment was finally put to a vote in the Senate in July 1979. With ninety-nine senators voting, the proposal received fifty-one votes—fifteen votes short of the sixty-six needed to send a proposed constitutional amendment to the states for ratification.[23] Failure on this vote ended further attempts in Congress to win approval of the direct-vote amendment.

By far the most democratic electoral reform proposal, the direct popular vote amendment is deceptively appealing. This plan would give every voter the same weight in the presidential balloting, in accordance with the one person, one vote doctrine. Every vote would count in a direct election. The large, competitive two-party states would lose some of their political clout and electoral advantage by the elimination of winner-take-all voting. Party competition might be increased within states, and perhaps nationwide. Voter turnout might increase. On paper, at least, the winner would gain more legitimacy as a result of a clear-cut popular triumph. Furthermore, the shortcomings of the present system, especially the constitutional requirement that presidential choice will be made by the House of Representatives if no candidate receives a majority of the electoral votes, would be replaced by a simple, direct, and decisive method. Would direct election strengthen the hand of the president as party leader?

The direct election plan is fraught with numerous potential boobytraps. Critics suspect that the new rules would change electoral behavior. The run-off proposal, for example, might encourage third-party, independent, or "spoiler" candidacies and seriously undermine the two-party system. The possibility that a defeated candidate from a national convention might obtain a ballot listing as a new party or an independent candidate cannot be easily dismissed.

Arthur M. Schlesinger, Jr., the historian, has expressed the fear that minor parties or single-cause candidates could magnify their strength under the direct vote plan.

Anti-Abortion parties, Black Power parties, anti-busing parties, anti-gun control parties, pro-homosexual rights parties—for that matter, Communist or Fascist parties—have a dim future in the Electoral College. In direct elections they could drain away enough votes, cumulative from state to state, to prevent the formation of a national majority—and to give themselves strong bargaining positions in case of a run-off.[24]

Thomas E. Cronin also raises another direct election specter: "The direct vote method could easily produce a series of 41 percent presidents."[25] Though we have elected fifteen minority presidents (that is, candidates elected by less than 50 percent of the popular vote), the present electoral college system—a two-stage process in which popular votes are transformed into electoral votes—magnifies the popular vote margin of the winner and strengthens the president-elect's mandate. Thus, even though there have been a number of cliff-hanger presidential election contests— Kennedy–Nixon in 1960, Nixon–Humphrey in 1968, and Carter–Ford in 1976—only once in the past century has a president failed to receive 55 percent of the electoral college vote.

Direct popular vote, if it were extremely close—say, within a few thousand votes nationwide—might easily lead to interminable recounts and challenges, leave open the possibility of electoral fraud in some states, and raise serious questions over the legitimacy of choice. Opponents insist that it would encourage unrestrained majority rule and probably political extremism. Lawyer Charles Black, a scholar not often given to exaggeration, has stated that direct election would be the most deeply radical amendment ever to enter the Constitution.[26] The present electoral college process, which rests on a federal system of choice, dampens electoral tensions, and for a century it has confirmed, without fail, a popular vote winner.

Opponents of the direct system also point out that the small states would be submerged and lose some of the power they presently enjoy in the federal system. Furthermore, the direct popular vote plan, among other things, necessitates some form of national administration of presidential elections, upsetting the present decentralized and economical state management of elections. Direct popular election would probably trigger demands for a uniform ballot in all states and uniform voter qualifications. Moreover, as Thomas E. Cronin cautions: "Once members of Congress attack details of this nature, they are also likely to regulate further the presidential primary process, the methods of voting, and hence, at least indirectly, to influence the national conventions."[27]

Some critics fear that the direct election plan would make the candidates more remote from the voters by transforming the campaigns into national telethons, since the sole object would be to reach as many potential voters in the large populous states in the most efficient manner possible. The late Theodore H. White, chronicler of a series of presidential elections, considered the direct election plan a revolutionary measure that would transform the entire system of elections and upset two centuries of American political history. Media professionals, White believed, would become the new political bosses, and state boundaries, which give us a sense of place in presidential politics, would give way to maps of major media markets:

This plebiscite proposal will withdraw from us a large and throbbing memory of our history—all those lovely maps of elections which tell school children as well as grownups how the country has swung section by section from mood to mood. Instead, we will have this boiling pot of 75 million votes stirred by a mixmaster, manipulators, and television—understandable only by statisticians and social scientists.[28]

State electoral victories would not be important, only the single national mandate would count. In defending the present system, columnist George Will observed some years ago: "The electoral college promotes unity and legitimacy by helping to generate majorities that are not narrow, geographically or ideologically, and by magnifying (as in 1960, 1968, 1976) narrow margins of victories in the popular vote."[29]

Defenders of the direct vote plan point out that three times in the nation's history (1824, 1876, and 1888) the electoral college has failed to give the popular vote winner a victory. "The vitality of federalism," columnist Neal Peirce writes, "rests chiefly on the constitutionally mandated system of congressional representation and the will and capacity of state and local governments to address compelling problems, not on the hocus-pocus of the 18th-century vote count system."[30]

In his first year of office, Jimmy Carter recommended that Congress adopt a constitutional amendment to provide for direct popular election of the president. In July 1979, as indicated earlier, the Senate voted fifty-one to forty-eight in support of Senator Bayh's direct election proposal—a simple majority but far short of the two-thirds majority needed for constitutional amendments. Opponents of the amendment consisted mostly of an alliance with southern conservatives and northern liberals. The voting on the proposed amendment, for example, produced such strange bedfellows as liberal Democratic Senator Edmund G. Muskie of Maine and conservative Republican Senator Strom Thurmond of South Carolina, both opposing the constitutional change. Some northern opponents were responding to black and Jewish groups who feared they might lose their "swing" vote power under the existing system.[31] Several senators from the small states, worried about possible diminution of their voting strength, also cast votes against the proposed amendment.[32]

NATIONAL BONUS PLAN FOR ELECTORAL COLLEGE TO REDUCE CHANCES OF DIVIDED GOVERNMENT

To strengthen the president's hand and reduce chances of a divided government, a Twentieth Century Fund task force in the late 1970s developed an ingenious "national bonus plan" to help assure that the popular vote winner would be the electoral college winner.[33] Under this plan, the electoral college would be retained, but it would also be weighted toward the popular vote winner. The plan would add to the existing 539 electoral votes a pool of 102 electoral votes (two for each state and the District of Columbia) and award these bonus delegates automatically to the candidate who won the most popular votes. These bonus votes would be added to the candidate's electoral college total won in the election. This candidate would be elected if these bonus votes, plus the regular electoral votes, totaled a majority (321 electors under the plan) in the electoral college. If not, a runoff election would be held between the two candidates winning the most popular votes. The national bonus plan would also do away with electors, electoral votes being automatically determined.

Advocates contend the plan would ensure that the national popular vote winner would also be the electoral vote winner—and thus the president-elect. Proponents argue that the chances of an electoral college deadlock (which would shift the election to the House of Representatives, as provided in the Constitution) would be sharply reduced. The "faithless" elector who votes against the decision of his or her own state would also be eliminated. One analyst, however, has commented: "By turning a close popular vote into a sizeable Electoral College victory, the national bonus plan presents the president-elect with an enlarged and to some extent unrepresentative mandate. In this sense, it may create unrealistic public expectations of him and his administration."[34]

Opponents of this plan say that this bonus plan would operate unfavorably against presidential candidates of minor parties and independent candidates. Election irregularities and fraud would present the same kind of problems for the national bonus plan as they do for direct election. Furthermore, many of the disadvantages of direct election would also apply to the bonus plan. The bonus plan, which would also require a constitutional amendment to implement, has enlisted very little support beyond academic seminars.

REPEAL OF THE TWENTY-SECOND AMENDMENT

Whether or not advocating repeal of an amendment added to the Constitution less than four decades ago constitutes reforming the presidency may be debatable. But it is this author's view that the Twenty-second Amendment two-term limitation on presidents should be repealed, chiefly because it makes a chief executive a lame duck the day after he is reelected. The Founding Fathers provided indefinite eligibility for presidents; the four-year term represented a compromise between those who favored the president serving during "good behavior," meaning indefinitely, so long as he comported himself within constitutional guidelines, and those who favored a seven-year term. Some Framers thought a second term should be banned. Thomas Jefferson and James Monroe, although neither attended the convention, favored periodic rotation in office.

Long after the Founding Fathers left Philadelphia, the length of presidential service continued to occupy national attention. Between 1789 and 1947, Thomas E. Cronin tells us, "No less than 270 resolutions to limit eligibility for reelection were introduced in Congress."[35] Why did the Twenty-second Amendment win approval after World War II, despite many previous rejections? The explanation can be traced to the special political conditions of the time. During the Eightieth Congress (1947–1948), Republicans dominated both houses, and they were determined not to see a repeat performance of four successive presidential victories by another FDR-type candidate.

To push the proposed amendment through Congress, GOP lawmakers were joined by some conservative Democrats, chiefly from the South, who had soured on the New Deal and Roosevelt. In less than four years, Republican-dominated legislatures in most of the states helped speed ratification of the two-term limitation. Proponents made a strong case that there is no indispensable man in a democracy; extended incumbency might lead to entrenched power and inflexibility. As one observer phrased it, the "Twenty-second Amendment protects us from periodic hardening of the governmental arteries!"[36]

Ironically, the Twenty-second Amendment, ratified in 1951, first applied to Republican President Dwight D. Eisenhower, who was barred from running in 1960. If Eisenhower had been eligible to run and wanted to seek a third term, most political pundits agreed that he would have easily won renomination and reelection.

This amendment is, according to some critics, antidemocratic, for it limits the national leadership choice of party and electorate alike. Furthermore, if the nation were in the midst of a major war or domestic crisis, it compels a rotation in office just when the electorate might wish to see an experienced president continue in office.

Though we have the experience of observing only presidents Eisenhower and Reagan in their second terms, most political experts seem agreed that the long-term effects of the amendment will undermine the effectiveness of most second-term presidents. Harry Truman, although not prohibited by the amendment from seeking another term, testified that any officer who is ineligible for reelection loses a lot of political clout. In the words of the plain-spoken man from Independence, the American people put the president "in the hardest job in the world, and send him out to fight our battles in a life and death struggle—and you have sent him out to fight with one hand tied behind his back because everyone knows he cannot run for reelection."[37] Truman added: "If he is not a good President, and you do not want to keep him, you do not have to reelect him. There is a way to get rid of him and it does not require a constitutional amendment to do it."[38] The late Clinton Rossiter, a leading authority on the presidency, predicted more than thirty years ago that the Twenty-second Amendment would prove to have permanently weakened the presidency. Everything in our history tells us, he wrote, "that a President who does not or cannot seek reelection loses much of his grip in his last couple of years, and we no longer can afford Presidents who lose their grip."[39]

On the other side of the ledger, presidential scholar Thomas E. Cronin has offered several major reasons why the two-term limit on presidents should be retained.[40] The two-term limit has a healthy effect on our two-party system. Requiring a changeover in presidents at least every eight years prevents political stagnation. The major parties, Cronin insists, are rejuvenated by facing the challenge of nurturing, recruiting, and nominating new national leaders. Eight years is enough time for a president and an administration to implement major policy changes. Most presidents witness a diminution of power in their second terms because of normal fatigue and the pressures of the job. Most of their innovative policies have been introduced in Congress and, if sufficiently attractive, enacted into law. A president who remains on the job for twelve or sixteen years would probably be able to stack, if not pack, the Supreme Court and fundamentally alter the composition of the entire federal judiciary. President Reagan, for example, appointed nearly half of the more than 700 federal judges during his eight years in the White House. Do we really want a president, Cronin asks, who could, by virtue of a large number of judicial appointments, gain control of two branches of the federal government?[41]

No political leader is indispensable. The Twenty-second Amendment would prevent the arrogance of power by a chief executive and reinforce the checks and balances in the future, without taking away the effectiveness of good presidents. Finally, Cronin argues, "The 22nd might, like impeachment, be needed only once a century, yet it would be there as a protection."[42]

What does the future hold for the Twenty-second Amendment? While most citizens support the two-term tradition, they sometimes view it as too restrictive to be cemented into the Constitution. However, there has been no groundswell to repeal the limitation. Possibly an emergency near the end of a popular president's second term might trigger a major repeal drive. But it seems doubtful if enough time could be found to repeal it before election, even discounting the additional obstacles that might arise if it became a partisan issue. Nor should the possibility be dismissed that a repeal drive might run head-on into an equally strong drive to adopt the widely publicized single, six-year presidential term.

FUTURE PROSPECTS FOR REFORM

Prospects for reform of the presidency in the immediate years ahead appear dim. Joint authors Neal R. Peirce and Lawrence D. Longley, strong advocates of direct election of the president of the United States, observed some years ago: "The cause of electoral reform has always suffered from two handicaps—the unwillingness of reformers to agree on a single system and the insistence of some on reforming the system for their own partisan advantage."[43] Indeed, the road to reform of presidential nominations and elections, as well as the institutionalized presidency, is littered with the wrecks of numerous previous attempts. The chief reason for the failure of these reforms is that nearly all of them would require constitutional amendments.

The amending process, as the Framers intended, is a formidable—but not impossible—barrier to change. To succeed, proponents of a constitutional amendment must form and maintain a broad national consensus. As explained by Peirce and Longley,

No constitutional amendment has much chance of ratification without the support or at least the acquiescence of all the major forces in the country—the controlling groups in each major political party, the spokesmen for each section of the country, and state and national party leaders. The stakes in any presidential election are so high that no political group will consent to a change in the electoral system if it seriously fears that its power and influence will be undercut.[44]

Though proposals to reform the presidency number in the hundreds, it is noteworthy that only four constitutional changes affecting the presidency—the Twelfth, Twentieth, Twenty-second, and Twenty-fifth Amendments—have been approved since the Bill of Rights was added to the Constitution in 1791. It is significant that all four amendments have dealt with mechanical problems—to provide for a joint ticket including presidential and vice-presidential candidates, to shift the date of the presidential inauguration, to establish the two-term limitation, and to deal with presidential disability as well as vice-presidential vacancies. But none of these amendments has altered the formal structure or power of the executive branch.

Still, if a proposed amendment generates strong popular support, it can sometimes pass in a breeze. The Twenty-sixth Amendment (which extends suffrage to eighteen-year-olds) quickly gained widespread support during the Vietnam War. It was approved by Congress and ratified in 1971 by the required thirty-eight states in less than four months. Proposed shortly after the Supreme Court ruled that states could prohibit eighteen-year-olds from voting in state elections, even though Congress had passed a law granting them votes in federal elections, the new amendment encountered no major organized opposition. With almost 500,000 American troops, consisting of a high percentage of eighteen- to twenty-one-year-olds still in Vietnam, the argument "if you are old enough to fight, you are old enough to vote" was virtually unassailable. Some proposed amendments, however, have languished in the states for years, and all of the most recent proposals, e.g., the Equal Rights Amendment (ERA), which had a seven-year time limit on ratification, plus another congressional extension of two years, have failed for lack of the requisite thirty-eight-state approval.

No proposed amendment to modify or change the institutionalized presidency has come to a vote in the House or Senate since the Senate failed to give its required constitutional two-thirds approval of the direct election of president amendment in 1979. Unless a major political earthquake occurs—for example, if a presidential candidate should lose the popular vote yet win the White House by capturing a majority of the electoral college vote, as happened in 1888 when Benjamin Harrison unseated President Cleveland—or unless a third-party candidate should garner enough electoral votes to force the presidential election into the House of Representatives, the prospects of presidential election reform do not seem promising.

THE FRENCH PRESIDENCY—A SOURCE OF POTENTIAL REFORMS OF THE AMERICAN PRESIDENCY

Reformers of the American presidency, seriously intent on overhauling the powers and duties of the chief executive, might wish to review the office of French president, whose powers and latitude of operation exceed those of the American. Influenced heavily in its formation by the late President Charles DeGaulle, the French president has several powers not available to the American chief executive:

- He is elected for a seven-year term, with no limit on the number of terms;
- He has the "sole power" to conduct foreign relations and negotiate and ratify treaties (except for certain types that require parliamentary approval);
- He can appoint the premier, equivalent to appointing the House and Senate leaders;
- He can dissolve parliament and call new elections (but he cannot do so a second time until after one year has elapsed);
- He can bypass parliament by passing laws via a national referendum or having the government "pledge its responsibility" for a bill. Under this system the bill is automatically enacted, unless the opposition introduces a motion of censure and prevails. If this happens, the government must resign;
- In times of national emergency, he can govern by decree.[45]

The French presidential election, it should be noted, does not coincide with parliamentary elections, usually taking place one to three months earlier. When President François Mitterrand was first elected in 1982, a majority of the French Assembly was in the hands of the opposing center-right parties. Consequently, Mitterrand promptly dissolved the Assembly and called for new parliamentary elections. In this election the French voters gave Mitterrand an absolute majority in the Assembly.

All these French structural features, except the separate dates for electing the president and Congress, would require constitutional amendments to be incorporated into the American system. Changing the timing of American elections, Lloyd Cutler points out, however, could be accomplished by an act of Congress, without amending the Constitution.[46] Under Article I, section 4 and Article II, section 1, Congress may determine the time for conducting both presidential and congressional elections; there is no constitutional requirement that the same date be set for both.

While the prospects for incorporating any of the French president's powers into the American Constitution are next to nothing, there can be no doubt that if they were accepted the American president would be a far more powerful party leader and chief executive than he is today.

SUMMARY

Although the numerous proposals for reforming the presidency outlined in the chapter may possess some merit, they by no means offer a panacea. Breaking down the barriers between the president and Congress by including members of Congress in the cabinet, for example, may merely shift the location of conflict, not remove it. James L. Sundquist has cogently noted, "When executives and legislators are disposed to cooperate, ample means for cooperation exist and additional formal mechanisms are scarcely needed."[47] Similarly, the six-year term might give the president ample time to learn the job—but what if he opts for one ill-advised policy after another? The country would be saddled with an incompetent chief executive for an additional two years. In the case of the no-confidence vote, the so-called cure (greater presidential–congressional cooperation) might well be worse than the ailment. The no-confidence vote, in all likelihood, would give Congress the opportunity continually to frustrate the president. More than likely, it would lead to a government of "revolving door" presidential elections. Government instability would probably be the chief result of this "reform." Clearly, institutional reform offers only the possibility, not the certainty, of improvement.

The most important lesson to be drawn from proposed reforms of the presidency is that for each remedy there are as many problems as there are solutions. No single all-purpose reform exists to help the president cope with the unrelenting demands placed on him. Indeed, a careful analysis of the various reform proposals suggests that most of the remedies merely exchange one set of difficulties for another—or worse yet, undermine the existing effectiveness of the American chief executive.

In retrospect, the record of the twentieth century shows that the nation has surged ahead most dramatically under the strong party leadership of three presidents—Woodrow Wilson, Franklin D. Roosevelt, and Lyndon Johnson—who had, in their first terms at least, the solid support of their party majorities in Congress. When the president and his party majority in Congress can work closely together, presidents have far more opportunities to move the country ahead and attain higher levels of social progress and reform. There is, of course, no foolproof method of guaranteeing that the electorate will choose wisely in picking a president and a congressional majority that will see eye to eye on public policy and act accordingly. But parties can serve as vehicles for mobilizing support for presidential programs in Congress. By the same token, the separation-of-powers system can continue to serve as a restraint on presidents who in their zeal to achieve their political goals may choose to ignore constitutional constraints and the rights of the minority opposition. In conclusion, no major overhaul of the presidency, it seems, is needed at the present time.

In the final chapter we assess the relations between the president and party in the last decade of the twentieth century.

NOTES

1. The most widely publicized proposal for establishing party government in the United States is found in the report of the Committee on Political Parties of the American Political Science Association, "Toward a More Responsible Two-Party System," *American Political Science Review* suppl., 44 (September 1950).

2. Leon D. Epstein, *Political Parties in the American Mold* (Madison: The University of Wisconsin Press, 1986), p. 35.

3. Ibid.

4. Ibid.; for the view that leadership rather than party constituted the central element of Wilson's program for political reform, see James W. Ceaser, *Presidential Selection: Theory and Development* (Princeton, NJ: Princeton University Press, 1979), pp. 197–212.

5. James MacGregor Burns, *Leadership* (New York: Harper and Row, 1978), Chap. 12, "Party Leadership."

6. Ibid., *The Deadlock of Democracy* (Englewood Cliffs, NJ: Prentice-Hall, 1963), p. 326.

7. Epstein, *Political Parties in the American Mold*, p. 36.

8. Charles M. Hardin, *Presidential Power and Accountability: Toward a New Constitution* (Chicago: University of Chicago Press, 1974).

9. Ibid.

10. Ibid.

11. Norman C. Thomas, "Reforming the Presidency: Problems and Prospects," in Thomas E. Cronin and Rexford G. Tugwell, eds., *The Presidency Reappraised*, 2nd ed. (New York: Praeger, 1977), p. 329.

12. Lloyd N. Cutler, "To Form a Government—On the Defects of the Separation of Powers," *Foreign Affairs* 59 (Fall 1980), pp. 126–143.

13. Ibid., p. 173.

14. Erwin C. Hargrove and Michael Nelson, *Presidents, Politics, and Policy* (Baltimore: The Johns Hopkins University Press, 1984), p. 270.

15. Ibid.

16. Donald L. Robinson, *To the Best of My Ability: The Presidency and the Constitution*, (New York: W. W. Norton, 1988).

17. Ibid., pp. 270–271.

18. Ibid., p. 272.

19. Edward S. Corwin, *The President: Office and Powers*, 4th ed., (New York: New York University Press, 1957), pp. 297–299.

20. Rowland Egger, *The President of the United States* (New York: McGraw-Hill, 1967), pp. 151–152.

21. James L. Sundquist, *Constitutional Reform and Effective Government* (Washington, DC: The Brookings Institution, 1986), p. 42.

22. United States, 96th Congress, 1st sess., S.J. Res. 28.

23. Neal R. Peirce and Lawrence D. Longley, *The People's President*, rev. ed. (New Haven, CT: Yale University Press, 1981), p. 205.

24. Cited by Thomas E. Cronin, *The State of the Presidency*, 2nd ed. (Boston: Little, Brown, 1980), pp. 361–362.

25. Ibid.

26. *Direct Election of the President* (Washington, DC: American Enterprise Institute, 1977), citing Black's testimony before the Senate Judiciary Committee in 1976, p. 392.

27. Cronin, *The State of the Presidency*, p. 64.

28. United States, Senate, 96th Congress, 1st sess., Hearings before the Subcommittee on the Constitution of the Committee of the Judiciary, (Washington, DC: GPO, 1979), p. 345.

29. George Will, "Don't Fool with the Electoral College," *Newsweek* 89 (April 4, 1977), p. 96.

30. Cited in Cronin, *The State of the Presidency*, p. 65.

31. Stephen J. Wayne, *The Road to the White House* (New York: St. Martin's, 1980), p. 21.

32. For further analysis of the proposed direct election amendment, see Thomas E. Cronin, "The Direct Vote and the Electoral College: A Case for Meshing Things Up!" *Political Science Quarterly* 94 (Spring 1979), pp. 144–163.

33. *Winner Takes All: Report on the 20th Century Fund Task Force on Reform of the Presidential Election Process* (New York, 1978); see also Thomas E. Cronin, "Choosing a President," *The Center Magazine*, Sept.–Oct., 1978, pp. 5–15.

34. Stephen J. Wayne, "Proposals for Reforming the Electoral College," in Robert Harmel, ed., *American Government: Readings on Continuity and Change* (New York: St. Martin's, 1988) p. 227.

35. Cronin, *The State of the Presidency*, p. 47.

36. Reo M. Christenson, cited in Cronin, *The State of the Presidency*, p. 72, n. 26.

37. Harry S. Truman, Senate Judiciary Hearings, 86th Congress, 1st sess., May 4, 1959, p. 7, cited in Cronin, *The State of the Presidency*, p. 7, n. 28.

38. Ibid.

39. Letter to Rep. Stewart L. Udall (D-AZ), *Congressional Record*, March 25, 1957, cited in Sundquist, *Constitutional Reform and Effective Government*, p. 48.

40. *The Christian Science Monitor*, February 27, 1987, p. 16.

41. Ibid.

42. Ibid.

43. Peirce and Longley, *The People's President*, rev. ed., p. ix.

44. Ibid., p. 179.

45. The discussion in this section draws heavily from Lloyd N. Cutler, "Modern European Constitutions and Their Relevance in the American Context," in *Reforming American Government*. The Bicentennial Papers of the Committee on the Constitutional System, edited by Donald L. Robinson (Boulder, CO: Westview, 1985), pp. 299–310.

46. Ibid., pp. 302–306.

47. Sundquist, *Constitutional Reform and Effective Government*, p. 205.

Chapter 9

Reassessing Presidential–Party Relations

A modern president may often prefer to operate in a "no party" environment. On the surface, at least, he finds that his posture as the "public president" attracts extensive media coverage and frequently generates favorable poll ratings. By "going public" the president seeks to avoid the constant coalition-building required in a badly fragmented Congress to obtain support for each measure sponsored by the administration. Still, as explained in this chapter, when it comes to "crunch time" on important measures the president wants enacted, he generally turns to his party for reinforcements. Public relations tactics and speeches to various interest groups cannot deliver the votes when they are most needed. The truth of the matter, it is emphasized in the chapter, is that the president and his party are mutually dependent upon each other. The president cannot demonstrate strong leadership unless he can count upon his party's support on Capitol Hill; the congressional party, in turn, needs the president's leadership and prestige to advance its programs.

The chapter concludes with the observation that the party can serve as an excellent braking device for "checking" and "balancing" the powers of the president. Over the course of their terms, few modern presidents have been able to resist the "arrogance of power." Fortunately, the constraining influence of the president's party can help keep the chief executive from exceeding his powers or making rash decisions that may come back to haunt him later.

DOMINANT PRESIDENTS AND WEAK PARTIES

In this era of the mass-media presidents, the national party organization is seldom heard from. Presidents Reagan and Bush and their predecessors, presidents Kennedy, Johnson, and Nixon, have completely dominated the TV networks' evening news programs and the front pages of the mass circulation dailies. The president's daily activities, especially speeches to national business, trade, fraternal, or labor organizations; discussions with foreign leaders visiting Washington; and international travels monopolize the national agenda. One of the few times the national party chairperson and the national committee of the president's party receive any significant news coverage occurs when it is time to pick the site of the next national nominating convention—and even then, the final choice of the convention city is the president's.

Presidents rarely address regular national committee meetings; indeed, with the exception of presidents Bush and Reagan, one would have to go back to the Kennedy era to find a traditional working relationship between the president and the national committee. President Carter, according to columnist David S. Broder, had to be reminded after seventeen months in office that he had never invited members of the Democratic national committee to the White House for an informal social hour.[1] In this era of global diplomacy and superpower politics, the president's time for party matters is strictly rationed. Intraparty issues in New Jersey, personality conflicts among party leaders in Wisconsin, or the scheduling of a president's speech in Louisiana will be completely overshadowed by the need to plan a summit meeting with the Soviet leader, a president's address to the meeting of NATO leaders in London, or an economic summit meeting—or to deal with another crisis in the Middle East.

Congressional leaders from the president's party (the Republican party for five of the six most recent terms) meet occasionally at the White House to review strategy for dealing with upcoming bills, usually introduced by members of the Democrat-controlled House of Representatives. In recent years, for example, Republican presidents Reagan and Bush have sent their annual budgets to Capitol Hill, only to hear that they were ''DOA''—dead on arrival—because the opposition Democrats chose to ignore this important document and draft their own version. In the spring of 1990, the minority Republicans in the House felt that the Bush-proposed 1991 federal budget (to take effect October 1, 1990) was so outdated by the fast-moving events in Eastern Europe and the Soviet Union that they decided against even asking for a vote on the Republican version.

Since virtually all decisions concerning prospective federal appointments are made by the White House staff, in consultation with leading members of Congress, the national party is no longer a major player in party patronage. Federal patronage now numbers only 4,000 to 5,000 federal positions. Contrast this case with President-elect Franklin D. Roosevelt's situation in 1933. FDR and his national party chairperson James A. Farley had, it has been estimated, approximately 75,000 patronage positions to fill—jobs especially attractive in light of the nation's 25 percent unemployment rate at the worst period of the Great Depression.[2] No wonder the role and influence of the national party were far more important in the New Deal era than in the present era of the civil service and merit system and the relatively low unemployment rate (5 to 7 percent annually).

IS THE PRESIDENT HIS PARTY'S WORST ENEMY?

The answer to this question depends upon which president we are talking about. If we are talking about Kennedy, Reagan, or Bush, the answer is no. All three of these presidents have taken an active interest in party affairs. In 1962, for example, Kennedy visited more than a dozen states in the mid-term election campaign—until the Cuban missile crisis with the Soviet Union cut short his barnstorming tour in mid-October. Kennedy did not hesitate to take an open stand as partisan leader of the Democrats, as his remarks show:

I do not intend to conceal the differences between our parties. . . . If the Democratic Party is charged with disturbing the status quo, with stirring up the great interests of this country, with daring to try something new, I plead "guilty," and if the Republican Party is charged with wanting to return to the past, with opposing nearly every constructive measure we have put forward, then they must plead "guilty" and the American people will make their judgment.[3]

President Kennedy was well satisfied with the results of his energetic 1962 political stumping. Instead of the anticipated loss of as many as thirty-nine House and five Senate seats, the Democrats lost only four House seats and gained three Senate seats; they also retained the same number of governorships—the best showing of any administration in off-year elections since 1934.

President Reagan was a good team player in the off-year election campaigns but less so during his own reelection campaign. In the 1982 off-year campaign, he made dozens of television and radio spot-ad announcements for congressional candidates, and he helped extensively with party fundraising. For the first time Reagan also used multistate radio satellite broadcasts to groups of GOP congressional supporters across the land. Even so, the GOP lost twenty-six House seats, although the party picked up one Senate seat.

During the 1984 reelection campaign, however, the Reagan White House—not the Republican national committee—independently managed his successful campaign. This bifurcated arrangement led the House Republican minority leader, Robert Michel, to blame Reagan's personal campaigning for a disappointing party performance in the House elections. Michel accused the Reagan White House of not helping enough to ensure more GOP gains in House, despite the Reagan landslide.[4]

George Bush, the first national party chairperson (1973–1974) to be elected president, has not needed any coaching on his party duties. During his first eighteen months in office, Bush campaigned actively for Republican gubernatorial candidates in Virginia and New Jersey in 1989 (they both lost) and participated in nearly a dozen major fundraising events within a ninety-day period in early 1990. Bush twice visited California, the most populous state in the Union and scene of a critical 1990 gubernatorial contest that would be a key factor in a congressional reapportionment struggle. Bush's vigorous campaign support, especially his fundraising activity, was a significant factor, most California analysts agreed, in helping Republican candidate Pete Wilson capture the governorship and thus protect GOP congressional interests in the post-1990 census reapportionment battle. If the GOP had lost the governor's seat in 1990, the Democrats, with control of both houses of the California legislature, would have been able to carve up and gerrymander the expected 52 congressional districts to their special advantage. This action would have given the Democrats a huge partisan advantage in the California congressional delegation, which will constitute more than 10 percent of the 435-member U.S. House of Representatives in 1992.

For presidents in the Lyndon Johnson–Richard Nixon tradition, it is scarcely an exaggeration to assert that they were their own parties' worst enemies. President Johnson treated the Democratic national committee with slightly disguised contempt. Soon after taking office, he placed Johnson loyalists (most Texans) in key positions on the national committee, but within a year he began shifting committee operations to the White House. One White House staffer recalls: "Shortly after his 1964 election it became clear that Johnson regarded the Democratic national committee as a debt ridden, presidentially irritating and irrelevant encumbrance."[5] Columnist David S. Broder observed that Johnson often acted as if party obligation and functions were the enemy, not the instruments, of responsible government.

Joseph A. Califano, Jr., one of Johnson's close aides, later recalled: "In my years on Lyndon Johnson's White House staff never once did I hear him say that he wanted to leave behind a strengthened Democratic Party."[6] In fact, Johnson left the Democratic national committee debt-ridden and in shambles long before he departed from the White House for retirement at his Texas ranch.

President Richard Nixon treated the GOP national committee in the same cavalier fashion as Johnson treated the Democrats—concentrating political power in the White House staff, running campaigns totally divorced from the party, relying on personal loyalists to fill the top executive-branch jobs, and virtually ignoring the national committee after his first year in office. Nor did Nixon hesitate early in his first term to fire GOP national chairperson Ray Bliss, widely acknowledged as a brilliant organizational tactician, because he apparently did not demonstrate sufficient loyalty to the White House.

Jimmy Carter's view of the Democratic national committee was not much better. After his victory in 1976, Carter recommended to Democratic Party national chairperson Robert S. Strauss that the size of the Democratic national committee staff be reduced by 70 percent. Shortly thereafter, the staff was cut down to only 20 full-time employees.[7] Meanwhile, Carter's campaign staffers held the chief positions at the Democratic national committee, and the Carter White House staff kept the entire national party apparatus on a short leash. In the 1980 presidential campaign, Carter used virtually all the money assiduously raised by the Democratic national committee over the past three years to underwrite his own reelection campaign, leaving virtually nothing to finance congressional or senatorial races or as "seed money" for future national party fundraising endeavors.

Until the major parties regain (if they ever do) a prominent voice in the selection of their presidential nominees, they cannot be overly sanguine about how they will be treated by future presidents. The chief reason for this pessimistic assessment is, as political scientist Robert Harmel emphasizes, "presidents themselves have very little incentive to lead their parties, since their election and subsequent powers are little tied to party-related resources."[8] Yet the late John D. Lees, a British observer of the American presidency, commented some years ago, "Whether they like it or not . . . Presidents and their parties are too interrelated to permit one to disown or divorce the other. Presidents in the future may become more selective about their participation in party activity but they are unlikely to ignore entirely the obligations or indeed the benefits of this relationship."[9]

PRESIDENTIAL NEGLECT OF STATE PARTY ORGANIZATIONS

In yesteryear, the "care and feeding" of state party organizations was a fairly high priority for presidents. After all, presidents owed their White House occupancy to the campaign help—spreading the candidate's message, registering voters, distributing campaign literature, and getting out the vote on election day—given them by the state organizations. It was not mere coincidence that as late as 1940, President Roosevelt chose New York's Bronx borough chairperson, Ed Flynn, to succeed James A. Farley (also a New Yorker) as Democratic national chairperson. New

York's forty-seven electoral votes were too important to be ignored in the upcoming presidential election to shop elsewhere for another national chairperson.

Twenty years later, President John F. Kennedy maintained close ties with Chicago Mayor Richard J. Daley, the Democratic boss, and with Governor David Lawrence, head of the powerful Pennsylvania Democratic organization. Each of these key preconvention supporters would always find the door of the Oval office open when he went to the nation's capital seeking federal help for his city or state. Furthermore, these powerful Democratic leaders could be counted on, in response to President Kennedy's requests, to exert pressure on their states' congressional delegations to support the president's legislative proposals. Throughout his brief term, Kennedy and the White House staff worked closely with state Democratic party organizations. Staunch Kennedy supporters will never forget that the day of his assassination the young president was visiting and speaking in Dallas in an attempt to reconcile the warring liberal and conservative wings of the Texas Democratic party.[10]

Since the 1970s, however, presidents have been far less concerned over the fate of their parties' state organizations. No longer do presidential candidates have to turn to state party leaders to deliver blocs of delegates at the national nominating conventions. The effect of the McGovern–Fraser Commission reforms, especially for the Democratic party, was to take the nominating process out of the smoke-filled rooms by stripping the party bosses and power brokers of their control over delegate-selection and turning it over to the voters in state presidential primaries. By the 1980s, over 80 percent of the national convention delegates ran pledged to specific candidates and were chosen by state voters. Moreover, the pledged delegates owed their allegiance to presidential candidates, not to the state party elite. To win the nomination in the 1970s, the presidential candidate had to establish his own political organization—managers, fundraisers, pollsters, media advisers, schedulers—and campaign tirelessly in the many primary states for the better part of two years or more. Especially in the early and populous primary states, the candidate had to rely heavily on expensive media campaigns to reach prospective voters. Television enabled the presidential contender to communicate directly with huge numbers of primary-state voters without the intermediary need of any state party organization workers.

PRESIDENTS FROM ONE-PARTY STATES

Until the publication of V. O. Key's monumental study, *Southern Politics*,[11] in 1949, political scientists and the general public did not fully appreciate how the Democratic one-party politics of states below the Mason-Dixon line differed from the traditional two-party situation found in most other states. Nor did they fully realize how different the impact of one-party politics was on the politicians from these states. As Key pointed out, one-party politics consisted chiefly of factional competition, flamboyant personalities, and issueless politics. Small wonder that presidents from one-party states enter the White House with a different perspective and understanding of how politics is conducted at the national level. Georgia Governor Jimmy Carter was the first southern president elected directly to the White House since General Zachary Taylor (a Whig from Louisiana) in 1848. The chief reason for this long interval was the pressure of nominating and electoral college politics, which gave a tremendous advantage to candidates from big northern swing states with fierce two-party competition: Wilson from New Jersey, Franklin D. Roosevelt from New York, Adlai Stevenson from Illinois, and John F. Kennedy from Massachusetts. Southerners, however, were often given a consolation prize—the vice presidency. Between 1944 and 1988, seven southern or border-state politicians received the Democratic vice presidential nomination: Truman, Barkley, Sparkman, Kefauver, Johnson, Eagleton, and Bentsen. To be sure, Lyndon Baines Johnson was a Texan, but Johnson reached the White House via the vice presidency following Kennedy's assassination in November 1963. Though Johnson and Carter, both Democrats, belonged to the same party, the similarities between these two chief executives ended there. Still, both men were influenced by the same political culture.

The first modern president from a one-party state, Lyndon B. Johnson was always skeptical of the Democratic party organization. His one-party Texas background undoubtedly produced this distrust. Until the 1950s, the Democratic party of Texas consisted mostly of public officeholders and the lawyers, lobbyists, and money men who worked hand in glove with them. The Texas Democratic party was, in effect, an empty shell. Traditionally, the governor picked the chairperson of the Texas State Democratic Executive Committee, usually a lawyer from the state capital in Austin. The party chairpersons took their marching orders from the governor, tried to remain on good terms with the Texas congressional delegation, and cultivated the big party contributors, who often became their clients.[12]

In this pre–civil rights era, tough voter registration requirements in Texas and throughout the South made it easy to exclude blacks and Mexican-Americans from voting. Consequently, there was little need for a host of precinct workers to haul voters to the polls. The notion of a cadre party or the state party chairperson, independent of the elected officeholders, was foreign to Johnson's view of politics. Small wonder that President Johnson in 1965 told Cliff Carter, his liaison man with the Democratic national committee, ''I'm damned if I can see why one guy and a couple of secretaries can't run that thing [the national committee].''[13] With this attitude toward his party, it is easier to understand how Johnson developed his concept of "consensus politics," to bring all the disparate elements within the Texas Democratic party under "a great big tent." Once in the White House, Johnson pursued with a vengeance consensus politics, rather than a conventional coalition-building type of politics. In the end, national columnist David S. Broder writes, Johnson's failure was not so much Vietnam but rather "his own flawed concept of presidential leadership and party responsibility in a democracy."[14] Perhaps Broder is being too charitable toward Johnson's failed presidency, but Broder is certainly correct in assessing the influence Johnson's one-party state background and its impact had upon Johnson's *modus operandi* in the White House.

He did not see political parties as necessary vehicles for communicating the often inchoate preferences of the voters to those in power. Nor did he see parties as instruments for disciplining the whims of the elected leaders and holding them accountable for their actions. Instead, he saw them as unwanted intruders on the process of consensus government.[15]

Georgia Democratic politics is certainly not a carbon copy of Texas Democratic politics. And Jimmy Carter, the second southern Democratic president of the twentieth century, was certainly not a clone of Lyndon B. Johnson. Carter's presidential operating style nevertheless reflected the same disturbing attitude displayed by Johnson toward his party. Carter approved the selection of former Maine Governor Kenneth Curtis as Democratic national chairperson to succeed Robert S. Strauss, who had brought the party back from exile after the McGovern disaster of 1972. But Curtis lasted less than one year. According to one source, Carter strategists thought Curtis "was giving the liberal carpers in the party too much rein."[16] From Inauguration Day, the Carter White House had kept the national committee on a check-rein, with a Carter staffer monitoring the national committee on a daily basis. Unlike Lyndon Johnson, who developed a national perspective over twenty years of Washington experience, beginning as the National Youth Administration director, then as congressman, senator, and vice president, before he reached the presidency, Carter's government experience was limited to one four-year term as a state senator and another four years as Georgia governor before he came to Washington. Even though Carter had been leader of the Georgia Young Democrats, the Democratic governor of Georgia, and in 1974 head of the congressional campaign organization for the Democratic national committee, he had always been an "outsider" within the party. He won his state senate seat on his second try, despite the opposition of the local Democratic organization. Similarly, he won the governorship on the strength of his independence from old-line Democrats. Thus, before reaching the White House, Carter had no elected experience in national politics or any close ties with the Democrats in Congress.[17] Indeed, Carter based his presidential campaign on his stand as an independent, anti-Washington candidate of the people, rather than the choice of the party professionals. Unfortunately, his victory reinforced his belief that the strategies and tactics of the Washington outsider that successfully brought him to the nation's capital would also be appropriate for governing the nation.

From the start, his provincial view of national government handicapped his relations with Congress, even though the Democratic majorities in both houses were almost as large as those of the Johnson years. When he tried to whipsaw Congress into passing his comprehensive energy program, as he had dealt with the Georgia legislature, Carter ran into a legislative swamp. More than a year passed before Congress passed a watered-down version of his energy proposal and sent it to the White House.

One veteran party-watcher has assessed Carter's party relationships this way:

A former governor of a one-party state where his principal adversaries were in his own party, Carter had little feeling for the presidential party role. He was generally perceived as an "outsider" among the Washington Democratic establishment and only occasionally addressed himself to party problems. From time to time he called upon party officials to lend support for his programs but offered little in return.[18]

Carter did not overcome his inability to negotiate and bargain with congressional leaders and take them into his confidence until late in his term—too late to reverse his downward spiraling popularity and win a second term.

NONPARTISAN VERSUS PARTY PRESIDENT

Have we reached the era of the nonpartisan presidency? Several leading students of the presidency and party suggest that we may be approaching this point. Political scientist Harold F. Bass, Jr., for example, argues that the current president–party relationship consists of "recurring and systematic presidential efforts to undermine the establishment and maintenance of a strong national party apparatus."[19] Clearly, recent presidential candidates have won the nomination and election without paying more than lip service to the national or state party organizations. The three most-recently elected presidents—Carter, Reagan, and Bush—all won the party nomination through the prodigious work of their own independent, candidate-centered organizations. Carter and Reagan operated their prenominating campaigns as "outsiders" running against Washington.

George Bush's prenominating campaign based its strategy on continuing the Reagan legacy, not on a Republican drive to retain the White House for the Grand Old Party. To underwrite their nominating drives, all three candidates raised all their own money, except for matching dollars provided under the Federal Election Campaign Act of 1974.

Their general election campaigns were all underwritten by Uncle Sam. Under the 1974 law—a reaction to the Watergate scandals—the federal government paid the full general election campaign bill—$21.8 million in 1976; $40.4 million in 1984; and $46.1 million in 1988. All three candidates could have, if they had chosen to exercise the option, refused to accept federal funds and raised all their campaign money themselves. None chose to do so. Indeed, Ronald Reagan, the arch-opponent of federal spending, holds the record for the acceptance of public funding of presidential nominating and general elections. In his three nominating races of 1976, 1980, and 1984 and his two general election campaigns of 1980 and 1984, Reagan accepted over $90 million in federal matching dollars for his primary races and the full-ride federal underwriting of his two general election campaigns.[20] Under these favorable financial conditions, who needs a party to win the presidency?

Before the Kennedy era, the national and state party organizations, for the most part, "ran" the presidential campaign; since then, however, the party's campaign function and its "educational" activity of arousing partisan interest in the electoral outcome have been largely supplanted by direct-to-the-people television appeals and slick Madison Avenue advertising campaigns produced by media specialists.[21] Presidential candidates count far more on their "personal image," polished and refined by their voice coaches and media consultants, than on their partisan affiliation to attract independent voters. Indeed, performing well in presidential debates, in which a single major gaffe before 100 million people watching on TV can cost the presidency, is worth far more than all the precinct workers in the country. Conversely, President Ford's statement, during the second presidential debate with Jimmy Carter in 1976, that Poland was not under the iron-fisted control of the Soviet Union may, in the minds of some pundits, have cost him the White House. (Recently, in light of the peaceful revolution of 1989 in Eastern Europe, Ford has jocularly insisted that he has been right all along!)

The nonparty presidential campaign has evolved not only because of television and public funding but also because it is easier, more efficient, and cost-effective. So much easier is the modern media campaign, with its heavy emphasis on 30-second "spot" ads that reach millions of voters every day, that presidents' campaign managers seldom give a thought to campaigning from the rear platform of a railroad observation car in Trumanesque style, except for a "photo-opportunity" on the networks' evening news programs. Public campaign finance funds—$46.1 million for each of the major party candidates in 1988—is a preferable alternative to hours spent by the candidates' fundraising teams collecting the needed money from party "fat cats." Since the 1974 campaign reforms limit individual contributors to $1,000, the task of raising $50 million or so for the general election campaign is a challenge most candidates choose not to face. A full-scale direct mail fundraising operation, similar to the ones used in the primaries, would have to be resurrected. In the pre-Watergate era, presidential candidates themselves sometimes had to spend hours of campaign time importuning big contributors.

Nor is there significant evidence available to suggest that the general public objects to the "nonparty" presidential campaign. Today's independently oriented electorate, eschewing "politics as usual," seems comfortable with media campaigning. With roughly one-third of the prospective voters listing themselves as independents and with split-ticket voting exceeding 50 percent of the electorate, the number of voters responding to partisan appeals has declined dramatically over the past quarter-century. As a result of these developments, presidential scholar Thomas E. Cronin has noted, "In this era of weaker party identification and rising independents, it is inevitable that presidents will strive to be impartial officeholders."[22] It might be added also that the likely prospect that a president will face a divided government (twenty years out of twenty-four years between 1968 and 1992) does not offer them an irresistible incentive to lead their parties since they believe their success in office depends far more on "going public," i.e., appealing to the American electorate via television, than relying on their party ties.

Since the age of Andrew Jackson, the presidency and the two-party system have generally complemented each other. Indeed, if the parties had not transformed the electoral vote system and if national conventions had not emerged as the nominating agency for presidential candidates, the American party system would in all likelihood have faint resemblance to the present structure. Similarly, without the office of president as a nationalizing force within our system, it seems unlikely that the federal system would have survived in its present form. Equally important, political parties have enabled our strong presidents, especially Woodrow Wilson, Franklin D. Roosevelt, Lyndon Johnson, and Ronald Reagan, to overcome some of the limitations of the constitutional separation of powers and to provide strong national leadership.

Though a number of factors—network television, independent campaign organizations, and government funding of presidential candidates—have all conspired to undermine the influence of political parties on American chief executives, party support still remains an essential ingredient in electoral success. Parties have been especially important, Robert Harmel tells us, "when the particularistic pulls of other forces have contributed to the factionalization of American politics and ultimately diminished presidential effectiveness."[23]

The symbolic support the president draws from his party enables him to go forth to the country with his plans and programs, knowing that a formidable army of the party faithful is prepared to reaffirm and back up his demands for action. No president, it seems clear, can expect to achieve his goals or withstand the assaults from the opposition without broad party backing. As Gary R. Orren has commented: "A President who must depend overwhelmingly on his personal image to sustain himself, who cannot count on the obligations of party elites to support him, is an isolated and vulnerable leader."[24] Political scientist David E. Price, now a congressman from North Carolina, has noted that strong party ties may be of decreasing importance for a contender seeking the presidential nomination, but they are "absolutely essential" for a president to lead Congress. In Price's words, "To neglect or bypass the party may be understandable in terms of the president's immediate desire for consensus or his need for control, but it is a shortsighted strategy that is likely, in the long run, to reduce the availability and potency of a critical instrument of governance."[25]

In the history of the American presidency, the record shows that the management of Uncle Sam's business "is considerably enhanced when the president commits time and resources to working closely with his party's establishment."[26] The truth of the matter is that the president and his party need each other. The president needs the party's support in order to enact a legislative program; the party needs the president's leadership and the prestige of his office to achieve its goals.

ARE WE APPROACHING AN ERA OF THE PRESIDENCY DIVORCED FROM PARTY?

Some observers have concluded that the opportunities for a president to use his own political party to advantage have declined perceptibly over the years. Conversely, the liabilities of close party ties and vigorous party leadership have grown.[27] Contributing factors most often cited are the decline in partisan identification as a cue for voting choice, the deleterious effects of party "reforms" of the presidential nominating process, and the fragmentation of power within Congress. These critics point out the president does not need the party any longer because he has virtually unlimited access to the electronic media, public financing of his reelection campaign, and several hundred dedicated White House staffers at his command that enable him to operate independent of his party. The president, in effect, has separated himself from his party.

The estrangement between the president and his party usually begins before the election, indeed before the nomination. In this era of candidate-centered campaigns, a presidential contender will begin his drive for the White House two or more years before the national convention. To have a serious chance of winning, he must establish his own team of campaign organizers, legal experts to handle state primary filings, pollsters, media consultants, schedulers, and accountants. This same team will stay with him through the nomination and, if successful in November, they are most likely to be found holding down key positions on the White House staff. During the preprimary phase of the campaign, the presidential contender will establish his own multicandidate political action committee (PACs) with high sounding names like "Fund of the Republic" or "America's Future" to pay all his staff costs and travel expenses and even to help fund some state legislative candidates or mayors who have aligned with him. Since these groups are established as multicandidate political action committees, this type of funding is a normal activity and perfectly within the law. Because the "long march" to the nomination and election is conducted independently of the national and state party organizations, the president incurs few obligations to his party; the party, in turn, owes him virtually nothing. Under these circumstances, the separation of the president and party is, unless the president takes action to build and reinforce his party ties, plainly evident.

Time demands, if nothing else, seriously limit the modern president's ability to include party matters on his schedule. Whereas a Lincoln, McKinley, or Teddy Roosevelt could devote several hours a day to party-related matters, the modern president's daily schedule may exceed a dozen hours. International issues, which consumed relatively little time in the earlier era, now crowd the agenda. Foreign heads of state arrive in Washington with amazing regularity. All of them must be given the red-carpet treatment—formal talks, receptions, dinners. Before World War II, the international community consisted of fewer than 50 countries; now more than 160 sovereign nations are members of the United Nations. To be sure, the president will not meet with every one of these national leaders during the course of a year, but scarcely a week passes that he does not play host to at least one "visiting fireman" at the White House, Camp David, or a mutually agreeable foreign site. As explained by one veteran foreign observer, "A President can no longer do his job by staying home." Whereas Herbert Hoover spent only three days abroad in his term of office and Franklin D. Roosevelt spent only nine days abroad in his first term, Richard Nixon spent fifty-nine days abroad in his first four years in office, and Jimmy Carter fifty-six.[28] President Bush has "outtraveled" all these presidents. In April 1990, for example, he undertook a series of three consecutive foreign policy consultations with Western leaders about changes in Eastern Europe and the upcoming summit meeting with Soviet President Mikhail S. Gorbachev. During a ten-day period, he visited Canadian Prime Minister Brian Mulroney in Toronto, British Prime Minister Margaret Thatcher in Bermuda; and French President François Mitterrand in Key Largo, Florida.

Understandably, high-level discussion on East–West relations, the future of the European Economic Community, the unification of Germany, and more frequent summit meetings with Soviet leaders push any pending party matters off the White House agenda for weeks—and perhaps months.

Priority domestic issues and travel also consume days and days of the president's time at the expense of major party questions. In October 1977, for example, President Jimmy Carter delivered eleven addresses in five cities on both coasts.[29] President Reagan made some twenty-five appearances around the country in 1983, not attending party festivities but promoting his views on "excellence in education," merit pay, and the need for classroom discipline.[30] President Reagan's staffers carefully managed his schedule to avoid overtaxing the aging president; consequently, they left only small slivers of time for party matters. No wonder some analysts suggest that we are rapidly approaching, if we have not already reached, an era in which the president and party go their separate ways.

SCENARIO OF A POSTPARTY PRESIDENCY

American voters have already caught glimpses of the postparty presidency. President Reagan, more than any other recent president, demonstrated how to operate the presidency effectively without benefit of his party. To kick off his tax reform proposal of 1985, Reagan did not talk with GOP congressional leaders or the Republican national committee. Instead, he traveled to Williamsburg, Virginia, to showcase the plan's theme as "the new American Revolution." The colonial setting in tidewater Virginia was ideal for the TV network evening newscasts, as Reagan reached an estimated 35 to 40 million viewers. No one remembers exactly what the president said, but in his address he laid the foundation for passage of the most important piece of legislation in his second term, though it was not signed into law until twelve months later.

George Bush has been an apt pupil of Ronald Reagan. In the two weeks prior to his meetings with Western leaders in April 1990, he addressed several nonpartisan but nevertheless formidable interest groups. Bush's message at the dinner honoring the twentieth anniversary of the Joint Center for Political and Economic Studies, a research group devoted to the role of blacks in America was: "The day will come—and it is not far off—when the legacy of Lincoln will finally be fulfilled at 1600 Pennsylvania, when a black man or woman will sit in the Oval Office."[31] Though the 1992 presidential election was still more than two years away, President Bush was busy in a "nonpartisan" way making inroads in the most Democratic ethnic voting group. Indeed, a *New York Times*/CBS poll in January 1990 showed that a remarkable 70 percent of blacks said they approved the job Bush was doing—more than twice as high as Reagan's most favorable rating.[32]

In another nonpartisan address in late March 1990, President Bush appealed for compassion toward people infected with the AIDS virus. Speaking at a conference sponsored by the National Leadership Coalition on AIDS, the president, for the first time, expressed support for a bill that would outlaw discrimination against people with AIDS and other diseases.[33] The president identified himself with those dealing with the dreaded disease that threatens the lives of countless thousands. Though critics within the AIDS organization found fault with Bush's limited involvement, Bush nevertheless moved into a front-line position on a major nonpartisan issue that could only help him at reelection time. As we move closer to the twenty-first century, we can expect to see postparty presidents identifying themselves with more nonpartisan issues—clean air, education, medical research, and the like—that have the support of Republicans, Democrats, and independents. This winning combination makes a first-term White House incumbent well nigh unbeatable.

THE PRESIDENT'S USE OF PARTY-RELATED ACTIVITIES TO ATTAIN MAJOR GOALS

Richard Rose, the respected British presidential scholar, has observed: "The extent to which a new President can change the direction of government is easily overestimated, especially by the President-elect."[34] Unfortunately, most recent presidents have been disinclined to rely heavily on their parties to attain major program goals. In fact, as one veteran presidential watcher has commented, "presidents have turned their creativity toward finding ways of conforming to (and, in fact, helping to shape) a new type of politics that is largely devoid of party influence."[35] Nevertheless, the relationship between presidents and political parties can still best be described as one of reciprocal needs and mutual dependence.[36]

President John Kennedy, though he had a strong distrust of party hacks like those found in some Boston precincts, nevertheless found time to devote to party-related activities that would help him achieve his long-term goals. His ambitious mid-term campaigning in 1962 is a case in point. Undoubtedly, he would have set an all-time presidential record in helping Democratic congressional candidates if the Cuban missile crisis had not erupted in mid-October. Similarly, his operatives at the Democratic national committee pushed a strong grass-roots campaign in the late summer of 1963 to stimulate employment in depressed areas of the country and to generate popular support for his tax reform proposals, especially the rapid plant depreciation concept to encourage business expansion. The Democratic national committee distributed thousands of copies of the Kennedy proposals to state committees. Kennedy mounted a cross-country speaking trip, with several stopovers in the Midwest. The present author recalls attending one of the Kennedy rallies in Duluth, Minnesota. Over five thousand Democratic–Farmer Labor (the official name of the Minnesota Democratic party) partisans gave Kennedy a rousing reception. One can only wonder if Kennedy would have continued to pursue these party-sponsored issue rallies if he had lived to run for a second term. Since then, presidents from both parties have been only lukewarm toward party-building activities to win support for their programs. To be sure, they have continued to devote time to fundraising activities to help their parties' congressional, senatorial, and occasional gubernatorial candidates—but not much more. With President George Bush, the only former national party chairperson to occupy the White House, now at the party controls it remains to be seen if such a seasoned party professional will decide to utilize the GOP machinery to push forward some of his programmatic goals.

PARTIES SERVE AS TOOL FOR "CHECKING" AND "BALANCING" THE PRESIDENT

The Madisonian system's institutional checks and balances within our three branches is generally understood, but it is sometimes overlooked that the political party itself serves as a tool for "checking" and "balancing" the powers of the president.[37] As two close students of the presidency have put it, "Parties can be a major means for reflecting popular impulses in ways that inform and channel uses of presidential power. Thus, they are potentially one means of holding the presidency within appropriate bounds."[38] The best known example is, of course, the refusal of Republican congressmen to support President Nixon during the final stages of the House Judiciary Committee's impeachment proceedings against the beleaguered president. When ranking GOP members refused to defend him, Nixon saw that his fate was sealed and promptly resigned. Beyond doubt, the Nixon experience demonstrated the danger of the absence of checks on a president by his party and the tragic consequences of excessive independence of presidents from the constraints of party and its meddling influence. Parties have usually served presidents in a positive manner. Parties have linked the people to the president by reflecting popular sentiment on important issues. Parties can serve as a compass to keep the president on a steady course, for without this organized support as buffer, the president is exposed to the obsessive demands of numerous special interest groups. Parties can supply ready-made coalitions in Congress to deliver votes and thus spare the president the onerous task of trying to put together a separate coalition for every vote.

Formerly, the president collected coalition support from his party in the various states while he was still running for office. Once he reached the White House, he could count on these partisans who had been through the heavy fire of battle. But with the decline of parties, the rapid growth of the mass media, and the rise of candidate-centered campaigns, the presidents have often neglected their parties. But when all else fails, and the president needs vital support to push his legislative agenda through Congress, his party will be his most dependable ally. As Robert Harmel reminds us, "Recent presidents have already learned that legislating by coalition is more difficult and more risky when there is not a substantial segment of party faithful who can be counted on to respond to a partisan appeal."[39] This political fact of life may encourage some future presidents to turn to their parties more frequently and thus strengthen the president–party relationship.

SUMMARY

With the rise of the mass media, the opportunities for presidential speechmaking have taken a quantum leap. Indeed, modern presidents, faced with the declining influence of political parties and fragmented leadership in Congress, seem to regard public speech as their most reliable ally. Still, presidential oratory can carry a president only so far. When it comes to decision-making time in the nation's capital, the president must, in the final analysis, turn to his party for broad-based support needed to implement his policies. Political scientist Robert McClure has put it well: "The irony is that without party as a meaningful organization this country's complicated government grinds to a halt, cannot deliver necessary national policies and cannot be a positive force for change. Party is the common organization that holds the disparate parts of society together."[40] Despite the intractable fragmentation of party politics in the United States, no known substitute has been found to replace the ability of political parties to facilitate consensus and redirect public policy.

Even in the divided government that has come to characterize our national government late in the twentieth century, the political party is central to the decision-making process because it serves as a vital communications link between the executive and legislative branches. Despite our separation of powers and the constant danger of gridlock, political parties also provide the lubrication to make the machinery of government move forward. Indeed, if presidents and lawmakers are disposed to cooperate, sufficient avenues for cooperation exist, and additional pathways are scarcely needed. Finally, the political party serves as an added insurance policy to protect the country against the potential threat of a plebiscitarian president—a leader who seeks to build a direct, unmediated relationship between himself and the American people.

NOTES

1. David S. Broder, *Washington Post*, June 14, 1978.
2. Laurin Henry, *Presidential Transitions* (Washington, DC: The Brookings Institution, 1960), p. 432.
3. *Congressional Quarterly Weekly Report*, October 19, 1962, p. 1973, quoted in Roger G. Brown and David M. Welborn, ''Presidents and Their Parties: Performance and Prospects,'' *Presidential Studies Quarterly* 12 (Summer, 1982), p. 307.
4. See Richard Vigurie, ''Reagan's Campaign Double-Crossed the GOP,'' *The New York Times*, November 12, 1984.
5. Joseph A. Califano, Jr., *A Presidential Nation* (New York: W. W. Norton, 1976), p. 151.
6. Ibid., p. 159.
7. Richard M. Pious, *The American Presidency* (New York: Basic Books, 1979), p. 126.
8. Robert Harmel, ''President-Part Relations in Context,'' in Robert Harmel, ed., *American Government: Readings on Continuity and Change* (New York: St. Martins, 1988), p. 391.
9. John D. Lees, ''The President and His Party,'' in Malcolm Shaw, ed., *Roosevelt to Reagan: The Development of the Modern Presidency* (London: C. Hurst, 1987), p. 82.
10. Theodore C. Sorenson, *Kennedy* (New York: Harper and Row, 1966), p. 843.
11. V. O. Key, Jr., *Southern Politics* (New York: Knopf, 1949).
12. David S. Broder, *The Party's Over* (New York: Harper and Row, 1971), pp. 65–66.
13. Ibid., p. 65.
14. Ibid., p. 56.
15. Ibid.; for another view of President Johnson's ''consensus politics,'' see Eric F. Goldman, *The Tragedy of Lyndon Johnson* (New York: Knopf, 1969), pp. 51–56.
16. Cragg Hines, *Texas Magazine* interview, quoted by Howard L. Reiter, ''The Gavels of August: Presidents and National Party Conventions,'' in Robert Harmel, ed., *Presidents and Their Parties: Leadership or Neglect* (New York: Praeger, 1984), p. 104.
17. Betty Glad, *Jimmy Carter in Search of the Great White House* (New York: W. W. Norton, 1980), pp. 123–226.
18. Ralph M. Goldman, ''The American President as Party Leader: A Synoptic History,'' in Harmel, ed., *Presidents and Their Parties*, p. 50.
19. Harold F. Bass, Jr., ''Presidential Responsibility for National Party Atrophy.'' Paper delivered at the 1977 Annual Meeting of the American Political Science Association, Washington, DC, August 1977, p. 1.
20. Frank J. Sorauf, *Money in American Elections* (Glenview, IL: Scott, Foresman, 1988), p. 221.

21. The discussion in this section relies heavily on Robert Harmel, "The Roots of President–Party Relations: Intellectual, Conceptual, and Contextual," in Harmel, ed., *Presidents and Their Parties*, pp. 10–16.

22. Thomas E. Cronin, "The Presidency and the Parties," in Gerald M. Pomper, ed., *Party Renewal in America* (New York: Praeger, 1981), pp. 176–193.

23. Harmel, "The Roots of President–Party Relations," p. 15.

24. Gary R. Orren, "The Changing Styles of American Party Politics," in Joel L. Fleishman, ed., *The Future of American Parties: The Challenge of Governance* (Englewood Cliffs, NJ: Prentice-Hall, 1982), p. 82.

25. David E. Price, *Bringing Back the Parties* (Washington, DC: Congressional Quarterly Press, 1984), p. 82.

26. Roger G. Brown, "The Presidency and the Political Parties," in Michael Nelson, ed., *The Presidency and the Political System*, (Washington, DC: Congressional Quarterly Press, 1984), p. 332.

27. Pious, *The American Presidency*, pp. 121–146.

28. Richard Rose, *The Postmodern President* (Chatham, NJ: Chatham House, 1988), p. 38. Rose's sources for these figures are William W. Lammer's "Presidential Attention Focusing Activities" in Doris Graber, ed., *The President and the Public* (Philadelphia: Institute for the Study of Human Issues, 1982), p. 160, and Elmer Plischke, "The President's Right to Go Abroad," *Orbus* 15 (4), pp. 755 ff.

29. Samuel Kernell, *Going Public: New Strategies of Presidential Leadership* (Washington, DC: Congressional Quarterly Press, 1986), p. 91.

30. Ibid., p. 3.

31. *The New York Times*, April 5, 1990.

32. Ibid., January 19, 1990.

33. Ibid., March 30, 1990.

34. Rose, *The Postmodern President*, p. 294.

35. Harmel, "President–Party Relations in the Modern Era," p. 260.

36. Lees, "The President and His Party," p. 46.

37. Thomas E. Cronin, "Presidents and Political Parties," in Thomas E. Cronin, ed., *Rethinking the Presidency* (Boston: Little, Brown, 1982), p. 300.

38. Roger G. Brown and David M. Wellborn, "Presidents and Their Parties: Performance and Prospects," *Presidential Studies Quarterly* 12 (Summer, 1982), p. 302.

39. Harmel, "President–Party Relations in Context," p. 392.

40. Cited in Raymond Tatalovich and Byron W. Daynes, *Presidential Power in the United States* (Monterey, CA: Brooks/Cole, 1984), pp. 72–73.

Selected Bibliography

BOOKS

Aldrich, John H.; Miller, Gary J.; Ostrom, Charles W., Jr.; and Rohde, David W. *American Government: People, Institutions, and Policies*. Boston: Houghton Mifflin, 1986.

Alexander, Herbert E.; and Bauer, Monica. *Financing the 1988 Election*. Boulder, CO: Westview, 1991.

Alexander, Herbert E.; and Haggerty, Brian A. *Financing the 1984 Election*. Lexington, MA: Heath, 1987.

Ambrose, Stephen E. *Eisenhower*. 2 vols. New York: Simon and Schuster, 1983, 1984.

Bailey, Thomas A. *A Diplomatic History of the American People*. 10th ed. Englewood Cliffs, NJ: Prentice-Hall, 1980.

Binkley, Wilfred E. *The Man in the White House*. Rev. ed. New York: Harper and Row, 1958.

Blum, John Morton. *The Republican Roosevelt*. Cambridge, MA: Harvard University Press, 1954.

Bone, Hugh A. *Party Committees and National Politics*. Seattle: University of Washington Press, 1958.

Broder, David S. *The Party's Over*. New York: Harper and Row, 1971.

Burnham, Walter Dean. *Critical Elections and the Mainsprings of American Politics*. New York: W. W. Norton, 1970.

Burns, James MacGregor. *Leadership*. New York: Harper and Row, 1978.

——. *Presidential Government*. Boston: Houghton Mifflin, 1966.

——. *The Deadlock of Democracy*. Englewood Cliffs, NJ: Prentice-Hall, 1963.

Califano, Joseph A., Jr. *A Presidential Nation*. New York: W. W. Norton, 1976.

Cannon, Lou. *Reagan*. New York: Putnam, 1982.

Ceaser, James W. *Presidential Selection: Theory and Development*. Princeton, NJ: Princeton University Press, 1979.

Chubb, John E.; and Peterson, Paul E., eds. *The New Direction in American Politics*. Washington, DC: The Brookings Institution, 1985.

Corwin, Edward S. *The President: Office and Powers*. 4th ed. New York: New York University Press, 1957.

Cotter, Cornelius P.; and Hennessy, Bernard. *Politics without Power: The National Party Committees*. New York: Atherton, 1964.

Cronin, Thomas E. *The State of the Presidency.* 2nd ed. Boston: Little, Brown, 1980.
———, ed. *Rethinking the Presidency.* Boston: Little, Brown, 1982.
Cronin, Thomas E.; and Tugwell, Rexford G., eds. *The Presidency Reappraised.* 2nd ed. New York: Praeger, 1977.
Davidson, Roger H.; and Oleszek, Walter J. *Congress and Its Members.* Washington, DC: Congressional Quarterly Press, 1981.
Davis, James W. *The American Presidency: A New Perspective.* New York: Harper and Row, 1987.
———. *National Conventions in an Age of Party Reform.* Westport, CT: Greenwood, 1983.
———. *Presidential Primaries: Road to the White House.* New York: Thomas Y. Crowell, 1967.
DeVries, Walter; and Tarrance, V. Lance. *The Split-Ticket Voter.* Grand Rapids, MI: Eerdmans, 1972.
Dodd, Lawrence C.; and Oppenheimer, Bruce I., eds. *Congress Reconsidered.* New York: Praeger, 1977.
Dolce, Philip C.; and Skau, George H., eds. *Power and the Presidency.* New York: Scribner's, 1976.
Edwards, George C., III. *At the Margins: Presidential Leadership of Congress.* New Haven, CT: Yale University Press, 1990.
———. *The Public Presidency.* New York: St. Martin's, 1983.
Edwards, George C., III; and Wayne, Stephen J. *Presidential Leadership.* New York: St. Martin's, 1985.
Egger, Rowland. *The President of the United States.* New York: McGraw-Hill, 1967.
Epstein, Leon D. *Political Parties in the American Mold.* Madison: University of Wisconsin Press, 1986.
Evans, Rowland, Jr.; and Novak, Robert D. *Nixon in the White House.* New York: Random House, 1971.
Fiorina, Morris P. *Congress: Keystone of the Washington Establishment.* New Haven, CT: Yale University Press, 1977.
Fleishman, Joel L., ed. *The Future of American Parties: The Challenge of Governance.* Englewood Cliffs, NJ: Prentice-Hall, 1982.
Freidel, Frank. *Franklin D. Roosevelt: A Rendezvous with Destiny.* Boston: Little, Brown, 1990.
Glad, Betty. *Jimmy Carter in Search of the Great White House.* New York: W. W. Norton, 1980.
Goldman, Eric F. *The Tragedy of Lyndon Johnson.* New York: Knopf, 1969.
Goldman, Ralph M. *The National Party Chairman and Committees.* Armonk, NY: M. E. Sharpe, 1990.
———. *Search for Consensus: The Story of the Democratic Party.* Philadelphia: Temple University Press, 1979.
Gosnell, Harold F. *Truman's Crises: A Political Biography of Harry S. Truman.* Westport, CT: Greenwood, 1980.
Gould, Lewis L. *The Presidency of Theodore Roosevelt.* Lawrence: University Press of Kansas, 1990.
Graber, Doris, ed. *The President and the Public.* Philadelphia: Institute for the Study of Human Issues, 1982.

Graff, Henry F., ed. *The Presidents: A Reference History*. New York: Scribner's, 1984.

Greenstein, Fred I. *The Hidden Hand Presidency*. New York: Basic Books, 1982.

———, ed. *Leadership in the Modern Presidency*. Cambridge, MA: Harvard University Press, 1988.

Grossman, Michael Baruch; and Kumar, Martha Joynt. *Portraying the President*. Baltimore: The Johns Hopkins University Press, 1981.

Hardin, Charles M. *Presidential Power and Accountability: Toward a New Constitution*. Chicago: University of Chicago Press, 1974.

Hargrove, Erwin C.; and Nelson, Michael. *Presidents, Politics, and Policy*. Baltimore: The Johns Hopkins University Press, 1984.

Harmel, Robert, ed. *Presidents and Their Parties: Leadership or Neglect*. New York: Praeger, 1984.

Hart, John. *The Presidential Branch*. New York: Pergamon, 1987.

Hart, Roderick P. *The Sound of Leadership*. Chicago: University of Chicago Press, 1987.

Hartmann, Susan M. *Truman and the 80th Congress*. Columbia: University of Missouri Press, 1971.

Henry, Laurin. *Presidential Transitions*. Washington, DC: The Brookings Institution, 1960.

Irish, Marion, ed. *Continuing Crisis in American Politics*. Englewood Cliffs, NJ: Prentice-Hall, 1963.

Jacobson, Gary C. *The Electoral Origins of Divided Government*. Boulder, CO: Westview, 1990.

Johnson, Lyndon B. *The Vantage Point*. New York: Holt, Rinehart, and Winston, 1971.

Jones, Charles O., ed. *The Reagan Legacy: Promise and Performance*. Chatham, NJ: Chatham House, 1988.

Kellerman, Barbara. *The Political Presidency*. New York: Oxford University Press, 1984.

Kernell, Samuel. *Going Public: New Strategies of Presidential Leadership*. Washington, DC: Congressional Quarterly Press, 1986.

Kessel, John H. *Presidential Parties*. Homewood, IL: Dorsey, 1984.

Key, V. O., Jr. *Southern Politics*. New York. Knopf, 1949.

King, Anthony. *The New Political System*. 2nd version. Washington, DC: American Enterprise Institute, 1990.

———, ed. *Both Ends of the Avenue*. Washington, DC: American Enterprise Institute, 1983.

Koenig, Louis W. *The Chief Executive*. 4th ed. New York: Harcourt Brace Jovanovich, 1981.

Latham, Earl, ed. *J.F. Kennedy and Presidential Power*. Lexington, MA: Heath, 1972.

Lazarsfeld, Paul; Berelson, Bernard; and Gaudet, Hazel. *The People's Choice*. New York: Columbia University Press, 1944.

Leech, Margaret. *In the Days of McKinley*. New York: Harper and Row, 1959.

Leuchtenburg, William E. *Franklin D. Roosevelt and the New Deal, 1932–1940*. New York: Harper and Row, 1963.

Light, Paul. *The President's Agenda: Domestic Policy Choice from Kennedy to Carter*.

Baltimore: The Johns Hopkins University Press, 1982.

Link, Arthur S. *Woodrow Wilson and the Progressive Era.* New York: Harper and Row, 1954.

Lowi, Theodore J. *The Personal President,* Ithaca, NY: Cornell University Press, 1985.

Mann, Thomas E., and Ornstein, Norman J., eds. *The New Congress.* Washington, DC: American Enterprise Institute, 1981.

Mayhew, David B., *Divided We Govern.* New Haven, CT: Yale University Press, 1991.

Meltsner, Arnold J., ed. *Politics and the Oval Office.* San Francisco: Institute for Contemporary Studies, 1981.

Mowry, George E. *The Era of Theodore Roosevelt.* New York: Harper and Row, 1958.

———. *Theodore Roosevelt and the Progressive Movement.* Madison: University of Wisconsin Press, 1947.

Nelson, Michael, ed. *The Elections of 1988.* Washington, DC: Congressional Quarterly Press, 1989.

———, ed. *The Presidency and the Political System.* Washington, DC: Congressional Quarterly Press, 1984.

Neustadt, Richard E. *Presidential Power: The Politics of Leadership.* New York: Wiley, 1980.

Nie, Norman H.; Verba, Sidney; and Petrocik, John R. *The Changing American Voter.* Cambridge, MA: Harvard University Press, 1976.

Ornstein, Norman J., ed. *The President and Congress.* Washington, DC: American Enterprise Institute, 1982.

Ornstein, Norman J.; Mann, Thomas E.; and Malbin, Michael J. *Vital Statistics on Congress, 1989–1990.* Washington, DC: American Enterprise Institute, 1990.

Pancake, John S. *Thomas Jefferson and Alexander Hamilton.* Woodbury, NY: Barron's Educational Series, 1974.

Parmet, Herbert S. *Eisenhower and the American Crusade.* New York: Macmillan, 1972.

———. *JFK: The Presidency of John F. Kennedy.* New York: Penguin, 1984.

Peirce, Neal R.; and Longley, Lawrence. *The People's President.* Rev. ed. New Haven, CT: Yale University Press, 1981.

Penniman, Howard R. *Sait's American Parties and Elections.* 5th ed. New York: Appleton Century Crofts, 1952.

Phillips, Cabell. The Truman Presidency. Baltimore: Penguin, 1969.

Pious, Richard M. *The American Presidency.* New York: Basic Books, 1979.

Pomper, Gerald M., ed. *The Elections of 1988.* Chatham, NJ: Chatham House, 1989.

———. *The Elections of 1984.* Chatham, NJ: Chatham House, 1985.

———. *Party Renewal in America.* New York: Praeger, 1981.

Price, David E. *Bringing Back the Parties.* Washington, DC: Congressional Quarterly Press, 1984.

Ranney, Austin. *Curing the Mischiefs of Faction.* Berkeley: The University of California Press, 1975.

Remini, Robert V., *The Life of Andrew Jackson.* New York: Penguin, 1990.

Robinson, Donald L. *Government for the Third American Century.* Boulder, CO: Westview, 1989.

———. *To the Best of My Ability: The Presidency and the Constitution.* New York: W. W. Norton, 1988.

———, ed. *Reforming American Government.* The Bicentennial Papers of the Committee on the Constitutional System. Boulder, CO: Westview, 1985.

Rose, Richard. *The Postmodern Presidency*. Chatham, NJ: Chatham House, 1988.

Roseboom, Eugene H. *A History of Presidential Elections*. New York: Macmillan, 1957.

Schlesinger, Arthur M., Jr. *The Imperial Presidency*. Boston: Houghton Mifflin, 1973.

Seligman, Lester G.; and Covington, Cary R. *The Coalitional Presidency*. Chicago: Dorsey, 1989.

Shaw, Malcolm, ed. *Roosevelt to Reagan: The Development of the Modern Presidency*. London: C. Hurst, 1987.

Sorauf, Frank J. *Money in American Elections*. Glenview, IL: Scott, Foresman, 1988.

Sorauf, Frank J.; and Beck, Paul Allen. *Party Politics in America*. 6th ed. Glenview, IL: Scott, Foresman, 1988.

Sorenson, Theodore C. *Kennedy*. New York: Harper and Row, 1966.

Sundquist, James L. *Constitutional Reform and Effective Government*. Washington, DC: The Brookings Institution, 1986.

Tatalovich, Raymond; and Daynes, Bryon W. *Presidential Power in the United States*. Monterey, CA: Brooks/Cole, 1984.

Thurber, James A., ed. *Divided Democracy: Cooperation and Conflict between the President and Congress*. Washington, DC: Congressional Quarterly Press, 1991.

Tulis, Jeffrey K. *The Rhetorical Presidency*. Princeton, NJ: Princeton University Press, 1987.

Wattenberg, Martin P. *The Decline of American Political Parties 1952–1988*. Cambridge, MA: Harvard University Press, 1990.

Wayne, Stephen J. *The Road to the White House*. New York: St. Martin's, 1980.

White, Theodore H. *America in Search of Itself*. New York: Harper and Row, 1982.

———. *Breach of Faith: The Fall of Richard Nixon*. New York: Atheneum, 1975.

———. *The Making of the President, 1972*. New York: Atheneum, 1973.

———. *The Making of the President, 1968*. New York: Atheneum, 1969.

———. *The Making of the President, 1964*. New York: Atheneum, 1965.

———. *The Making of the President, 1960*. New York: Atheneum, 1961.

Wills, Garry. *Nixon Agonistes: The Crisis of the Self-Made Man*. Boston: Houghton Mifflin, 1969.

Wilson, Woodrow. *Congressional Government*. Boston: Houghton Mifflin, 1885.

———. *Constitutional Government in the United States*. New York: Columbia University Press, 1908.

Witcover, Jules, *Marathon*. New York: Viking, 1977.

Woodward, C. Vann. *Reunion and Reaction*. Boston: Little, Brown, 1951.

ARTICLES

Alexander, Herbert E. "The Price We Pay for Our Presidents." *Public Opinion* 11 (March/April 1989), pp. 46–48.

Alston, Chuck. "Bush Ladles Gravy for GOP Mashed-Potato Circuit," *CQ Guide to Current American Government*, Spring 1991, Washington, DC: Congressional Quarterly, 1991), pp. 94–96.

Binkley, Wilfred E. "The President as Chief Legislator." *Annals of the American Academy of Political and Social Science* 307 (September 1956), pp. 92–105.

Broder, David S. "Bush Gets Big Prize, But It's a Split Decision." *Washington Post National Weekly Edition*, November 14–20, 1988, p. 10.

Brown, Roger G.; and Welborn, David M. "Presidents and Their Parties: Performance and Prospects." *Presidential Studies Quarterly* 12 (Summer 1982), pp. 302–316.

Calvert, Randall L.; and Ferejohn, John A. "Coattail Voting in Recent Presidential Elections." *American Political Science Review* 77 (June 1983), pp. 407–419.

Campbell, James A. and Sumners, Joe A., "Presidential Coattails in Senate Elections," *American Political Science Review*, 84 (June 1990), pp. 513–524.

Ceaser, James W.; Thurow, Glen E.; Tulis, Jeffrey; and Besette, Joseph M. "The Rise of the Rhetorical Presidency." *Presidential Studies Quarterly* 11 (Spring 1981), pp. 158–171.

Cronin, Thomas E. "Choosing a President." *The Center Magazine*, Sept.–Oct. 1978, pp. 5–15.

———. "The Direct Vote and the Electoral College: A Case for Meshing Things Up!" *Political Science Quarterly* 94 (Spring 1979), pp. 144–163.

Cutler, Lloyd N. "To Form a Government—On the Defects of the Separation of Powers." *Foreign Affairs* 59 (Fall 1980), pp. 126–142.

Dahl, Robert A. "Myth of the Presidential Mandate." *Political Science Quarterly* 105 (Fall 1990), pp. 355–372.

Davis, Eric L. "Legislative Liaison in the Carter Administration." *Political Science Quarterly* 94 (Summer 1979), pp. 287–300.

Dowd, Maureen; and Friedman, Thomas L. "The Fabulous Bush and Baker Boys." *New York Times Magazine*, May 6, 1990, pp. 34–37, 58–67.

Greenstein, Fred I. "Eisenhower as an Activist President: A Look at New Evidence." *Political Science Quarterly* (Winter 1979–80), pp. 575–600.

Hibbs, D. A., Jr. "On the Demand for Economic Outcomes: Macroeconomic Performances and Mass Political Support in the United States." *Journal of Politics* 44 (May 1982), pp. 426–462.

Huntington, Samuel. "The Democratic Distemper." *The Public Interest* 41 (1975).

Kempton, Murray. "The Underestimation of Dwight D. Eisenhower." *Esquire*, September 1967, p. 110.

Manley, John F. "Presidential Power and White House Lobbying." *Political Science Quarterly* 93 (Summer 1978), pp. 255–275.

Orren, Gary R. "The Nomination Process: Vicissitudes of Candidate Selection." In Michael Nelson, ed., *The Elections of 1984*. Washington, DC: Congressional Quarterly Press, 1985, pp. 27–82.

Ostrom, Charles W., Jr.; and Simon, Dennis. "Managing Popular Support: The Presidential Dilemma." *Policy Studies Journal* 12 (1984), pp. 677–690.

———. "Promise and Performance: A Dynamic Model of Presidential Popularity." *American Political Science Review* 79 (June 1985), pp. 334–358.

Quirk, Paul J. "The Cooperative Resolution of Policy Conflict." *American Political Science Review* 83 (September 1989), pp. 905–921.

Ragsdale, Lyn. "The Politics of Presidential Speechmaking, 1949–1980." *American Political Science Review* 78 (December 1984), pp. 971–984.

Sidey, Hugh. "Totaling Up One Year." *Time* 135 (February 5, 1990), p. 23.

Sundquist, James L. "Needed: A Political Theory for the New Era of Coalition Government in the United States." *Political Science Quarterly* 103 (Winter 1988–89), pp. 613–636.

Vance, Cyrus R. "Reforming the Electoral Reforms." *New York Times Magazine*, February 22, 1981, pp. 16, 62–69.

Will, George. "Don't Fool with the Electoral College." *Newsweek* 89 (April 4, 1977), p. 96.

MONOGRAPHS

"Toward a More Responsible Two Party System." *American Political Science Review* 44 (September 1950), supp.

Winner Take All: Report of the Twentieth Century Fund Task Force on Reform of the Presidential Election Process. New York: Twentieth Century Fund, 1978.

Index

Acheson, Dean, 57
Adams, Brock, 133
Adams, John, 5, 107, 120, 138
Adams, John Quincy, 7, 107
Adams, John T., 100–101
"Agency agreements," 112
Agnew, Spiro T., 71, 84, 110
Albertazzie, Ralph, 170
Aldrich, John H., 170, 213
Aldrich, Nelson, 46, 123
Alexander, Herbert E., 40, 117, 140, 213, 217
Alston, Chuck, 140, 217
Ambrose, Stephen E., 60, 75, 86, 94–95, 213
Amendments, constitutional, 187–188
American Liberty League, 165
Americans for Democratic Action, 25
Anderson, Robert, 86
Anti-Federalists, 2, 120–121
Anti-Masonic party, 5
Arthur, Chester A., 107
Arvey, Jacob, 24–25
Attlee, Clement R., 97–98
Atwater, Lee, 34, 105–106
Authorization for Use of Military Force against Iraq Resolution, 77

Babcock, Charles, 111
Backdoor lobbying, 49–51
Bailey, John, 104
Bailey, Thomas A., 171, 213

Baker, Howard, 54
Baker, James, III, 34, 73, 82, 109, 128
Baker, Ross K., 41
"Bank War," 45
Barkley, Alben, 199
Bass, Harold F., 116–117, 201, 210
Bauer, Monica, 117, 140, 213
Bayh, Birch, 180–181, 183
Beck, Paul Allen, 116, 217
Bennett, William J., 106
Bentsen, Lloyd, 199
Berelson, Bernard, 41, 215
Besette, Joseph M., 170, 218
Bipartisan leadership, 55–58, 78
Bingham, Jonathan, 177
Binkley, Wilfred E., 8, 18, 213, 217
Black, Charles, 182
Bliss, Ray, 105, 197
Blough, Roger, 165–166
Blum, John Morton, 171, 213
"Boll weevils," 46, 49–50, 72, 168
Bone, Hugh A., 139–140, 213
Bork, Robert, 54
Brady, Nicholas F., 128
Brauer, Carl M., 156, 171
Brezhnev, Leonid, 145
Broder, David S., 53–54, 61, 93, 95, 117, 157, 171, 194, 196, 200, 210, 213, 217
Brown, Roger G., 31, 41, 117, 125, 139, 210–211, 218
Buchanan, James, 107, 119

Budget-deficit reduction, 77
Budget and Impoundment Control
   Act, 90
"Bully pulpit," 10, 99, 160
Bundy, McGeorge, 57
Burnham, Walter Dean, 17, 41, 213
Burns, James M., 120–121, 125–126,
   139, 174, 190, 213
Bush, George, 1, 15, 16, 22, 33, 35,
   36, 38, 47, 58, 64, 66, 71, 73–74, 76,
   78, 80, 82–83, 85, 87, 88, 92–93,
   97–98, 103, 105–107, 109–112, 114,
   128, 135, 137, 146–148, 151, 154–156,
   159, 168–169, 193–196, 201–202,
   205–208
Butler, Paul, 101
Butler, William M., 101

Cable News Network (CNN), 15, 29
Calhoun, John C., 122
Califano, Joseph A., Jr., 117, 196,
   210, 213
California, 8, 33, 70, 98, 114, 147, 196
Calvert, Randall L., 41, 218
Campbell, James W., 38, 42
Candidate-centered campaign, 30, 40,
   111, 115, 201, 205, 209
Cannon, Clarence, 50
Cannon, Joe, 46, 123
Cannon, Lou, 140, 213
Carpenter, John A., 45, 60
Carswell, E. Harold, 76
Carter, Cliff, 199
Carter, Jimmy, 15, 21, 26, 28, 33,
   36–37, 43, 47, 48, 52, 55, 85, 98,
   105, 107, 109, 113–115, 135, 143,
   145–146, 150–152, 158, 166, 179,
   183, 194, 197, 199–201, 205–206
Ceaser, James W., 170, 190, 213, 218
Central Intelligence Agency, 34
Chambers, William Nesbet, 17
Cheney, Richard, 127
Chinese Emergency Immigration Act,
   82
Chubb, John E., 139, 170, 213
Churchill, Winston, 148
Citizens for Eisenhower–Nixon, 70

Citizens for Johnson and Humphrey,
   136
Civil Rights Acts of 1964 and 1965, 54
Civil War, 6, 8–9, 44
Clay, Henry, 7, 122–123
Clean Air Act, 90–91
Cleveland, Grover, 9, 46, 64, 85, 99,
   107–108, 122, 138, 188
Co-partisan government, 67
Coalition-building, 43, 130–132, 144,
   209
Cohen, Ben, 51
Colson, Charles, 55
Committee to Re-Elect the President
   (CREEP), 30, 109, 136
Confederate Party system, 15
Congress, 2, 4, 6, 8, 9–10, 11, 13–14,
   32–33, 65–67, 69, 73, 76–77
Congressional Caucus, 3–5, 23, 119,
   122
Congressional Government, 10
Congressional party, 120, 123–124, 193
Congressional Quarterly, 79–80
Congressional Reform, 48
Conlan, Timothy J., 90–92, 95
Connally, John, 136–137
"Consensus politics," 156–157, 200
Conservative party (Great Britain),
   12–13, 21
Constitutional Convention, 2–3
Contra aid, 73
Coolidge, Calvin, 101, 107, 119, 142
Corcoran, Tommy, 51
Corwin's Legislative Cabinet, 180
Corwin, E.S., 172, 191, 213
Cotter, Cornelius P., 41, 61, 105,
   116–117, 213
Council of States, 3
"Court packing" plan, 11
Covington, Cary R., 130–131, 140–141,
   167, 170, 172, 217
Cranston, Alan, 41
Cronin, Thomas E., 16, 18, 102–103,
   116, 182, 185–186, 190–191, 203,
   211, 214, 218
Cross-party coalitions, 74–78
Cuban missile crisis, 84, 114, 153,

Cuban missile crisis (*continued*)
195, 207
Curtis, Kenneth M., 109, 200
Cutler Plan, 177-178
Cutler, Lloyd N., 177-178, 189, 191,
218

D'Amato, Alfonse M., 82
Dahl, Robert A., 17, 218
Daley, Richard J., 198
Dana, Charles A., 9, 18
Davidson, Roger H., 60, 73, 94-95, 214
Davis, Eric L., 60, 218
Davis, James W., 17-18, 40, 60-61,
94-95, 214
Daynes, Byron W., 211, 217
Deaver, Michael K., 129
DeGaulle, Charles, 188
Democratic National Committee, 5,
97-118, 194, 196-197, 200, 207-208
Democratic-Republicans, 2-3, 6, 120
Dern, George, 34
DeVries, Walter, 171, 214
Dewey, Thomas E., 25, 69
Dillon, C. Douglas, 57
Direct election of president, 180-183
Direct-mail fundraising, 12
Dirksen, Everett M., 53-54, 68, 86
Divided government, 12, 16, 44, 46,
56-59, 63-95, 124, 143, 155, 159,
168, 203, 209
Dodd, Lawrence C., 94, 214
Dolce, Phillip C., 17, 60, 214
Dole, Robert, 72-73, 104-105, 110-111
Douglas, William O., 25
Dowd, Maureen, 117, 218
Duffy, Michael, 41
Dukakis, Michael, 21, 66, 112

Eagleton, Thomas, 110, 199
Eaton, Charles A., 68
Edwards, George C., III, 41, 48, 60,
146, 170, 214
Egger, Rowland, 191, 214
Eightieth Congress, 25, 69, 85, 165, 185
Eisenhower, Dwight D., 12, 16, 24-25,
27, 36-37, 46, 51, 56, 64, 69-70,

Eisenhower, Dwight D. (*continued*)
72-75, 82, 84-87, 92, 101-102, 104,
107, 109, 113, 136, 141, 147-148,
150-152, 156, 165, 185
Electoral College, 4-7, 17, 23, 38,
180-184
Elving, Ronald D., 94
Epstein, Leon D., 126-127, 139, 173,
190, 214
Equal Rights Amendment, 188
"Era of Good Feelings," 69
Euchner, Charles C., 88, 95
European Recovery Administration, 56
Evans, Rowland, 70, 94, 117, 214
Executive Office of the President,
115, 130

Factions, 2
Factional Types of Presidential Parti-
sanship, 107-108
Fahrenkopf, Frank, 105
Fair Deal, 69
Fair Labor Standards Act (1938), 11
Farley, James A., 27, 34, 55, 98, 101-
103, 108, 115, 194-195, 197
"Favorite son" candidates, 126
Federal Election Commission (FEC),
22, 27, 30, 111-112, 137
Federal Election Campaign Act of
1974, 19, 22, 27-28, 40, 90, 111, 133,
135-136, 202-203
Federal matching dollars, 127, 136
Federalist, The, 2, 17
Federalists, 2, 120-121
Ferejohn, John A., 41, 218
Ferguson, Homer, 68
Ferrell, Robert H., 117
Fillmore, Millard, 107-108
Fiorina, Morris P., 37, 41, 93, 214
"Fireside chats," 142-143
Fleishman, Joel L., 211, 214
Flynn, Edward J., 102, 197
Ford, Gerald R., 15, 26, 38, 53, 55,
64, 71-72, 85, 88, 103, 107, 110, 114,
117, 129, 151-152, 157-158, 202
Formosa Straits Resolution, 75, 153
French Presidency, 188-189

Friedel, Frank, 18, 60–61, 116, 214
Friedersdorf, Max, 49, 52
Friedman, Thomas L., 117, 218
Fundraising, 132–137, 195–196

Gallup opinion poll, 30, 87, 150–155
Garfield, James A., 107
Gaudet, Hazel, 41, 215
Gilded Age, 10, 45, 99
Glad, Betty, 170, 210, 214
"Going public," 88, 141–169, 193, 203
Goldman, Eric F., 210, 214
Goldman, Ralph M., 106–109, 117,
    139, 210, 214
Goldwater, Barry, 87, 110, 129, 136
Gonzales, Henry, 114
Goodell, Charles, 71
Gorbachev, Mikhail, 73, 87, 143, 146,
    206
Gorman, Arthur P., 99
Gorton, Slade, 132–133
Gosnell, Harold F., 40, 214
Gould, Lewis L., 116, 214
Graber, Doris, 211, 214
Graff, Henry F., 18, 59, 61, 117, 215
Gramm–Latta bill, 50
Grant, Ulysses S., 9, 44, 85, 107
Great Depression, 24
Greece, 56, 68
Greenspan, Alan, 57–58, 91
Greenstein, Fred, 94, 116, 140, 156,
    171, 215, 218
Grenada, 153
Grossman, Michael Baruch, 140, 170,
    215
Gruenther, Alfred, 86

Haggarty, Brian A., 40, 213
Hall, Leonard, 104, 109, 115, 136
Halleck, Charles, 86
Hamilton, Alexander, 2–3, 51, 120
Hanna, Mark A., 98, 100, 103, 108, 115
Hardin, Charles M., 175–177, 190, 215
Harding, Warren G., 100–101, 107,
    119, 142
Hargrove, Erwin C., 171, 178, 191, 215
Harmel, Robert, 116–117, 191, 197,
    203–204, 209–211, 215

Harmon, Richard, 60
Harrison, Benjamin, 107, 119, 188
Harrison, William Henry, 23, 45,
    107–108
Hart, John, 61, 215
Hart, Roderick T., 141, 169, 215
Hartmann, Susan M., 94, 215
Hatfield, Mark, 71
Hayes, Rutherford B., 44, 46, 64, 107
Hague, Frank, 24
Haynesworth, Clement, 76
Heclo, Hugh, 131, 140
Helms, Jesse, 73
Hennessy, Bernard, 41, 61, 105, 116–
    117, 213
Henry, Laurin, 210, 215
Herter, Christian A., 68
Hibbs, D. A., Jr., 170, 218
Hill, David B., 99
Hill–Burton Act, 71
Hobby, Oveta Culp, 86
Hoffman, Paul, 56
Hoover, Herbert, 24, 107, 142, 205
House of Representatives, 5, 7, 12,
    23, 36, 65
House Rules Committee, 53
Hughes, Richard, 114
Hull, Cordell, 34
Humphrey, Hubert H., 20, 110, 128,
    136
"Hundred Days" legislative program,
    11
Huntington, Samuel, 140, 218

Ickes, Harold, 34
Ignatious, David, 117
Impeachment, 9, 208
Imperial Presidency, 7–8, 168
Incumbency, 37, 65
Independent voters, 29, 37, 65, 161–
    162, 169, 203
"Independent" or "separated" presi-
    dent, 63, 88–89, 93
Intermediate Nuclear Forces Treaty
    (INF), 73, 87, 154
Iran hostage crises, 26, 150
Iran-Contra affair, 54, 87
Iraq, 77–78

Irish, Marion, 139, 215

Jackson, Andrew, 1, 3–4, 6–8, 44–45, 80, 98, 107, 119–120, 122, 138, 180, 203
Jackson, Henry M. "Scoop," 110
Jackson, Jesse, 22
Jacob, Charles E., 116
Jacobson, Gary C., 66–67, 93–94, 215
Jaworski, Leon, 145
Jefferson, Thomas, 1–3, 6–7, 44, 98, 107, 120–121, 138, 167, 184
Johnson, Andrew, 9, 72, 99, 107–108, 123
Johnson, Lyndon B., 20, 25–26, 31, 36, 38, 41, 44, 46, 49, 51, 53–54, 59, 69, 78, 82, 84–85, 104, 107, 109–110, 123, 128, 136, 150–152, 156–157, 168, 179, 190, 194, 196, 199–200, 203, 215
Johnson, Richard T., 117
Joint Center for Political and Economic Studies, 206–207
Jones, Charles O., 67, 88, 95, 118, 215

Kaifu, Toshiki, 147
Kefauver, Estes, 20, 25, 199
Kellerman, Barbara, 18, 215
Kemp–Roth tax bill, 50–51
Kempton, Murray, 156, 171, 218
Kennedy, David M., 61
Kennedy, Edward R. (Ted), 26, 110, 114–115, 128–129
Kennedy, John F., 3, 15, 20, 36–37, 43, 47, 49, 51–52, 54, 57, 70, 78, 81–82, 84, 86, 98, 101, 104, 107, 109–110, 114, 123–124, 128–129, 147, 151, 153, 156, 165–166, 194–195, 198–199, 207–208
Kennedy, Robert F., 25, 128
Kernell, Samuel, 60, 142–143, 170, 172, 211, 215
Kerney, Edward N., 140
Kessel, John, 127, 139, 215
Key, V. O., Jr., 198–199, 210, 215
Khrushchev, Nikita, 86
"King Caucus," 3, 5, 38
King, Anthony, 13, 18, 41, 60, 95, 215

Kleindienst, Richard, 76
Knowland, William, 69
Knox, Frank M., 56
Koenig, Louis, 18, 61, 215
Korean War, 165
Kroll, Jack, 24
Kumar, Martha Joynt, 140, 170, 215
Kuwait, 77

Labour party, 12–13, 97–98
Lame ducks, 87, 184
Lammers, William W., 211
Lance, Bert, 27
Latham, Earl, 172, 215
Laxalt, Paul, 31, 105, 109, 111
Lazarsfeld, Paul, 41, 215
Leader of all the people, 155–159
Leech, Margaret, 215
Lees, John A., 117, 197, 210–211
Legislator-in-chief, 52
Leuchtenburg, William E., 75, 94, 171, 215
Light, Paul 60, 216
Lincoln, Abraham, 1, 3, 6, 8–9, 20, 44–45, 78, 98–99, 107–108, 113, 122, 138, 159, 168, 205
Link, Arthur S., 163, 171, 216
Lodge, Henry C., Jr., 86, 110
Longley, Lawrence D., 186–187, 191, 216
Louisiana Purchase 8
Lowi, Theodore, 3, 17, 89, 95, 167–168, 172, 216
Lugar, Richard, 31

Madison, James, 2, 88, 107
Majors, John, 147
"Malaise" speech, 145
Malbin, Michael J., 95, 216
Manatt, Charles, 27
Manley, John F., 60, 94, 218
Mann, Thomas E., 95, 144, 216
Mansfield, Mike, 54
Marshall Plan, 56, 68
Mass membership interest groups, 139
Mayhew, David R., 89–90, 95
McCarthy, Eugene, 20, 25, 128
McCarthy, Joseph, 68, 125

McCloy, John J., 57
McClure, Robert, 209
McCombs, William F., 100, 115
McCormick, Vance, 100
McGovern, George, 21, 37, 110, 136, 200
McGovern–Fraser Commission, 198
McGrath, J. Howard, 103
McKinley, William, 35, 78, 107, 108, 205
McLenmore Resolution, 11
McNamara, Robert S., 57
Meese, Edwin, III, 129
Meltsner, Arnold J., 140, 216
Michel, Robert, 30–31, 195–196
Midterm elections, 83–85
Miller, Gary J., 170, 213
Miller, William E., 110, 115
"Misery" index, 153
Mitterand, Francois, 147, 188–189, 206
"Mixed" caucus-primary system, 20, 23
"Mixed" conventions, 5
Moe, Terry, M. 128, 139
Mondale, Walter F., 21, 22, 27, 30
Monroe, James, 69, 107, 184
Morton, Rogers, 103–104, 110
Morton, Thruston, 103, 110
Mosbacher, Robert, 34, 128
Mowry, George E., 40, 60, 216
Mulroney, Brian, 147, 206
Murray, Philip, 24
Muskie, Edmund G., 110, 136, 183

National Association of Manufacturers, 165
National Bonus Plan for Electoral College, 183–184
National Leadership Coalition on AIDS, 207
National Nominating Convention, 1, 4–6, 19, 21, 23, 27, 35, 97, 119, 122
National Party Chairman, 97–99, 108–112, 194
National Progressive League for Roosevelt, 34

National Republican Party, 23, 121
Nelson, Michael, 40–41, 93, 118, 139, 191, 211, 215–216
New Freedom Policy, 160
New Hampshire primary, 25, 34, 70, 86, 149
Neustadt, Richard E., 71, 88, 94, 149, 154, 170, 216
Nicaraguan Contra aid, 73, 88–89
Nie, Norman H., 41, 216
Nixon, Richard M., 15, 22, 26, 30, 36–38, 57, 64, 70–71, 73, 75–76, 82, 84–86, 88, 90–92, 103–105, 107, 109–110, 129, 143–145, 149, 151–152, 157–158, 165, 168, 194, 196–197, 205, 208
Nofziger, Lyn, 50, 129
"Nonfederal accounts," 112
Nonpartisan president, 201–204, 207
Northern Securities Case, 163
Novak, Robert D., 70, 94, 117, 214

O'Brien, Lawrence, 51–52, 110
O'Donnell, Kenneth, 104
O'Dwyer, William, 24–25
Off-year elections, 38, 86
Office of Congressional Relations, 51–52, 59
Office of Education bill, 71
Office of Management and Budget. 48, 77
Office of Media Liaison, 132
Office of Political Affairs, 129
Office of Public Liaison, 55, 131–132
Office of White House Communications, 55
Oleszek, Walter, 60, 73, 94, 214
O'Neill, Thomas P. (Tip), 48, 49, 54
Oppenheimer, Bruce I., 94, 214
Oregon territory, 8, 45
Ornstein, Norman J., 60, 95, 170, 216
Orr, Kay, 147
Orren, Gary R., 204, 211, 218
Ostrom, Charles W., Jr., 150, 170, 213, 218

Packwood, Robert, 31

Panama Canal tolls, 11
Pancake, John S., 139, 216
Parliamentary system, 1, 10–14, 17,
    21, 97, 119, 173–177
Parmet, Herbert S., 61, 117, 216
Participatory democracy, 21, 26
Party "decomposition," 22, 54
Party government, 64
Party identification, 162, 204
Party "purge" of 1938, 58
Party reform, 40
Patronage, 8–9, 11, 14–15, 24, 35, 45,
    49, 58, 70, 113–114, 194–195
Peirce, Neal, 183, 186–187, 191–192
Pendergast, Paul, 42
Penniman, R., 116–117, 216
Percy, Charles, 71
"Permanent" campaign, 113
Persian Gulf War, 74, 83, 148, 154
Persons, Wilton B., 51
Pessen, Edward, 60
Peterson, Paul E., 139, 170, 213
Petrocik, John R., 41, 216
Phillips, Cabell, 61, 93, 171, 216
Photo opportunities, 16, 88–89, 169,
    202–203
Pierce, Franklin, 107
Pika, Joseph, 140
Pious, Richard M., 14, 18, 42, 117,
    210–211, 216
Platt, Thomas C., 46
Plebiscitarian presidency, 7, 21, 120
Plebiscitary nominating system, 20–22
Pletcher, David M., 18, 60
Plischke, Elmer, 211
Plural executive, 3
Polakoff, Ian, 59
Policy escalation, 91, 93
Political Action Committee (PAC), 37,
    205
Polk, James, K., 6, 8, 44–45, 107, 122,
    138
Polls, 65–66, 68, 87, 92, 151–152
Pomper, Gerald M., 41, 116, 211, 216
"Postage stamp" presidencies, 9, 138
Presidential campaign spending,
    134–35

Presidential coattails, 35–38, 40
Presidential electors, 3–5
Presidential Models for Running
    National Party Organization, 106–108
Presidential party, 119–139
Presidential primaries, 19–22, 25–26,
    32, 34, 39, 40, 65, 122, 126, 129,
    182, 198
Presidential renomination, 24–26, 40
Price, David E., 41, 171, 204, 211, 216
Progressive (or Bull Moose) party, 24,
    108, 126
Progressive movement, 12, 100
Public presidency, 141–172
Public Utility Holding Company Act,
    165

Quasi-party leader, 15, 17, 59
Quirk, Paul J., 95, 218

Radical Republicans, 9, 99, 123
Ragsdale, Lyn, 170, 218
Ranney, Austin, 17, 18, 35–36, 41, 60,
    216
Raskob, John, 102
Rayburn, Sam, 46, 53, 69, 123
Reagan, Ronald W., 1, 3, 12, 15, 22,
    26, 30–31, 33, 36, 38, 45, 49–50,
    52–54, 57–58, 64, 66, 71–73, 76,
    82, 85–89, 91–92, 98, 103, 105, 107,
    109, 111, 115, 123–124, 129, 132,
    135, 137, 143–144, 146, 149–155,
    166–168, 185, 193–195, 201–203,
    206
Reconstruction, 44
Reed, Thomas B., 123
Rehnquist, William H., 76
Reiter, Howard, 210
Remini, Robert V., 7, 17, 216
Republican Citizens, 86
Republican Congressional Campaign
    Committee, 123
Republican National Committee, 12,
    50, 72, 86, 97–118, 137, 146, 195,
    206
Responsible parties school, 173–174
Rhetorical presidency, 142–143

Richards, Richard, 103, 109
Robinson, Donald L., 93, 178–180, 191–192, 216
Robinson's "federal council," 179–180
Rockefeller, Nelson A., 70, 110
Rockman, Bert A., 115, 118
Rohde, David W., 151–152, 170, 213
Romney, George, 70
Roosevelt, Franklin D., 1, 3, 11, 12, 15, 20, 27, 34–36, 38, 44, 46–47, 50–51, 55–56, 59, 74–75, 78, 80–81, 83, 85, 98, 101, 103, 107, 112–113, 123–124, 126–127, 133, 142–143, 147–148, 154–156, 165, 190, 194, 199, 203, 205
Roosevelt, Franklin D. Jr., 24
Roosevelt, James, 24, 25
Roosevelt, Theodore, 3, 10, 20, 24, 35, 44, 46, 59, 87, 99–100, 107–108, 113, 123, 138, 160, 163, 205
Rose, Richard, 18, 33, 41, 207, 211, 217
Roseboom, Eugene H., 17, 217
Rossiter, Clinton, 86, 123, 139, 185–186
Rostenkowski, Dan, 124
Rowan, Hobart, 172
Rowe, James, 51
Rules Committee, 53, 91
Rusk, Dean, 57
Russell, Richard B., 25, 123

Salinas, Carlos, 147
Schlesinger, Arthur M., Jr., 7–8, 18, 167, 181, 217
Scott, Hugh, 71
Scowcroft, Brent, 127
Scranton, William, 86
Selected Service Act of 1940, 75
Seligman, Lester G., 130–131, 140–141, 167, 170, 172, 217
Senate Campaign Committees, 30–31
Separation of powers, 3, 4, 6, 8, 13–14, 17, 43, 59, 63–64, 91, 120, 123–124, 138, 175, 180, 190
Shaw, Malcolm, 117, 210, 217
Sherman, General William T., 9
Shriver, R., Sargent, 110
Sidey, Hugh, 170, 218
"Silent majority," 157
Silver Democrats, 108

Simon, Dennis M., 150, 170, 218
Simpson, Alan K., 47, 82
Six-year presidential term, 189
Skau, George H., 17, 60, 214
Skowronik, Stephen, 115, 118
Slavery question, 8, 9, 45
Social Security Act, 11, 90–91
"Soft" money, 112, 137
Sorauf, Frank J., 41, 116, 210, 217
Sorenson, Ted, 114, 117, 210, 217
Southern Democratic GOP Coalition, 47, 52–53, 74–76, 78–80
Soviet Union, 73, 145, 152
Sparkman, John, 199
"Special interests," 163–166, 208–209
Split-ticket voting, 14, 65–67, 161–164, 203
"Spoils" system, 7, 45
Spooner, John C., 46
St. Lawrence Seaway project, 56
Stalwarts, 100
Standard Marketing Area (SMA), 29
State Legislative Caucuses and Conventions, 5
State of the Union Message, 142
State party activity, 113–115, 197–198
Stevenson, Adlai E., 20, 136, 199
"Stewardship theory," 10
Stimson, Henry, 56
Stone, Harlan F., 56
Strategic Arms Reduction Treaty (START), 113
Strauss, Robert S., 58, 105, 197, 200
"Subcommitteeization," 48, 54, 143–144
Summerfield, Arthur, 27, 109
Sundquist, James L., 80, 93–95, 189, 191–192, 217–218
Sumners, Joe A., 38, 42
Sununu, John, 34, 82, 83, 106, 137
Swanson, Claude, 34
Symington, Stuart, 98

Taft, Robert A., 68–70, 123
Taft, William Howard, 24, 100, 107
Taft–Hartley Labor Relations Act, 69
Tarrance, V. Lance, 171, 214
Tatalovich, Raymond, 211, 217

Tax Reform Act of 1986, 31, 72, 91,
   166–167, 206
Taylor, Zachary, 70, 107, 199
Television, 15–17, 20, 23, 28–29, 65,
   112–113, 133, 143–145, 148–149, 163,
   202
TerHorst, J. F., 170
Texas, 45, 199–200
Thatcher, Margaret, 206
Thirteenth Amendment, 9
Thomas, Norman C., 177, 190
Thurber, James A., 95, 217
Thurmond, Strom, 183
Thurow, Glen E., 170, 218
Tilden, Samuel B., 44
Tillman Act (1907), 108
Titular leader, 98
"Toward a More Responsible Two-
   Party System," 190, 219
"Tribune of the People," 7, 17
Truman, Harry S., 24–25, 36, 44, 47,
   50, 56, 67–69, 98, 103, 107, 113, 123,
   133, 148, 151–152, 156–157, 165,
   185, 191, 199
Tugwell, Rexford G., 190, 214
Tulis, Jeffrey, 170, 217, 218
Turkey, 56, 68
Twentieth Century Task Force, 183–184
Twenty-fifth Amendment, 181
Twenty-second Amendment, 25,
   85–87, 93, 185–186
Twenty-second Amendment, proposed
   repeal, 184–187
Twenty-sixth Amendment, 187
Two-thirds rule, 122
Tyler, John, 45, 72, 107–108

Underwood Tariff Act, 11, 163
Union party, 8–9
United States Chamber of Commerce,
   50

Van Buren, Martin, 8, 23, 107
Vance, Cyrus, 41, 218

Vandenberg, Arthur H., 56, 68
Verba, Sidney, 41, 216
Versailles Treaty, 160–161
Vetoes, 45, 47, 54, 63, 71–72, 74, 76,
   80–83, 87, 92–93, 168
Vice presidents, 32–33, 83, 115, 199
Vietnam War, 12, 84, 153, 157, 179,
   187, 200
Virginia Plan, 3

War Democrats, 8–9
War Powers Act of 1973, 90
Washington, George, 1, 2, 5, 17, 51,
   106–107, 120
Watergate scandals, 30, 72, 76, 102,
   109, 145, 154, 157
Wattenberg, Martin P., 171, 217
Wayne, Stephen J., 48, 60, 191, 214,
   217
Ways and Means Committee, 11, 47
Webster, Daniel, 23, 122–123
Weinberger, Casper, 129
Wellborn, David M., 210, 211, 218
Wexler, Anne, 55
Whig party, 5, 23, 108, 121–122
White, Hugh, 23
White, Theodore H., 29, 41, 116–117,
   139–140, 182–183, 217
Whitten, Jaime, 124
Will, George, 183, 191, 219
Wills, Garry, 156, 171, 217
Wilson, Pete, 114, 147, 196
Wilson, Woodrow, 1, 3, 10–11, 18,
   20, 24, 35, 38, 46, 59, 80, 85, 94,
   100, 107, 113, 123–124, 126, 138,
   142, 148, 155, 160, 163, 171, 173–174,
   190, 199, 203, 217
Witcover, Jules, 117, 171, 217
Woodward, C. Vann, 59, 217
World Almanac, 29, 41

Yates, Sidney, 54
Yeutter, Clayton K., 106

About the Author

JAMES W. DAVIS is Professor Emeritus of Political Science at Western Washington University. He is the author of *The American Presidency: A New Perspective* (1987), *National Conventions in an Age of Party Reform* (Greenwood Press, 1983), and *Presidential Primaries: Road to the White House* (Greenwood, 1980).

DATE DUE

Demco, Inc. 38-293